Extraterritorial Jurisdiction in Theory and Practice

Extraterritorial Jurisdiction in Theory and Practice

Editor

Dr. Karl M. Meessen

KLUWER LAW INTERNATIONAL

LONDON – THE HAGUE – BOSTON

Published by Kluwer Law International Ltd
Sterling House
66 Wilton Road
London SW1V 1DE
United Kingdom

Sold and distributed in the USA and Canada
by Kluwer Law International
675 Massachusetts Avenue
Cambridge MA 02139
USA

Kluwer Law International Ltd incorporates
the publishing programmes of
Graham & Trotman Ltd,
Kluwer Law & Taxation Publishers
and Martinus Nijhoff Publishers

In all other countries, sold and distributed
by Kluwer Law International
P.O. Box 85889
2508 CN The Hague
The Netherlands

ISBN 90-411-0899-8

© Kluwer Law International 1996
First published 1996

British Library Cataloguing in Publication Data is available

Library of Congress Cataloguing-in-Publication Data
Extraterritorial jurisdiction in theory and practice / editor, Karl M.
Meessen.
    p. cm.
    Contains the edited transcript of a symposium held in Dresden, Oct
8–10, 1993.
    Includes index.
    ISBN 9041108998
    1. Exterritoriality–Congresses. 2. Conflict of laws–Congresses.
3. International and municipal law–Congresses. I. Meessen, Karl
Matthias.
K7075.E885 1996
341.4–dc20   96-20674
                                                                    CIP

Typeset in 10/12pt Galliard by BookEns Ltd, Royston, Herts.
Printed and bound in Great Britain by Hartnolls Ltd, Bodmin, Cornwall.

Table of Contents

Foreword

This book contains the edited transcript of a symposium held in Dresden between 8 and 10 October 1993, on extraterritorial jurisdiction. This symposium, over which I had the honour to preside, was an offshoot of the work of the Committee of the International Law Association on the Legal Aspects of Extraterritorial Jurisdiction of which I am chairman. The symposium, so ably organised by Karl Meessen, Rapporteur of the ILA Committee, was deliberately designed to examine jurisdictional questions which have arisen or are arising in fields other than the traditional problem areas of export controls and antitrust. Participants in the symposium, who were not confined to members of the ILA Committee, represented differing (sometimes opposed) intellectual approaches to the nature and role of law in the regulation of human society. One quality does however shine through: each of the principal contributors was an acknowledged expert in the area of activity which he was requested to survey – whether antitrust in the insurance field, international taxation, bank deposits, customary international law, criminal law, environmental law, international mergers and acquisitions, or banking and securities. Here we have, then, an informal enquiry into the impact and consequences of attempts to assert extraterritorial jurisdiction and regulatory controls over widely disparate human activities.

These transcripts are raw in the sense that they have not been edited other than to remove grammatical infelicities. They accordingly and inevitably betray from time to time the signs of quick and spontaneous reactions to fresh ideas or points of view, at least in the case of the record of discussions following the presentation of individual papers. It is this feature of the transcripts which is so interesting, since it demonstrates that a genuine dialogue was engaged. I think I may accordingly speak for all participants in saying that the symposium was stimulating and thought-provoking; and that all of those who took part learnt much from the frank and open presentation of differing viewpoints in an atmosphere of lively and good-humoured interchange.

For many of us who travelled to Dresden on this occasion, it was the first opportunity to see this city with its rich artistic and cultural history, a city so tragically devastated some 50 years ago. But if we could not fail to be horrified by the savage destruction wrought on an historic city, we were also able to see the progress which was being made in restoring Dresden to some at least of its former glories, and to sense the spirit of hope in which this major task of reconstruction is being undertaken.

Sir Ian Sinclair
8 November 1995

List of Contributors

Andrea Bianchi

Andrea Bianchi, LL.M. (Harvard), Ph.D. (Milan). Assistant Professor of International Law at the University of Siena since 1990. His publications on extraterritorial jurisdiction include: *L'applicazione extraterritoriale dei controlli all'esportazione. Contributo allo studio dei fenomeni di extraterritorialità nel diritto internazionale* (Padova, 1995); 'Extraterritoriality and Export Controls: Some Remarks on the Alleged Antinomy Between European and U.S. Approaches', 35 *German Yearbook of International Law* 366–434 (1992); 'Esportaziano e transito di materiali di armamento: profili di diritto internationale', 75 *Rivista di diritto internazionale* 65–90 (1992); (together with F. Francioni), 'Italy', in K. Meessen (ed.), *The International Law of Export Control* (London, 1992) 105–115.

Gary Born

Gary Born is the Managing Partner of Wilmer, Cutler & Pickering's London office. He is a member of the Bar of the District of Columbia. He is the author of *International Civil Litigation in United States Courts* (Kluwer), presently in its third edition, and *International Commercial Arbitration in the United States* (Kluwer). He has also authored numerous other publications, particularly in the field of extraterritoriality.

Ulrich Bosch

Ulrich Bosch is senior vice president and counsel (Syndikus) of Deutsche Bank AG (head office), Frankfurt am Main, where he is in charge of international financial and capital markets law amongst other matters. He studied law and economics at the universities of Tübingen, Geneva and Bonn, passed his state law examinations in Cologne and Munich and has a doctorate in law from the

University of Bonn. Dr. Bosch has been a company lawyer and attorney-at-law since 1971 and joined Deutsche Bank in 1976. He has occasionally written and given presentations of various aspects of banking and capital markets law, including international lending, securities legislation, financial derivatives, corporate governance and extraterritoriality issues in litigation involving the US and Germany.

Philip Bovey

Philip Bovey was educated at Rugby and Cambridge, where he read history. He qualified as a solicitor in 1974 after training with the City of London firm of Slaughter and May. He has worked in a number of government departments including the Cabinet Office and Foreign and Commonwealth Office and since 1985 has been under secretary (legal) in the Department of Trade and Industry. His responsibilities include overseas trade (including sanctions and export controls), consumers, competition, business law, and deregulation.

Ulrich Drobnig

Ulrich Drobnig was born in 1928; and undertook law studies in Tübingen and at New York University, New York (Dr. jur. (Hamburg) and Master of Comparative Jurisprudence (NYU)). He is a temporary research associate at the University of Michigan and Cornell University Schools of Law; and a teaching fellow at the University of Chicago Law School. Other positions held are as a research associate and (since 1979) director at the Max Planck Institute for Foreign Private and Private International Law, Hamburg; and professor, at the University of Hamburg, in the Faculty of Law.

Francesco Francioni

Francesco Francioni is a Dr. jur., University of Florence, 1966 and attained a LL.M. at Harvard, 1968. He is the Professor of International Law and Vice-Rector at the University of Siena.

Ernesto M. Hizon

Ernesto M. Hizon, a lawyer from the Philippines, is a Dr. jur. (Doctoral) Candidate in International and Foreign Comparative Law at the Johann Wolfgang von Goethe University in Frankfurt, Germany. From 1991 to 1994, he was a Hanns Seidel Foundation Scholar in Germany, and worked in 1993 and 1994 as a research assistant at the Chair for Public International Law, European Law and International Economic Law at Augsburg University. He has published articles on European and International Trade Law in Europe and in the US. He graduated with a LL.M. at the Johann Wolfgang von Goethe University in 1992 *magna cum laude*, and holds A.B. Economics and Bachelor of Laws degrees from the Jesuit Ateneo de Manila University. At present, he is Senior Fellow, Asia Program at the Center for International Environmental Law (CIEL) based in Washington, D.C., where he is also involved in Trade and Environment research.

Mr Hizon also obtained a masters degree in Business Economics from the Center for Research and Communication (CRC) in Manila on a CRC Foundation scholarship. Prior to his international experience, he worked for two years as a law clerk to a justice of the Philippine Supreme Court and practiced law for two Manila law firms for four years. At the same time, he was Adjunct Professor of Business Law at the De La Salle University in Manila. As an undergraduate economics and law student, he edited the university newspaper and was the associate editor of the *Ateneo Law Review*.

Michael D.C. Johnson

Michael Johnson worked in the British civil service from 1960 to 1995. For over 20 years he specialised in international trade policy and economic relations, including GATT and the Uruguay Round of multilateral trade negotiations. He was for many years responsible for the UK's bilateral commercial relations with the US, and handled many of the most serious disputes which arose from UK objections to the assertion by the US of extraterritorial jurisdiction, including the Westinghouse uranium antitrust litigation and the dispute in 1982 over the provision of technology for the Soviet gas pipeline. He was the administrator who advised British ministers on the passage through Parliament of the Protection of Trading Interests Act 1980. He is now an independent adviser and lecturer on international trade policy.

Pieter J. Kuyper

Pieter J. Kuyper is presently one of the legal advisers to the European Commission. As such he is specially charged with matters relating to international trade, in particular the WTO. He has represented the EC in several GATT and WTO panel procedures. He has also advised on matters of competition policy, export controls, Community jurisdiction and extraterritoriality. He has regularly published law review articles and submitted contributions to volumes of essays on these subjects.

Cynthia C. Lichtenstein

Professor Cynthia Crawford Lichtenstein received her Dr. jur. from Yale Law School and her Masters of Comparative Law from the University of Chicago Law School. She became a member of the Bar of New York and practiced with the New York firm of Milbank, Tweed, Hadley and McCloy, primarily in the area of international banking. She entered teaching in 1971 at Boston College Law School where she is Professor of Law. From 1985 to 1994 she returned to Milbank, Tweed as a consultant. She has served as president of the American Branch of the International Law Association, is presently chair of the ILA International Securities Regulation Committee and, most recently, was named on the roster of governmental and non-governmental panelists approved by the Dispute Settlement Body of the WTO on 27 September 1995.

Andreas F. Lowenfeld

Andreas F. Lowenfeld is Herbert and Rose Rubin Professor of International Law at New York University School of Law. He is the author, among other works, of *International Litigation and Arbitration* (1993) and *International Litigation and the Quest for Reasonableness* (1996). Professor Lowenfeld served as associate reporter of the American Law Institute's *Restatement (Third) of the Foreign Relations Law of the United States* (1980–97) and has also served as a rapporteur for the Institut de Droit International (1991–95). Prior to joining the faculty of New York University, Professor Lowenfeld was assistant legal adviser and deputy legal adviser in the US Department of State (1961–66).

Harold G. Maier

Professor Harold G. Maier is David Daniels Allen Distinguished Professor and Director of Transnational Legal Studies at Vanderbilt Law School Nashville, Tennessee. He has published numerous articles on extraterritorial jurisdiction and private international law. Professor Maier was counselor on international law to the office of the legal adviser, US State Department in 1983–84 where he served as liaison with the American Law Institute reporters during the preparation of the *Restatement (Third) of Foreign Relations Law of the United States*. He has been visiting professor at The University of Pennsylvania, The University of North Carolina, and George Washington University, and has been a guest scholar at the Brookings Institution in Washington, D.C.

Rutsel Silvestre J. Martha

Dr. Martha is Minister Plenipotentiary to the Permanent Representation of the Kingdom of The Netherlands to the European Union. Formerly, he was a Counsellor in the Legal Department of the International Monetary Fund (Washington D.C.) and legal adviser to the Central Bank of the Netherlands Antilles. In 1989, he was awarded the Dr. Mitchell B. Carroll Prize of the International Fiscal Association for his book *The Jurisdiction to Tax in International Law*.

Campbell McLachlan

Campbell McLachlan is a Partner in Herbert Smith, solicitors, London. He has a PhD from the University of London and holds the diploma *cum laude* of the Hague Academy of International Law. He is Secretary of the International Bar Association's International Litigation Committee and rapporteur of the International Law Association's International Civil and Commercial Litigation Committee. He has had extensive experience of extraterritoriality issues in practice, and has written widely on private international law, including on issues of jurisdiction and crossborder court orders.

Karl M. Meessen

Jean-Monnet Professor of Public Law, European Law, International Law and International Commercial Law at the Friedrich-Schiller-Universität, Jena (Germany); formerly Professor of Law and President, of the University of Augsburg (Germany); Visiting Professor at the University of Chicago, the University of Paris II and at the Graduate Institute of International Studies, Geneva (Switzerland).

Yoshio Ohara

Yoshio Ohara is Professor Emeritus, Kobe University and a professor in the Faculty of Law at Kanagawa University. From October 1991 to October 1994 he held the position of executive director of the Japan Association of International Economic Law. His academic qualifications are as follows: LL.B., Tokyo (1953); M.C.L., Columbia (1959); LL.M., Harvard (1960); and LL.D., Tokyo (1994). His publications include 'International Application of the Japanese Antimonopoly Act', *Swiss Review of International Competition Law*, No. 28 (1986) (Geneva); *International Business and National Jurisdiction: International and Comparative Law Analysis on Extraterritorial Application of Competition Law in the U.S., Germany, the EC and Japan and the U.S. Export Control Legislation* (Yubikaku Publishing Co, Tokyo, 1993), a dissertation in Japanese.

Aurelio Pappalardo

Aurelio Pappalardo was born in 1936 (Trapani, Italy) and attended Law School from 1953 to 1957, Catholic University, Milan. He is a member of the Italian Bar; a research fellow at the University of Chicago (1967/68); and from 1960 to 1986 was an official with the Commission of the European Communities (Antitrust Department). Since 1987 he has been practising law in Brussels (Studio Legale 'Pappalardo e Associati', a law firm specialising in EC law). Since 1969 he has also been a part-time professor of EC competition law at the College of Europe, Bruges, Belgium; and since 1986 a member of the Law School Faculty of the University of Liege, Belgium. His publications include several articles and comments on EC law provisions, mostly in the field of antitrust (some of which treat the question of extraterritorial application of EC rules).

Paul Peters

Paul Peters (Netherlands), is a former international law adviser and economist of companies of the Royal Dutch/Shell Group in the UK, Venezuela and the Netherlands.

Adelheid Puttler

Adelheid Puttler is a Dr. jur. (University of Augsburg, Germany), LL.M.

(University of Chicago), and holds the Diplôme International d'Administration Publique (Ecole Nationale d'Administration, France). From 1983 to 1988 she was assistant professor of law (Akademische Rätin) at the University of Augsburg; since 1988 she has been a legal adviser in the department of European affairs at the Bavarian Ministry of Economics; and from 1991 to 1994 was assigned to the Federal Constitutional Court of Germany (Bundesverfassungs-gericht) as a research lawyer. Adelheid Puttler is currently working on her habilitation thesis at the University of Augsburg. In 1989 she published 'Völkerrechtliche Grenzen von Export-und Reexportverboten', a treatise on questions of extraterritorial jurisdiction of export control law. She has authored further publications in the field of European and German law.

Edward B. Sherman

Edward Sherman is currently director of capital market development at Ezra Zask Associates in New York, where he is involved in researching investment opportunities in the Russian Federation. Before that he served as assistant to the international competition policy director at the EC Commission to the European Union. He graduated from the University of Pittsburg School of Law, *magna cum laude* in 1992, where he worked on the *Law Review*. After law school he clerked for the US federal district court for the eastern district of Pennsylvania.

Ian Sinclair

Sir Ian Sinclair is currently in practice at the international law Bar in London, and acting as counsel in several cases before the International Court of Justice involving land and seabed boundaries or other international legal disputes. He was in the legal branch of the British Diplomatic Service for 34 years, ending up (from 1976 to 1984) as legal adviser to the Foreign and Commonwealth Office. In that capacity, he took part in many international negotiations with the US government on the practical problems raised by disputed exercises of extraterritorial jurisdiction. He also participated in several academic conferences on the problem, including the International Law Association conference in London in 1983 on 'The Extraterritorial Application of Laws, and Responses thereto'. He was a member of the International Law Commission from 1981 to 1986 and has been a member of the Institut de Droit International since 1987 (Associate Member, 1983–87). His publications include *Vienna Convention on the Law of Treaties* (2nd edn, 1984), the *International Law Commission* (1987), and many articles and notes in international legal journals.

H.-Peter v. Stoephasius

Hans-Peter v. Stoephasius is a Dr. jur., and Professor für Staats- und Verwaltungsrecht, Fachbereich 3, at the Fachhochschule für Verwaltung und Rechtspflege in Berlin, Alt Friedrichsfelde, 60, 10315 Berlin, tel: 030-5161-

4347. He was the head of sector 'European Cartel Law', at the Federal Cartel Office in Berlin. His publications include *Extraterritorial application of the EEC-Cartel-Law on enterprises outside the EEC* (German), (Diss. Göttingen, 1971) and 'International jurisdiction of the EEC Commission in cartel proceedings' (German), *WRP* 1972, 568.

Andreas Weitbrecht

Andreas Weitbrecht was born in 1947 and undertook law studies at Bonn University, First State Examination 1974 (Cologne), Second State Examination 1979 (Bavaria). He was Assistant Professor of Law (Akademischer Rat) at Augsburg University from 1979 to 1985. He attained a LL.M., University of California (Berkeley) in 1984. Dr. jur., University of Augsburg 1986 ('The Prohibition of Transnational Mergers'), and in 1986 gained admission to the German Bar. He is presently Counsel at Wilmer, Cutler & Pickering, Brussels, practising, *inter alia*, in the areas of German and EC antitrust and aviation law. He has authored numerous publications in German, European and international economic law.

Chapter I

Jurisdictional Issues Before National Courts: The *Insurance Antitrust* Case

Andreas F. Lowenfeld

Rather than presenting a comprehensive treatment of this subject, which has occupied me for a substantial part of my professional career, I thought it might be appropriate to discuss the recent decision of the US Supreme Court in the *Insurance Antitrust* case, known formally as *Hartford Fire Insurance Co v California*,[1] which is interesting for our purposes for what it says about the application of US law to the London insurance market, in particular the reinsurance market at Lloyd's. After about half a century of application of US law to transnational activities – on initiative of private litigants, government agencies and, in this case, states of the United States, the *Insurance Antitrust* case was the first case in which the US Supreme Court seriously addressed the reach of American law in the context of economic regulation. I believe ours is the first international conference on the question of jurisdiction since the issue of the decision on the final day of the Supreme Court 1992-93 term, and we may see from the results of the decision and the 5-4 split among the justices where further work by scholars may usefully be pursued.[2]

---

[1]   113 S. Ct. 2891 (1993).
[2]   The present writer served as a member of the legal team that represented the Lloyd's defendants before the Supreme Court. However, the discussion herein is presented, as much as possible, from the point of view of a scholar and not an advocate, and in no way purports to speak for the Lloyd's parties or its permanent counsel.

1.   The Facts of the Case

The case concerned the provision of commercial general liability insurance and reinsurance in the US. Commercial general liability insurance covers both factories making products sold to the public and facilities such as daycare centres and kindergartens, which may be the target of claims by persons alleging injury. The background of the case was a perception widely (but not universally) shared that there was an insurance crisis in the US, compelling a variety of facilities to shut down because they could not obtain insurance;[3] the reason that they could not obtain insurance, so the theory went, was that potential insurers could not obtain adequate reinsurance.

Plaintiffs in the action, brought in the federal district court in San Francisco in 1988, were the attorneys general of 19 states of the US, plus a number of private plaintiffs, led by the Attorney General of California.[4] The basic charge was that the defendants had agreed (unlawfully agreed) first to eliminate occurrence-based or 'long-tail' coverage in favour of the exclusive issue of claims-made policies, and secondly to eliminate 'sudden and accidental' pollution from liability policies.[5] The defendants were four major domestic insurance companies, several domestic reinsurance companies, brokers, and insurance associations, plus a number of foreign reinsurers and their principals, in particular a number of underwriting agencies at Lloyd's.

For present purposes, the significant complaint was that the London defendants had violated US antitrust law by refusing, in England, to offer reinsurance to American companies except on terms to which the London defendants had jointly agreed, thus harming parties for whom the state attorneys general acted as *parens patriae*. The defence was that the London underwriters had acted in England in full compliance with English law and policy.

The English defendants did not deny that their actions had effects in the US – indeed direct and substantial effects. They argued, however, that their conduct was legal in the state where it took place, that they operated in full compliance with a regime of regulation and self-regulation as prescribed by the UK Parliament and that, under principles of international law and comity as spelled out particularly in two major decisions of US courts of appeals – *Timberlane*

---

[3]   For contrasting views on this point, see e.g., 'Symposium: Perspectives on the Insurance Crisis', 5 *Yale L. J.* on Regulation 367 (1988); also George L. Priest, 'The Current Insurance Issues and Modern Tort Law', 96 *Yale L. J.* 1521 (1987).

[4]   Interestingly, it was the attorneys general and not the insurance commissioners who filed the action; in many instances, the state insurance commissioners were opposed to bringing the suit. But since the action was brought under federal law and no allegations were made of violations of state law, the insurance commissioners were not responsible for the decisions to file or join the suit.

[5]   An insurance policy based on occurrence during the effective period of the policy has the effect that the issuer cannot close its books on policies written for a given period until long after the end of the term of the policy. In the 1980s insurers and reinsurers that had written occurrence-based policies for the United States, found themselves confronted with massive claims arising

Lumber Co v Bank of America, N.T. & S.A.[6] and *Mannington Mills Inc v Congoleum Corp*[7] — as well as two generations of Restatements of the Foreign Relations Law of the United States,[8] jurisdiction to apply US law should not be exercised in this case.

2. Two Views in the Lower Courts

In the much discussed *Timberlane* case, it will be recalled, Judge Choy had written that the 'effects doctrine' as formulated by Judge Learned Hand in *Alcoa*[9] is incomplete, because it fails to consider the interests of other nations in the application or non-application of US law.[10] Judge Choy had proposed a three-part test — first, determine whether challenged conduct had had *some* effect on the commerce of the US — the minimum contact to support application of US law; secondly, see if a greater showing could be made that the conduct in question imposed a burden or restraint on US commerce, i.e. whether the complaint stated a claim under the antitrust laws; and thirdly, determine 'the additional question which is unique to the international setting of whether the interests of, and links to, the United States ... are sufficiently strong, *vis-à-vis* those of other nations, to justify an assertion of extraterritorial authority'.[11] Judge Choy then proceeded to set out a list of seven factors by which to judge the third or 'ought to' question, based on a list of factors proposed some years earlier by Professor Kingman Brewster.[12] Other courts and the Restatement modified the criteria somewhat,[13] but for the most part adopted the approach of the *Timberlane* case.

In *Insurance Antitrust*, the district judge, evaluating the complaint in the light of *Timberlane*, dismissed the action, on the basis that 'the *conflict* with English law and policy which could result from the extraterritorial application of the [US] antitrust laws in this case is not outweighed by other factors'.[14] The Court of Appeals, going through the same factors, acknowledged the 'significant

---

cont.

out of the use of asbestos in the construction of buildings, and also with claims arising out of underground chemical pollution. Defendants contended that whatever they had done was intended only to staunch the losses arising as a result of such claims. Plaintiffs asserted that nevertheless the agreements were unlawful under US antitrust law.

[6] 549 F.2d 597 (9th Cir. 1976).

[7] 595 F.2d 1287 (3d Cir. 1979).

[8] Restatement (Second) ss. 403, 415 (1987).

[9] *US v Aluminum Co of America*, 148 F.2d 416 (2d. Cir. 1945).

[10] *Timberlane*, 549 F.2d 597, 611–12.

[11] *Id.* 597, 613.

[12] Kingman Brewster, *Antitrust and American Business Abroad* 446 (1958), quoted in *Timberlane* 549 F.2d 597, 614 note 31.

[13] See e.g. *Mannington Mills Inc v Conaoleum Corp* 595 F.2d 1287, 1297-98; *Restatement Third of Foreign Relations Law s. 403 (2)*.

[14] Re Insurance Antitrust Litigation 723 F. Supp. 464, 490 (N.D. Cal. 1989).

conflict' with English law and policy,[15] but held that the conflict was outweighed by the 'significance of the effects on American commerce, their foreseeability and their purposefulness'.[16] Accordingly, the Court of Appeals reinstated the action.[17] Thus, when the Supreme Court granted review, much of the argument on the international aspect of the case focused on the relative importance under *Timberlane* of conduct – clearly in England, versus effect – largely in the US. Since both lower courts had accepted that there was a conflict between US and English law, not much argument focused on defining the conflict.[18] In the Supreme Court, however, it was precisely the existence of conflict that divided the majority, and that proved decisive to the outcome of the case.

3.   Two Views in the Supreme Court

In many ways, the decision of the Supreme Court was a disappointment, not so much in outcome as in the scope of the decision. Justice David Souter, for the majority of five, wrote: The only substantial question in this case is 'whether there is in fact a true conflict between domestic and foreign law'.[19]

Justice Souter went on to acknowledge the argument of the London reinsurers, supported by the British government, that applying the Sherman Act to their conduct would conflict significantly with English law. But English law did not *require* the agreements that were the basis of the challenge under the Sherman Act. All that English law did was to establish a regulatory, and largely self-regulatory, regime with which the challenged conduct was consistent. 'This', said Justice Souter, citing the Restatement,[20] 'is not to state a conflict .... No conflict exists, for these purposes, "where a person subject to regulation by two states can comply with the laws of both" '.[21]

I want to come back to the Restatement in the penultimate section of this

---

[15]   *Re Insurance Antitrust Litigation* 938 F.2d 919, 933 (9th. Cir. 1991).

[16]   *Id.* 919, 934.

[17]   The Court of Appeals also held that the domestic defendants, who had relied on immunity from antitrust legislation granted by the so-called McCarran-Ferguson Act, 15 U.S.C. s. 1012 (b), had lost their immunity by conspiring with foreign non-exempt parties (938 F.2d 919, 928). The Supreme Court unanimously reversed this holding.

[18]   The US government, which had declined to become involved in the case earlier, submitted a brief *amicus curiae* on behalf of the plaintiffs, primarily devoted to the domestic aspects of the case. The brief of the Solicitor General also argued, however, that application of US law should be stayed only in case of a direct conflict, defined as existing only if:
  (1) the foreign government has directed the defendants to engage in the challenged conduct; or
  (2) the defendants would have frustrated clearly articulated policies of the foreign government if they had not engaged in the disputed conduct.

[19]   113 S. Ct. 2891, 2910. The phrase in quotation marks refers to the opinion of Justice Blackmun in *Société National Industrielle Aérospatiale v US District Court* 482 US 522, 555 (1987).

[20]   Restatement (Third) of Foreign Relations Law, s. 403 comment e, s. 415, comment j.

[21]   113 S. Ct. 2891, 2910.

paper. For the moment, I want to point out only that Justice Souter's opinion seems to equate 'conflict' with 'foreign compulsion'. For conflict, i.e. for inconsistent interests of states, *Timberlane* taught that one should evaluate or balance the interests; for foreign compulsion, in contrast, we had understood since the *Nylon* and *Light Bulb* cartel cases of the early 1950s that no person would be required to carry out an act in another state that is prohibited by the law of that state,[22] in other words that the territorial preference would make balancing unnecessary. But Justice Souter said nothing about the controversial subject of balancing – either for or against – and barely mentioned *Timberlane*. 'We have no need in this case,' he concluded, 'to address other considerations that might inform a decision to refrain from the exercise of jurisdiction on grounds of international comity'.[23] For Justice Scalia and the four-person minority, the case looked entirely different. Justice Scalia started with two presumptions – first, that legislation of Congress, unless a contrary intent appears, 'is meant to apply only within the territorial jurisdiction of the United States'; and secondly, that 'an act of Congress ought never be construed to violate the law of nations if any other possible construction remains', a quotation going back to Chief Justice Marshall,[24] and that customary international law includes limitations on a nation's exercise of its jurisdiction to prescribe.[25] The first point, of course, begs the question whether one looks at conduct (in London), or effect (in the US). If one looks at effect, then application of the Sherman Act would not be extraterritorial.[26] In any event, Justice Scalia conceded that there were numerous precedents for application of the Sherman Act to conduct outside the United States. The second point, about customary international law, led Justice Scalia to the series of court of appeals decisions from *Alcoa*[27] to *Timberlane*[28] and *Mannington Mills*,[29] plus decisions by the US Supreme Court in a series of seamen's cases cited to the Court by the English defendants,[30] as well as to the Restatement. 'Whether the Restatement precisely reflects international law in every detail matters little here,' he wrote, 'as I believe

---

[22] See the decree in *US v Imperial Chemical Industries* 105 F. Supp. 215 (S.D.N.Y. 1952), as quoted in *British Nylon Spinners Ltd v Imperial Chemical Industries Ltd* [1953] ChD 19, 28 (UK Ct. App.), [1955] 1 ChD 37, 53 (Chancery Ct.); *US v General Electric Co* 115 F. Supp. 835, 878 (D.N.J. 1953). See also Restatement s. 441.

[23] 113 S. Ct. 2891, 2911.

[24] 113 S. Ct. 2891, 2919, quoting *Murray v The Charming Betsy* 6 US (2 Cranch) 64, 118 (1804).

[25] *Ibid.*

[26] The Restatement, for instance, looks at jurisdiction based on effect in the territory of the state exercising jurisdiction as an aspect of territorial jurisdiction, s. 402 (1)(c), subject, like other exercises of jurisdiction, to the requirement of reasonableness as set forth in s. 403.

[27] Note 9 above.

[28] Note 6 above.

[29] Note 7 above

[30] 113 S. Ct. 2891, 2919–20, citing *Lauritzen v Larsen* 345 US 571 (1953); *Romero v International Terminal Operating Co* 358 US 354 (1959); *McCulloch v Sociedad Nacional de Marineros de Honduras* 372 US 10 (1963), all emphasising the traditional international law looking to the national law of an ocean-going ship's flag or registry 113 S. Ct. 2891, 2919–20.

this case would be resolved the same way under virtually any conceivable test that takes account of foreign regulatory interests'.[31] Justice Scalia went through the approach of the Restatement, including the factors set out in s. 403(2). 'Rarely', he concluded, perhaps exaggerating in order to emphasise his difference from the majority, 'would these factors point more clearly against application of United States law'.[32]

Further, on the conclusion by the majority that a true conflict would exist only if compliance with US law would constitute violation of the other state's law, Justice Scalia wrote:

> That breathtakingly broad proposition, which contradicts the many cases discussed earlier, will bring the Sherman Act and other laws into sharp and unnecessary conflict with the legitimate interests of other countries – particularly our trading partners.[33]

4.   Some Observations

I want to leave you with three sets of observations. First, on the state of American law on our favourite subject; secondly, on the status and usefulness of the Restatement, which both the majority and the dissent claimed to rely on but interpreted so differently; and finally on the concept of conflict, which I believe needs more exploration.

A.   *The Status of US Law*

I think it is now clear beyond doubt that the Supreme Court – majority and minority – understands that the reach of a nation's law is a subject of *international* law – public customary international law.

In contrast to the European Court of Justice, which is still reluctant to pronounce the 'E' word,[34] the US Supreme Court takes the 'effects doctrine' for granted. It has no doubt that a state may apply its law, i.e. exercise its jurisdiction to prescribe, on the basis of effects caused by the challenged activity in its territory, even when no part of the activity was carried out in its territory. Perhaps if the effect in the US is slight, unintended, and not foreseeable – say a securities fraud centred on the Frankfurt Stock Exchange which had an adverse impact on an American bank that had lent money to the victim of the fraud – the Supreme Court might regard the effect as too remote to support application of US law. But certainly direct, substantial, and foreseeable effect coupled with intent or presumed intent is no longer contestable in the US, and was in fact not contested in the *Insurance Antitrust* case.

---

[31]   113 S. Ct. 2891, 2920–21.
[32]   *Id.* 2891, 2921.
[33]   *Id.* 2891, 2922.
[34]   See the *Woodpulp* case, Case 89/85, Decision of 27 Sept. 1988, (1988) E.C.R. 5193.

The 'foreign compulsion defence' seems to be recognised by the Supreme Court, and even expanded somewhat. A mandatory law at the place of conduct will, I think, trump the law at the place of effect.[35] In the case of true compulsion, the territorial still prevails over the extraterritorial.

The previous 'leading cases', notably *Timberlane* and *Mannington Mills* and also some of the securities cases,[36] seem to have lost some of their significance. While the lower courts in *Insurance Antitrust*, and the litigants in most cases raising the issue of the reach of US economic regulation, sought to place themselves within the *Timberlane* factors, the text on which the Supreme Court focused – and split – was the Restatement, as discussed below.

Does the Supreme Court now reject balancing? Justice Souter did not say so explicitly, though perhaps one can infer that meaning from his statement that the only substantial question is whether there is a true conflict. But if that question were to be answered yes, i.e. if in a future instance a true conflict were found to exist, there would still need to be a way to resolve the conflict. I suspect that some form of evaluation of the respective interests of the concerned states could not be avoided. I would predict that an expressed interest by the US government in law enforcement would weigh more heavily than a private action.[37] In the actual case we saw an intermediate group of plaintiffs, officials of some but not all (or even a majority) of the states of the US, acting as *parens patriae*. But it must be said that my belief in the future of balancing is only a prediction, and has no direct textual support in the majority's opinion.[38]

B. *The Split over the Restatement*

Not for the first time – see, for instance, the two opinions in *Aerospatiale*[39] – both the majority and the dissent in the Supreme Court used the Restatement (Third) of Foreign Relations Law as a principal source of support, and reached quite different conclusions. I suppose in some sense this suggests a failing on the part of the authors of the Restatement, though it is a failing shared with Aristotle, the Bible, the Koran, the American Constitution, and other authorities

---

[35] I do not here address law related to litigation activity, such as banking secrecy, requirements of non-disclosure of economic information, and the like, which are subject to somewhat different evaluation.

[36] For instance *Leasco Data Processing Equipment Corp v Maxwell* 468 F.2d 1326 (2d Cir. 1972), also, e.g. *Bersch v Drexel Firestone Inc* 519 F.2d 974 (2d. Cir. 1975) *cert. denied*, 423 US 1018 (1979); *IIT v Vencap*, 519 F.2d 1001 (2d Cir. 1975).

[37] The official position of the Justice Department is that when it has spoken, i.e. in an action brought on behalf of the US, 'the issue of comity does not arise'. See, e.g. brief for the US as *amicus curiae* in *Hartford Fire Insurance Co v California* 27. I do not believe this is sound, nor that the Supreme Court would accept it.

[38] Of course, the several citations to the Restatement could be marshalled in support of a contention that the Court agrees with that work's basic approach, but I think the evidence supports only a prediction, not a conclusion in this direction.

[39] *Société Nationale Industrielle Aerospatiale v US District Court for the Southern District of Iowa* 482 US 522 (1987).

with much longer life expectancies than a Restatement of the law of international relations. I do think, however, that the effort on the part of the reporters to distinguish between overlap of jurisdiction and clash of prescriptions, which went through many drafts and several votes, did not emerge as clearly as we might have liked. I trust that a small effort here at clarification will not be regarded as out of order.

The scheme of the Restatement with respect to jurisdiction to prescribe has several stages:

(1) Section 402 sets out the basic foundations of jurisdiction – territoriality and nationality – but states that jurisdiction on either basis is subject to s. 403, i.e. the condition that the exercise of jurisdiction not be unreasonable.

(2) Section 403(2) sets out a series of factors to be evaluated in determining whether or not exercise of jurisdiction over a person or activity would be unreasonable. Among these factors are:

'(g) the extent to which another state may have an interest in regulating the activity; and

(h) the likelihood of conflict with regulation by another state.'

Both of these factors call for at least a yellow light in the decision process of the first state, whether undertaken by a legislature, a regulatory agency, or a court. Putting the point another way, the more strongly these factors are present in the second state, the greater is the need to justify the exercise of jurisdiction by the first state on the basis of its strong interest, as measured against the other factors set out, particularly s. 403(2)(a), (b), and (c).[40] The fact that another state has an interest in regulating the activity in question is relevant, even when the objectives of the regulation are entirely consistent (s. 403(2)(g)); the likelihood of conflict (s. 403(2)(h)), i.e. a difference in values, objectives, or regulatory techniques of the two states, weighs more heavily in questioning the reasonableness of exercise of jurisdiction by the first state, but as comment d to s. 403 states, neither subpara. (g) nor subpara. (h) is conclusive that it is unreasonable for the first state to exercise jurisdiction. 'Nor', to quote further from comment d, 'is it conclusive that one state has a strong policy to permit or encourage an activity which the other state wishes to

---

[40] These read, respectively:

(a) the link of the activity to the territory of the regulation state, i.e., the extent to which the activity takes place within the territory, or has substantial, direct, and foreseeable effect upon or in the territory;

(b) the connections, such as nationality, residence, or economic activity, between the regulating state and the person principally responsible for the activity to be regulated, or between that state and those whom the regulation is designed to protect;

(c) the character of the activity to be regulated, the importance of regulation to the regulating state, the extent to which other states regulate such activities, and the degree to which the desirability of such regulation is generally accepted.

prohibit'. But though not *conclusive*, these factors are not insignificant or irrelevant to consideration of the reasonableness of the exercise of jurisdiction. Justice Scalia understood this. Justice Souter apparently did not.

(3) Section 403(3) addresses the situation when, under the criteria of s. 403(2), it would not be unreasonable for each of two states to exercise jurisdiction, both states have done so, and their prescriptions clash. Thus the situation contemplated by s. 403(3) cannot arise until both states have passed the threshold imposed by s. 403(2). In the critical passage in the majority's opinion in *Insurance Antitrust* previously quoted, Justice Souter writes: '*No conflict exists for these purposes* where a person subject to regulation by two states can comply with the laws of both.' (italics added).[41]

The words in quotation marks, as Justice Souter indicates, come from comment e to s. 403, addressed to subs. (3). The illustration there given is of a multinational corporation required to keep its books on a cash basis by one state, and on an accrual basis by the other state. The situation to which subs. (3) is directed does not apply, because while it may be a nuisance, keeping two sets of books is not impossible, and therefore neither state is obliged to evaluate the other's interest with a view to yielding its jurisdiction to the other. But the Restatement does not say that no conflict exists as long as a person can comply with the law of both states. In place of the words that I have italicised, the sentence quoted by Justice Souter begins 'It (i.e., subsection (3)) does not apply . . . .'.

Thus, the misquotation is not just a matter of a few words, but of approach. In the Restatement's scheme, there may well be conflict between the values and objectives of the two states without presenting the intolerable situation of the person caught between incompatible commands – conflict between state interests defined in s. 403(2)(g) and (h). However one appraises the conflict present in *Insurance Antitrust*, to which I turn in the last section, it is clear to me that Justice Scalia understood, and Justice Souter misunderstood the approach of the Restatement.

Just a few more words about the majority's reliance on the Restatement are in order. In addition to the basic scheme set out in ss. 402 and 403, the Restatement contains a series of sections illustrating exercise of jurisdiction to prescribe in particular areas – tax, securities regulation, multinational corporations and, in s. 415, competition law. The majority opinion in *Insurance Antitrust*, just before the quotation reproduced above, quotes from comment j to s. 415 as follows: '[T]he fact that conduct is lawful in the state in which it took place will not, of itself, bar application of the United States antitrust laws.'[42]

---

[41] 113 S. Ct. 2891, 2910.
[42] 113 S. Ct. 2891, 1910.

Here (except for omission of the introductory word 'Ordinarily') the quotation is complete. But the key is the phrase 'of itself'. One cannot tell, merely from the fact that state B does not prohibit or punish a given activity, whether it has a strong interest in continuance of the activity, or in non-interference in the activity by state A. But unless foreign compulsion is the only criterion,[43] one cannot draw the opposite inference either. I would now add that the fact that a state does not require a given conduct or activity does not, of itself, demonstrate that the state is disinterested in continuance of the conduct or activity.

The question remains whether there is a conflict (a conflict of state interests) which under international law needs to be evaluated. While I am not as certain as Justice Scalia how such an evaluation comes out, I am clear that to say that the *Insurance Antitrust* case presented no conflict at all is quite mistaken, and certainly at odds with the scheme of the Restatement.

C.   *Evaluating Conflict of Jurisdictions*

It seems clear that if the British government had *ordered* the London underwriters to stop selling long-tail policies and to exclude sudden and accidental pollution from liability policies that they reinsured, Justice Souter would have viewed the case as presenting a 'true conflict'. Though one cannot be sure, there is good reason to believe that he, or at least some of his colleagues in the narrow majority, would have come around to the position of the dissenters that the US should defer to the UK's strongly expressed interest, and accordingly should decline to uphold exercise of jurisdiction to apply US law to the challenged activity. The question that I want to leave with you is what lesser expression of interest on the part of the British government would or should tip the balance against application of US law, assuming that you accept the argument that I have made throughout this paper that it is an error to confuse the foreign compulsion defence with the question of conflict of jurisdiction.

Consider the following proposals:

(1) Suppose that English law had provided that any agreements among underwriters concerning the terms and conditions of reinsurance policies had to be submitted to the Minister of Trade for approval, and that the agreements here challenged had been submitted and approved. That would not rise to the level of compulsion, but it would be unequivocal evidence of the British government's exercise of jurisdiction to prescribe. I am not sure that this would meet Justice Souter's threshold of conflict, but it would make Justice Scalia's conclusion that the UK had established 'a comprehensive regulatory scheme governing the London reinsurance

---

[43] Cf. *US v First National City Bank* 396 F.2d 897 (2d Cir. 1968).

markets . . .' which conflicted with the application of US antitrust law more convincing.

(2) Suppose, alternatively, a statutory scheme according to which agreements among underwriters had to be submitted to the Minister and would go into effect 30 days after submission unless *dis*approved, and that the agreements in question had been so submitted and not disapproved. This, too, would be an exercise of jurisdiction to prescribe, and an expression of the values and priorities of the UK, but with somewhat lesser involvement of the government.

(3) What about a scheme providing for approval (or non-disapproval) by an industry committee serving under delegation from the government?

I am not ready to propose an answer to each of these statements, or to other possible variations. My point is that there is a significant space between such indifference on the part of state B to a given activity carried on in its territory as to remove all doubt about the reasonableness of the exercise of jurisdiction by state A, and such compulsion by state B as would be required to create a 'true conflict' as defined by the majority in *Insurance Antitrust*. Moreover, while I have long been sceptical about assertions by governments of state B – including statements in *amicus curiae* briefs – that they have 'a strong interest in the above-entitled case', I am also sceptical about someone in state A – typically the US – passing judgment on the manner in which economic regulation or administrative law is practiced in other states, whether by compulsion, 'administrative guidance', industry committees, or whatever.

In determining whether state A should exercise jurisdiction over an activity significantly linked to state B, one important question, in my submission, is whether B has a demonstrable system of values and priorities different from those of state A that would be impaired by the application of the law of A. I am not suggesting that if the answer to this question is yes, A must stay its hand. The magnitude of A's interest, the effect of the challenged activity within A, the intention of the actors, and the other factors that I hope will not disappear from view remain important. My message to this Conference, and to the international legal community generally, is that conflict is not just about commands, but about interests, values, and priorities. While measuring and weighing the elements of transnational conflict is not easy, the very effort to do so in the long run cannot but promote harmonisation and the rational allocation of jurisdiction that should be the goal of us all.

Sir Ian Sinclair:

I am most grateful to you, Andy. That was a very useful analysis of this recent case before the Supreme Court which I was in fact aware of and which will be familiar to most around this table. Some I know have strong views on it and in particular Gary Born who brought the case to my attention. So perhaps Gary might want to comment on it.

Gary Born:

As usual I agree with much of what Andy says. Nevertheless, I have some different perspectives on a couple of points. One is that the Supreme Court concluded that the foreign parties conceded the jurisdictional issue; in particular, the Court concluded at oral argument the British reinsurers admitted that there was statutory jurisdiction. Given the way that the US Supreme Court looked at the legal issue – these days, that is relatively formalistically – that was, in my view, a fatal concession because it put the foreign insurers in the position of needing to rely on what the court imputed as a fairly fuzzy doctrine of international comity to overcome the statutory pronounced presumption.

Andreas F. Lowenfeld:

That is because the oral argument was made basically by an antitrust lawyer and not an international lawyer.

Gary Born:

I'm not sure.

Andreas F. Lowenfeld:

Were you there?

Gary Born:

No, but I looked at the transcript and the Court cites from the transcript in its opinion. I'm sure you wouldn't have made that concession. In any event, if you have a situation in which the court does not believe that jurisdiction has been conceded, I think that Justice Scalia's analysis in dissent is a lot more likely to be persuasive. Simply put, if jurisdiction, rather than comity, is the issue, I think a much stronger case can be made against the extraterritorial application of US law.

Second, one of the more interesting things that the Supreme Court has done over the last two or three years is to have embraced the territoriality presumption whole-heartedly. In the *EEOC v Aramco*, Title VII of the civil rights employment discrimination statute pretty clearly was intended to apply outside the US. Nevertheless, the Supreme Court limited the statute to US territory relying on the territoriality presumption and citing things like *Charming Betsy* and similar decisions.

Andreas F. Lowenfeld:

Congress immediately amends the . . .

Gary Born:

That's right but in a different regulatory context, like antitrust, I think it is less likely that one would get that sort of congressional action. The only other point that I would like to make is that I think Justice Souter's opinion was in fact much more negative on the question of what comity means and in the circumstances in which it can be incorporated.

Unlike Andy, I don't think you can fairly rely on the *Insurance Antitrust* cases for the proposition that international law and international comity are part of the US law and automatically get incorporated into some statute. Indeed, Justice Souter went out of his way to say almost exactly the opposite. He said he was not at all certain that international comity would ever be a valid basis for overcoming a positive statutory command, but that even assuming it were, comity meant only what most international lawyers had always thought was foreign sovereign compulsion. It seems to me that we have the very troubling prospect that at least the five justices including Justice Souter and a majority, might well say, no, comity simply isn't an appropriate consideration for US courts.

Andreas F. Lowenfeld:

I have never liked the word comity, because I think that comity is something different from obligation. You are quite right, that Souter moves on more to comity, but do you think I exaggerate the acceptance of the basic propositions?

Gary Born:

I think that there is a significant chance that the current court will generally refuse to apply 'comity' and that, if it does, 'comity' will be given a very narrow meaning. Still, I think there is both a silver lining and a black cloud on the horizon in the case. I think the silver lining is that if someone comes in and argues vigorously that the antitrust laws must be construed in light of the territoriality presumption and the restrictive use of jurisdiction that were reflected in traditional and contemporary private and public international law, that argument has a reasonable chance of succeeding. The negative argument that may pop up on the horizon is that if that argument loses the fluffy notion of comity it is unlikely to succeed. I think that the US courts are just not interested in that at this stage.

Harold G. Maier:

One of the problems with these cases is that we tend to start with labels and wind up with policy rather than the other way around. The real question is whether this is the kind of US statute that ought to be applied in this type of circumstance. Once that question is answered, we can attach the appropriate labels. We ought to affix the label to describe why a policy does or doesn't make sense. For years, Andy and I have been arguing about what is 'comity' and what isn't. I do not care what one calls 'comity'. There are some contexts in which the US courts don't apply statutes to foreign events because it would not be in the US interest to do so in light of what other countries might do in response in later cases.

The decision Andy discussed suggests that the court is not taking the position that where Congress gives a direct command, the court will refuse to follow the statute anyway. If the courts should do that, I think we have real problems, but I don't see the courts going that far. The court, after all, has to follow the command of its legislature. If the legislature's command is clear, the court has to do what the legislature ordered.

Unlike Gary, I do not think that the command was clear in the *Aramco* case. My sense is that there might have been an implicit feeling on Congress's part, if they thought about it at all, which I doubt, that this legislation would have been applied abroad. All the court would have had to do in *Aramco* was to find that the statute applied to an American employer operating abroad on the basis of the nationality principle and it would have avoided the whole analytical problem.

Andreas F. Lowenfeld:

One point if I might just add that was not in the Supreme Court's opinion but was in the arguments. The arguments said the British are out of it anyhow because the European Community is undertaking a big investigation about insurance and the notion that the debate between the British and the Americans is really in the long term about a value judgment is obsolete. Now, that did not come up in the opinion but it was argued, particularly in the briefs by the state attorneys general, and with some force. We ignored it because we really didn't know how to answer that.

Philip Bovey:

There was a particularly nice footnote which said that there was no requirement on the British government to be logical. There isn't a statute that required it.

Andreas F. Lowenfeld:

I thought the British government's brief by the way was like one of those things you get when you rent a car, you push a button and then the whole contract gets typed out. They've done the same brief over and over and didn't really specify the interest in any meaningful way.

Philip Bovey:

But you see it's interesting, of course, I've found that they know what the connection is but I simply want to make a personal declaration: that I am not and never have been a name at Lloyd's ...

Andreas F. Lowenfeld:

Lucky you!

Philip Bovey:

. . . but quite clearly obviously this is dealing in part with asbestos or some sort of potential asbestos.

Andreas F. Lowenfeld:

Sure!

Philip Bovey:

Obviously. Is something falling to the ground?

Cynthia Lichtenstein:

That is exactly what I wanted to ask. In thinking about a definition of conflict of law, of a conflict, when you say 'law' do you mean the law of the UK or do you mean what should be their law since the UK is a member state of the European Community?

Philip Bovey:

Well, I was going to get us to concentrate initially on the matter of what Andy was saying. What do we mean by 'conflict' and what do we mean by conflict with the laws and policies of another state, particularly when the law is reflected, deliberately reflected, in an absence of restitution upon an empty regulation? I meant that, this is where I think the shoe really pinches, really hurts. When state A has taken a deliberate policy decision that it will not seek to regulate this kind of activity. State B, in this case the US, has taken the deliberate policy decision that it will regulate. Now when the two conflict which one is going to prevail? I think this really . . .

Andreas F. Lowenfeld:

I think it is always hard to prove. Maybe, for example, if you have a statute and you apply it and you have lots of legislation.

Gary Born:

But the absence of a statute is just as significant.

Andreas F. Lowenfeld:

Well, I agree but then . . . I remember advising a former student who was representing the Dominican Republic in some controversy. I've just forgotten exactly what the controversy was. The American Civil Aeronautics Board was seeking to impose truth in advertising on travel agents in the Dominican Republic and I said to my former student who was advising them, 'pass a statute or regulation, I don't care what you do, but show that you are regulating these agents, because otherwise the Americans are going to say there is a vacuum and we can fill it'.

Philip Bovey:

The self-regulation at Lloyd's was actually a complete red herring. Because what let them off antitrust law in the UK was not that there was self-regulation at Lloyd's but that they were in the insurance business because there is a general exclusion from antitrust for all insurance in the UK just as there is in the US.

I am sure it was psychologically important to the Supreme Court and certainly to the arguments further down that this was Lloyd's and self-regulation and I am equally certain that it was important to the defendants because I don't think they would have behaved in the same way. Supposing they had gone to the European Commission and actually, when you say it ought to be our law, it is our law. Article 85 is our law.

Andreas F. Lowenfeld:

It's directly applicable, like it or not.

Philip Bovey:

But supposing they had gone to the Commission and got an individual exemption with the Commission having weighed out the particular aspects of it. Now they still wouldn't have been compelled to do it because a Commission exemption does not make it compulsory but it does show that an independent governmental body has addressed the issues.

Andreas F. Lowenfeld:

But it depends on what you mean by it. If they had gone to the European Commission or the Board of Trade or whatever it is in London and said we are having a meeting on Friday and we're going to change the reinsurance form to exclude long-tail claims and sudden pollution claims and here is the draft of our agreement. Will you approve it? If the minister or the Commission had approved it, I think the answer is quite clear, the case would come out the other way. But if it is just generally, we have this market and we meet all the time and it really does not fit the competition laws, then it is still doubtful.

Philip Bovey:

But the difference is the approval and not the compulsion.

Cynthia Lichtenstein:

There is a problem with that because the gravamen of the US complaint was not the form itself but the pressure on other insurers. If they continued to use the former form they could not get reinsurance. It was the boycott, not the form.

Andreas F. Lowenfeld:

That is right. There is no doubt there was a meeting and it is also true that some of the people from Lloyd's came to the US and gave speeches and sort of cheered on the form. So that there is some doubt about the real effects and whether they dominated the market. There is no doubt that there was an agreement. I think that you are quite right. My view is that compulsion is too strong and won't stand up.

But specific approval is different from general exemption which is what we have, general exemption plus self-regulation. I would like to see a case where it comes up the other way around. Where the US deregulates.

For example US airlines. I hung around Frankfurt Airport for three hours today, because there was nothing else to do and it was astonishing how many American airlines are there and we know that the Germans are getting angry about that. Now, there is already an interim capacity agreement, but suppose that some German or European regulation comes along when the US has substantially deregulated. Will the US accept European regulation of American airlines? That will show a true conflict, in my view, though the American approach is one of values, not compulsion.

Karl M. Meessen:

To wait for a specific regulatory action on the part of the foreign state is quite an odd proposition in my opinion since it solicits this kind of blocking statute and the enactment of all sorts of laws covering certain conduct. I wonder, and that's actually my question to you, Andy, why didn't they rely to a greater extent on *Aerospatiale* in the insurance case? After all, in *Aerospatiale* there was no foreign legislation in any way prohibiting certain types of taking evidence in the US. The conflict in *Aerospatiale* was just, if you like, a philosophical one. It's a different approach, that civil law countries take, with England somewhere in between the two, to handling the taking of evidence. Even in the majority opinion of *Aerospatiale*, I think they were more open-minded in their recognition of this foreign resentment against the imposition of the American approach than I gather from the insurance case, and I must say I find the Souter opinion quite deplorable.

Final question to you Andy: even if there had been specific approval or anything backing the Lloyd's business conduct of not extending reinsurance policies, in those cases – even if that had been the case Justice Souter may have recognised that there was a comity issue. But whether he would have weighed it the way you would have liked to have him weigh the issues, that is not really clear to me in reading the opinion.

Andreas F. Lowenfeld:

Well let me answer the third question first. I think that you are right. Justice Souter might not have changed, but then he probably would not have gotten a majority. I think Justice Blackmun, for example, who dissents in *Aerospatiale* would have then joined Scalia. Step back a minute about the US Supreme Court, and maybe Gary has a different view, but I think in the period of the Burger Court, in the 1970s and early 1980s, we had a series of pro-international decisions. We had *Zapata* on forum clauses,[44] *Scherk* on arbitration even in a securities case,[45] we had *Mitsubishi*,[46] which even in the antitrust context enforced an arbitration clause. The Court began to shift in the two cases involving the Hague Service and Evidence Conventions, *Schlunk*[47] and *Aerospatiale*.[48] It shifts a little bit more. In cases not in the economic area, the case involving the Haitian refugees, the kidnapping in Mexico and the search in Mexico. There are three cases where the Supreme Court says: well, international law is nice but not for us – and now they don't say that in this case. So I'm a little more optimistic than Gary. I was trying to think how you could use *Aerospatiale*. We, of course, cited *Aerospatiale* but we didn't make much of it because we thought in the end all you can really say is well everybody says that you should consider the foreign interests, not that they should trump. *Aerospatiale*, in my view was very badly argued because the French and the Germans were *amici* and soon said the treaty was compulsory when it clearly wasn't and that irritated the Court.

Karl M. Meessen:

That is indeed the reason why I did not say so in my opinion submitted to the Court.[49]

---

[44]   *The Bremen v Zapata Off-Shore Co* 407 US 1 (1972).
[45]   *Scherk v Alberto-Culver Co* 417 US 506 (1974).
[46]   *Mitsubishi Motors Corp v Soler Chrysler-Plymouth Inc* 473 US 614 (1985).
[47]   *Volkswagenwerk Aktiengesellschaft v Schlunk*, 486 US 694 (1988).
[48]   *Société Nationale Aérospatiale v US District Court* 482 US 522 (1987).
[49]   25 *ILM* 832 (1986).

Chapter II

Extraterritorial Taxation in International Law

Rutsel Silvestre J. Martha

1. Introduction

This paper deals with the question(s) whether and if so in what manner public international law relates to extraterritorial taxation by nation states. It explores the practice of states, judicial decisions, awards of international tribunals and writings of publicists. It is mainly based on my book *The Jurisdiction to Tax in International Law*.[50] A brief discussion of the development of international law with respect to the jurisdiction to tax will serve to state the general principles concerning jurisdiction as an attribute of sovereignty. Thereupon the extraterritorial taxation of nationals and aliens (including legal persons such as corporations) will be addressed.

2. Panorama of Extraterritorial Tax Practices

In the practice of international taxation the question of extraterritoriality appears to concentrate on the worldwide versus the source taxation of income,[51] rather

---

[50] Martha, *The Jurisdiction to Tax in International Law*, No. 9 in the Series on International Taxation (Kluwer Law & Tax Publishers); see also A.H. Qureshi, 'The Freedom of a State to Legislate in Fiscal Matters and International Law', *Bulletin of Intl Fiscal Documentation* 14–21 (1987) and for a compilation of texts, cases and materials, A.H. Qureshi, *The Public International Law of Taxation* (1944).

[51] Cf. K. Vogel, *Worldwide vs Source Taxation of Income – a Review and Re-evaluation of Arguments*, Part I, *Intertax* 216–229 (1988), Part II, *Intertax* 310–320 (1988) and Part III, *Intertax* 393–402 (1988).

than the taxation of nationals versus aliens or residents versus non-residents. This is mainly due to the fact that practically all countries levy income tax while none of these countries forgoes taxing domestic source income, irrespective of whether such income is derived by nationals, aliens, residents or non-residents. However, national legislations differ considerably with regard to the definition of domestic source income, which raises questions of extraterritoriality in their own right. Even less consistency exists in the practice of states with regard to the taxation of foreign source income. Besides the fact that taxation of foreign income is inherently extraterritorial, the problem of extraterritoriality is' exacerbated by the fact that no established universal rule of conventional or customary international law exists concerning the delimitation between domestic source income and foreign source income, or even the attribution of income to the particular taxpayers.

In Latin American countries, and also in some European, Asian, and African countries, the so-called territoriality of income tax legislation is traditionally emphasised, which, in essence, amounts to source-based taxation. However, as the UN ad hoc group of experts on tax treaties found out, in recent Latin American legislation and treaties, the principle of territoriality has somewhat receded. In any case, even amongst countries which confine themselves to taxing domestic source income only and do not tax foreign income at all, there may be considerable differences in practice. For instance, Argentina, Hong Kong, Kenya, Zambia and Uruguay tax both natural persons and corporations only with respect to their domestic source income. But Brazil and France tax natural persons on their worldwide income, yet they confine the taxation of corporations to their domestic source income. It may also happen that the so-called secondary withholding tax dividend income received by foreign shareholders of a foreign corporation from sources within the taxing state is deemed to be domestic source income.

The taxation of corporations and natural persons on their worldwide income is mostly found in the practice of industrialised countries. Some of these countries, however, do not tax certain classes of foreign income. This is the case in the Netherlands where foreign income which is derived from, *inter alia*, dividends and permanent establishments abroad is exempted from taxation, provided that such income is taxable in the country where it arose. Similarly, Australia exempts foreign income other than dividends, interests and royalties, subject to the same condition of taxability abroad. Other countries, such as Switzerland, exclude unconditionally foreign business income derived through foreign-based permanent establishments, or income from foreign real estate. There are also countries (e.g. Germany) which allow domestic parent companies with subsidiaries in developing countries to claim a credit for the amount of tax which would have been due on the dividends if the subsidiary were a domestic company. The same effect is achieved in countries where dividends are exempted from the parents' corporation tax.

Finally, by treating legally independent subsidiaries of domestic corporations as independent taxable entities, countries do not consider income of foreign-based subsidiaries as taxable in the country of residence of the parent until remitted to the parent. Major exemptions are made to the latter as a consequence of anti-tax-avoidance techniques such as lifting of the corporate veil, the German Organschaft or the Californian unitary taxation. In addition to the extraterritoriality that emanates from the foregoing tax practice, issues of extraterritoriality occasionally arise where countries attempt to directly or indirectly enforce their tax laws beyond their territory. Moreover, international aviation and offshore mining have led to the practice of extraterritorial taxation of aliens for their use of the airspace, and the extraterritorial taxation of offshore mineral activities.

Except in the latter cases, the criticism of extraterritorial taxation is rarely based on arguments derived from positive public international law. Mainly equity considerations and considerations of an economic nature are invoked. This may be attributed to the view held by some that public international law contains no rules governing the jurisdiction to tax.[52] However, the better view would seem to be that general international law contains no conflict rules to regulate the preference in cases of concurrent fiscal jurisdiction nor does general international law adequately deal with the disparity between fiscal concepts, such as the definitions of income, permanent establishment, residence, etc.[53]

Moreover, problems of extraterritorial taxation find solutions to a substantial degree under double taxation treaties.[54] Therefore, issues related to the jurisdiction to tax in international law are of limited relevance to the day-to-day international tax experience, and problems of international law seem to be confined to issues arising under the law of treaties, particularly the interpretation of treaties.[55]

It will be seen that the question of whether extraterritorial taxation is permissible under international law should be given an affirmative answer. However, this is far from saying that the jurisdiction to tax is unfettered. In this respect, those who deny or question the role of public international law in matters of taxation are proved wrong. Many publicists have emphasised that a nation's taxing power is primarily a problem of international law.[56] Tribunals, including the US Supreme Court[57] and the German Supreme Tax Court[58] confirm the foregoing.

---

[52] E.g. Wurzel, 'Foreign Investment and Extraterritorial Taxation', *Colum. L. Rev.* 209 (1937), M. Norr, 'Jurisdiction to Tax and International Income', 17 *Tax Law Review* 431 (1962).

[53] Martha, *op. cit.*, note 50 above, Ch. 4, s. XIII.

[54] See comprehensively, K. Vogel, *Double Taxation Conventions* (1991).

[55] E.g. J. M. Mössner, 'Zur Auslegung von Doppelbesteuerungsabkommen', in *Liber amicorum I. Seidl-Hohenveldern*, 430 *et seq.* (1988); see also sources cited Martha, *op. cit.*, note 50 above, at 14 note 37.

[56] E.g. K. Friedrich, *Gibt es eine Völkerrechtliche Grenze für die Höhe der Besteuerung* 16 (1972).

[57] In *Burnet v Brooks* 288 US 378 the US Supreme Court declared: 'We determine national power in relation to other countries and their subjects by applying the principles of jurisdiction recognized in international relations'.

[58] See H.-W. Bayer, 'Das Völkerrecht in der Rechtsprechung des Bundesfinanzhofs', 38 *Steuer und Wirtschaft* 61 (1981).

3.   Fiscal Sovereignty in International Law

In his article contributed to the 1952 *British Yearbook of International Law*,[59] Albrecht asserted that state jurisdiction to tax 'is justified in international law as an attribute of statehood or sovereignty, limited by international law and exercised in varying manners according to the policies of the states possessed of it'.[60] The US-Mexican Claims Commission, in its award of 10 October 1930 in the case of *George Cook v United Mexican States*, held: 'The right of the State to levy taxes constitutes an inherent part of its sovereignty'.[61] This also reveals that jurisdiction and sovereignty are not synonymous. Accordingly, Mann states that 'jurisdiction is an aspect of sovereignty, it is coexistent with it, and indeed, incidental to but also limited by, the State's sovereignty'.[62] Therefore he points out that jurisdiction should be conceptually distinguished from sovereignty, because the doctrine of jurisdiction deals with the question of whether and under what circumstances a state has the right of regulation, and sovereignty is the concept by virtue of which jurisdiction is exercised; as Lord MacMillan said, jurisdiction is 'an essential attribute of sovereignty'.[63] Or, as Professor Brownlie prefers to say, '[j]urisdiction is an aspect of sovereignty and refers to judicial, legislative, and administrative competence'.[64]

It is therefore clear that, in principle, fiscal jurisdiction cannot exist without sovereignty. The norm of international law dictates that jurisdiction is an attribute of sovereignty, and based thereon a sovereign (i.e. a state) may exercise jurisdiction. This caused Professor Ryser to note:

> Il existe donc apparemment une relation entre l'étendue de la juridiction fiscale et les limites de la souveraineté étatique. Mais où se trouvent ces limites? Sont-elles définies de manière précise et contraignante?[65]

This is indeed the right question because if jurisdiction is an attribute of sovereignty then it must be the case that the limits of fiscal jurisdiction are similar to those of national sovereignty. Consequently, identifying the limits of sovereignty is tantamount to identifying the limits of every type of jurisdiction, including tax or fiscal jurisdiction.[66]

Sovereignty is basically a unitary concept which in the course of time and in the light of the objects of regulation has come to represent personal sovereignty,

---

[59]   A.R. Albrecht, 'The Taxation of Aliens Under International Law', 29 *BYIL* 145 (1952).
[60]   *Ibid.*, 148.
[61]   *Cook v Mexico*, 4. RIAA 595 (1930).
[62]   F.A. Mann, 'The Doctrine of Jurisdiction in International Law', *Studies in Intl L.* 9 (1973).
[63]   *The Cristina* (1938) A.C., 485, 496, 497.
[64]   I. Brownlie, *Principles of Public International Law*, 299 (4th edn, 1990); R. Jennings and A. Watts, *Oppenheim's International Law*, 136, 456 (Vol. I, Part 1) (9th edn, 1992).
[65]   W. Ryser, 'Extraterritorialité et Droit Fiscal', 39 *Außenwirtschaft* 136 (1984).
[66]   Mann, *loc. cit.*, note 62 above, at 9, but see *Oppenheim's International Law*, *op. cit.*, note 64 above, at 136, 457.

territorial sovereignty, and functional sovereignty.[67] Rather than being phenomena *sui generis*, they are in fact three modalities of one genus, although caution should be exercised with respect to the third modality.

Still one basic rule remains – which for some is a customary rule – that must serve as the most fundamental and basic test in matters of international taxation: A state may only fiscally attach those persons and objects subject to its supremacy. The personal sovereignty of a state is the supremacy it has over persons (natural or juridical), and comprises the right to extend its laws to regulate conduct or attach legal consequences to the conduct of these people wherever they may be.[68]

Territorial sovereignty constitutes the second yardstick to determine the limit of sovereignty and comprises the power of a state to exercise supreme authority over all persons and things within its territory.[69]

Functional sovereignty is a rather new concept, which is actually a direct result of the developments during the present century in the area of the law of the sea. However, it is also closely linked to the growth of international organisations.[70]

Personal, territorial, and functional sovereignty are, or will be seen as, conceptual antecedents of the fiscal jurisdiction of states. These types of sovereignty can reside conjunctively or disjunctively, in one or several entities which are therefore entitled to jurisdiction. Once stated, it becomes possible to deduce the fundamental elements of international taxation, and thus discern the rules governing extraterritorial taxation.

4. The Limits of Fiscal Jurisdiction

The question then becomes how to establish the limits of fiscal jurisdiction. For that purpose, the concepts of personal, territorial and functional sovereignty must be introduced from which the fundamental elements of international taxation can be deduced.[71] These elements become the crucial tests for determining the extent (legitimacy) of (state) jurisdiction in matters of taxation.

The first element, called 'fiscal attachment', serves to explain the relationship between the holder of fiscal jurisdiction (the state or international organisation, as the case may be) and the fiscal subject or object of taxation, which determines the legality of the exercise of fiscal jurisdiction.[72] This concept of attachment,

---

[67] Martha, *op. cit.* note 50 above, Ch. 2, s. VI; B. Conforti, *International Law and the Role of Domestic Legal Systems* 133–152 (1993).

[68] *Oppenheim's International Law*, *op. cit.*, note 64 above, at 138; Conforti (*op. cit.*, note 67 above, at 150), however, adheres to a more restricted definition.

[69] *Id.*, para. 137.

[70] See generally, W. Riphagen, 'Some Reflections on Functional Sovereignty', *Neth. YBIL* 227 (1974).

[71] Martha, note 50 above, Ch. 2, s. VII.

[72] A.A. Knechtle, *Basic Problems in International Fiscal Law*, 35–36 (1979).

when applied to legal subjects (i.e. natural and juristic persons), can be said to exist either as a consequence of personal sovereignty (nationality), territorial sovereignty (residence or presence in territory short of residence) or functional sovereignty. This type of attachment is called 'personal fiscal attachment'.[73] When the relationship between the state and the fiscal subject is indirect, i.e. through the object of the tax which is located in the taxing state, it is called an 'economic fiscal attachment' (property and source of income within the taxing state).[74] Finally, there are areas where international law allows states to exercise certain functional powers in connection with specific rights: that is the case with the continental shelf, the exclusive economic zone, the 'area', i.e. the seabed and subsoil of the high seas, and arguably, the flight information regions. In these cases, one speaks of 'functional fiscal attachment'.[75]

The second element is called fiscal liability, which expresses the extent of the tax liability or, to put it differently, the scope of the holder of fiscal jurisdiction's taxing power in relation to a specific fiscal subject. Fiscal liability can be either unlimited, i.e. the holder of fiscal jurisdiction can assess the worldwide income in its tax assessment, or limited, i.e. the taxing state has the right to tax only the income derived from sources within its territory. Unlimited fiscal liability corresponds with personal fiscal attachment based on nationality and residence.[76] Limited fiscal liability corresponds with personal fiscal attachment short of residence, economic fiscal attachment[77] and functional fiscal attachment.[78] Thus, as a rule, the type of fiscal attachment throws light not only on the subjective side of the fiscal relationship, but also on the extent of the fiscal liability.

5.   The Rules of Fiscal Jurisdiction Reflected in State Practice

The rules of fiscal jurisdiction under general international law, established on the basis of the foregoing exercise and confirmed by state practice, can be summarised as follows:

(1) Notwithstanding the questioning of nationality as a proper basis for fiscal attachment, from an international law perspective, a state is fully entitled to tax its nationals wherever they may be. Practice reveals that there are very few states that use this entitlement. Such entitlement extends to the liberty of states to tax the income of their citizens irrespective of the source of such income and irrespective of where they are located.[79] The question here is, of course, how to determine who is the national of a

---

[73] *Ibid.*, at 36.
[74] *Id.*
[75] Martha, note 50 above, at 55 and 165 *et seq.*
[76] Knechtle, note 72 above, at 36.
[77] *Id.*
[78] Martha, note 50 above, at 55.
[79] *Cook v Tait* 265 US 47 (1924).

certain state. As to the nationality of natural persons, international law essentially leaves this to national law to determine.[80] On the other hand, international law holds that the nationality of juridical persons, e.g. corporations, is that of the state of incorporation.[81]

(2) The jurisdiction of a state to tax aliens (natural persons and juristic persons) is based on territorial sovereignty and takes the form of fiscal attachment on the basis of residence, fiscal attachment short of residence and economic fiscal attachment. In the first case, the alien can be taxed in the same way as nationals may be taxed, i.e. taxation on worldwide income.[82] In the absence of residency, an alien may only be taxed on the income derived from sources within the taxing state.[83] Non-resident aliens may also be taxed on property located within the taxing state and it is not important that there is no physical contact between the taxing state and the taxed person himself.[84]

(3) In addition to the entitlement to tax on the basis of nationality and territoriality, international law recognises, prospectively, the right to tax on a functional basis.[85] This right, however, as it turns out, does not follow from the 1958 Geneva Convention on the Continental Shelf.[86] This treaty does not confer functional fiscal jurisdiction; this is contrary to what has been assumed by some without proper testing.[87] Yet, prospectively, the 1982 Montego Bay Convention on the Law of the Seas does confer such right under the regimes of continental shelf and the exclusive economic zone respectively.[88] An analysis of the relevant state practice in the fiscal area reveals that it would be unwarranted to assert that the 1982 Convention crystallised or generated customary international law on the matter.[89] The 1982 Montego Bay Convention introduces an additional phenomenon: original fiscal jurisdiction of a territorial nature attributed to an international organisation.[90] The International Seabed Authority, as conceived under the 1982 treaty, will be entrusted with jurisdiction over the seabed and subsoil of maritime

---

[80] *Nationality Decrees Issued in Tunis and Morocco* PCIJ Series B, No. 4.
[81] 'Barcelona Traction (Second Phase)', *ICJ Rep.* (1970); see, however, *Oppenheim's International Law* note 64 above, para. 380 (Vol. I, Parts 2 and 4).
[82] Martha, note 50 above, at 90–93.
[83] *Imperial Tobacco Co of India v Commissioners of Income Tax* 27 ILR 103 (1958).
[84] E.g. *Johnson v Commissioner of Stamp Duties* (1956) A.C. 331, 352, per Lord Keith of Avonholme.
[85] Martha, note 50 above, Ch. 3, s. XI.
[86] *Ibid.*, at 115–129 and 165–174; see also *Oil Tanker Officer Liability Case* 74 ILR 204 (1987).
[87] E.g. Conforti, note 67 above, at 144.
[88] Martha, note 50 above, at 129–133.
[89] *Ibid.*, at 165–170; for a description of the taxation of offshore business activities, see A.A. Skaar, *Permanent Establishment – Erosion of a Tax Treaty Principle*, 419 *et seq.* (1991).
[90] See generally, International Fiscal Association, *Taxation of Income Arising from the International Seabed* (1982); W. Hauser, 'An International Fiscal Regime for Deep Seabed Mining: Comparisons to Land-Based Mining', 19 *Harvard Int L. J.* 759 (1978); and Martha, note 50 above, at 133–138.

areas outside national jurisdiction and will exercise powers that have fiscal implications. As to jurisdiction over flight information regions, the principle and practice are still inconclusive.[91]

It may strike the observer that the conclusions under (2) very much resemble the practice of the majority of states. One exception is with regard to unitary worldwide taxation which will be discussed later. The conclusions under (1) are more disputable but are nevertheless valid as a matter of international law. Some of the conclusions under (3) defy certain untested assumptions with respect to the jurisdiction over maritime zones.

6.   Suppressing Extraterritorial Tax Practices

It is believed that some general conclusions can be drawn from the study of state practice with respect to extraterritorial taxation, which can be helpful at the practical level of international taxation. To be specific, certain regulative principles for the pursuit of the suppression of extraterritorial taxation can be extracted from it:

(1) The concept of excess of fiscal jurisdiction could be used for defining the area of negotiation. For, it is clear, that a position based on illegally exercised jurisdiction cannot be the subject of negotiations except for the purpose of undoing it. Once illegally based jurisdiction is taken away, a clear picture of the legally genuine interests of the states concerned can be drawn.

(2) The idea that international law often presupposes national legal orders by operating through incomplete norms affords an indication as to how to suppress extraterritorial taxation caused by distortions in fiscal categories, such as residence, nationality, income, etc. The message here is that tax treaties should unify the concepts by providing exhaustive definitions that are not dependent on national regulations or concepts.

(3) Finally, modern undertakings aimed at relieving the burden of double taxation should also contemplate the new areas in which states are about to be allowed to exercise tax jurisdiction, namely in the maritime areas within national jurisdiction. Similarly, the fiscal competence of certain international organisations should also be taken into account.

This approach has also some practical instructions that can be used by any legislator, tax enforcer, attorney or tribunal (domestic or international) facing situations involving extraterritorial taxation. These instructions are in the form of

---

[91] *Pan American World Airways Inc v The Queen* 129 D.L.R. 3(d) 257 (1981); Martha, note 50 above, at 138–139.

four questions which were used by the Permanent Court of International Justice in the *Lotus* case:[92]

(1) Does the case come within the sovereignty of the claiming state on the basis of either personal, territorial or functional sovereignty?

(2) If it is found to be within the state's sovereign sphere, (in order to verify the legality of the assertion) is there at the relevant time any prohibitive rule developed *a posteriori* that limits the state's jurisdiction in tax matters?

(3) Alternatively, if it is found to be outside the sovereign sphere of the state claiming tax, is there a permissive rule developed *a posteriori* allowing it to exercise fiscal jurisdiction?

(4) Has a rule been developed *a posteriori* (even in the event that the state's personal, territorial or functional sovereignty was correctly involved) which takes the matter outside the 'domestic jurisdiction' (i.e. the material sphere of validity) of the state in question or which provides a conflict rule of international law that denies exercise of fiscal jurisdiction in a case such as the one under consideration?[93]

7. Detecting Excessive Extraterritorial Tax Practices

In a decision of 22 March 1983, a German court for the first time acknowledged that a state's jurisdiction to tax its nationals is unlimited, but then continued to say that the taxation of aliens is subject to the limitations of public international law.[94] The court refers explicitly to the lectures of Dr Mann at the Hague Academy in 1964[95] and sets forth some tests that are similar, to a large extent, to the tests employed by the American Legal Institute in the Third Restatement and which resemble the above analysis of the *Lotus* case. If it is accepted that the exercise of jurisdiction can be illegal, then one must be able to determine in many cases where states have attempted to tax without the necessary legal basis in international law. I will briefly refer to a few cases that I have found where the US Supreme Court and other states have made statements containing assertions of illegal extraterritorial taxation. One instance is a case where the United States withdrew the nationality of a non-resident national and still taxed this person on his worldwide income. The US Court of Appeals for the First Circuit held this to be illegal.[96] Another situation involved a Turkish expatriate naturalised in the US as a US citizen and living in the US, who was still taxed by Turkey on his

---

[92] P.C.I.J., Series A No. 10.
[93] See Martha, note 50 above, at 38–41.
[94] *Case concerning the German-Austrian Legal Cooperation Treaty* 22 March 1983, in *Decisions of the Bundesverfassungsgericht – Federal Constitutional Court – Federal Republic of Germany*, Vol. 1, Part II, at 471 (1992) = 63 BVerfGE 343 (1983).
[95] See note 62 above.
[96] *US v Lucienne D'Hotelle* 558 F.2d 37 (1st Cir. 1977).

worldwide income. Upon a demand from the US government, Turkey stopped taxing this person.[97] There was also a situation where the taxing state would try to assess a scope of taxation much larger than would be justified on the basis of a link between the taxing state and the taxpayer. It concerned the case where a US citizen travelled to Germany and was receiving money from her father for six months' travel and then was assessed on her worldwide income because of the money that she was receiving. This case was also settled by diplomatic action.[98]

I have already mentioned the problem of worldwide unitary taxation. As you all know, this has been criticised by the European Community. The UK also invoked international law and asserted that this was a case of excess fiscal jurisdiction. I came to a different conclusion. In the case of unitary taxation the taxpayer is a US corporation and, therefore, the US can tax this US corporation on its worldwide income. However, the problem with worldwide unitary taxation is that the technique employed to determine the worldwide income of the corporation is so abusive that it amounts effectively to the extraterritorial taxation of non-resident corporations. In my view, this is not a matter of excess of jurisdiction[99] but rather a situation that would probably qualify under the doctrine of abuse of rights. This point is made because one of the problems that are still out there in international tax practice is that, while there is broad agreement on the basis of taxation as well as the scope of taxation, there are no uniform concepts. Therefore, there can exist double residence corporations which are taxed twice despite the tax treaty. We also have double nationality involving worldwide taxation. Situations exist where income is not defined, causing a disparity between the legal concepts. This leads to extraterritorial taxation. Most of those situations are normally sorted out by international double taxation treaties. However, double taxation treaties do not always address all these issues. The case of worldwide unitary taxation is a good example. Except for one treaty between the US and the UK, there are no treaties that attempt to address the definition of income so as to exclude the implementation of worldwide unitary taxation. Even the UK–US treaty has not been accepted by the US Senate. It consented to the treaty but excluded the clause addressing the issue of worldwide unitary taxation.

Two interesting cases that have dealt with the matter of taxation on the continental shelf should be mentioned. The first case involved the UK Finance Act 1970.[100] The UK taxes foreign non-resident aliens who are wage earners on the continental shelf of the UK. In this case the tax was imposed on a non-resident employer to withhold the taxes. The employer went to court and the House of Lords held in favour of the UK. The question that was not settled and

---

[97] J.B. Moore, *Digest of International Law*, Vol. III, at 691.
[98] *Ibid.*, Vol. II, at 60–61.
[99] Cf. Qureshi, note 50 above.
[100] *Clark (Inspector of Taxes) v Oceanic Contracters Inc* 78 ILR 527–550; for an analysis, see F.A. Mann, *Further Studies in International Law* 19–20 (1990) and Conforti, *op. cit.*, note 67 above, at 144–145; Martha, note 50 above, at 112–115.

not addressed was whether a non-resident alien working on the continental shelf was taxable at all. The UK did not need to address this issue at all in this case. However, this question was addressed in a decision by the German Finance Court involving an alien officer on an oiltanker which was anchored on the German continental shelf. The alien officer was taxed on his worldwide income by the German taxing authority.[101] He challenged the tax and the German court concluded that the continental shelf was not a part of the territory of Germany and that the rights conferred by UN Continental Shelf Convention of 1958 did not include the jurisdiction to tax. Therefore, the tax was disallowed.[102] I might add that, contrary to the 1958 Convention, the 1982 Convention does explicitly confer jurisdiction to tax on the coastal state with respect to the economic zone and the continental shelf.

8. Concluding Remarks

The issue of extraterritoriality in the area of taxation is solved, as said before, rather satisfactorily by treaties, unlike other areas involving extraterritorial jurisdiction. Tax lawyers recognised very early that under international law situations of concurrent jurisdiction may arise and that general international law does not contain rules to settle conflicts of concurrent jurisdiction.[103] Hence a practice has developed to settle issues of extraterritorial taxation by double taxation treaties. It is probably true that most of the problems of extraterritorial jurisdiction that we witness in other areas of law should and ought to be solved in this way. In this respect, I disagree with those who suggest that the court of one country can unilaterally settle issues of conflicts of jurisdiction involving extraterritoriality by adopting, for instance, the concept of comity, or rule of reason or whatever rule has been suggested. I am therefore convinced that the International Law Association will serve the international community better by suggesting that problems of extraterritorial jurisdiction should and ought to be solved by treaties and not by unilateral measures. The practice under double taxation treaties is a useful example indeed.

Sir Ian Sinclair:

Thank you very much. I will just make two brief comments myself then I'll pass the floor to Gary Born who will make a comment in this matter. I think that we are mostly public international lawyers at this table rather than tax lawyers and I think that public international lawyers would all agree a) that there is nothing certain in life but death and taxes and b) that all tax authorities without exception want to plunder as much from the taxpayer as they possibly can.

---

[101] See note 83 above.
[102] But see Conforti, *op. cit.*, note 67 above, at 145.
[103] Cf. Vogel, note 51 above, 4.

Gary Born:

And I can guarantee that the third comment is that the taxpayers want to make sure that the taxing authorities plunder as little as possible. I am not a tax lawyer and I am not a public international lawyer either so please bear with me. I'd like to talk, just a little, about the unitary tax issue. As you know, the principal culprit in unitary tax over the last ten years or so has been the state of California in the US. The state of California has imposed a system of worldwide unitary taxation at various times on both domestic corporations and foreign corporations. That activity has produced a firestorm of controversy on each of four levels: It has produced countless diplomatic notes from various trading partners of the US. It has produced legislative activity both in California and at the federal level in the US. It has produced litigation in the various US courts, California and the US Supreme Court, and it has produced efforts to alter various US tax treaties with its trading partners.

When the US and the UK concluded their tax treaty, the UK bargained very hard to obtain a provision forbidding the states of the US from using a unitary tax method and, as the previous speaker mentioned, the US Senate refused to accept that article, art. 9(4) of the Tax Treaty. The treaty went into effect between the US and the UK with the UK's request for a prohibition against state unitary taxation being rejected. Litigation in the US ensued in the US courts with the US Constitution, particularly the due process clause and the commerce clause, being used as weapons against the unitary tax imposed at the state level. That litigation culminated in the decision in 1983 called *Container Corp* in which the US Supreme Court, as to domestic companies, rejected the argument that the Constitution forbids unitary taxation. According to the US Supreme Court, the world is a very complicated place. You have these multinational corporations with operations and subsidiaries all over the world. They derive income in numerous different ways and pass their products and their profits around the world between their various subsidiaries and affiliates in highly fluid and complex ways. According to the Court, imposing an income tax in any particular jurisdiction requires allocating appropriate amounts of income and expenses to that jurisdiction; given the interrelated and complex character of international commerce, making this allocation is very hard.

One way to make the allocation is to use the taxpayers' accounting records, which assign income and expense to various subsidiaries in various locations. Where the accounting records involve transactions between related entities not reflecting market value, adjustments can be made. In shorthand, this approach is referred to as separate arm's-length accounting. This is the approach that the US federal government and most of its trading partners use.

California said it was not quite sure it wanted to take a company's word for what it had earned within the state and that a more sensible way to look at how much a company earned within the state was to look at the worldwide profits of the entire corporate group and to use some sort of apportionment formula to attach to the state of California the appropriate amount of income. The apportionment formula that California used was a three factor test that looked at sales, payroll and property within the state and took that proportion of in-state sales, payroll and property and compared it to worldwide sales, payroll and property, took the fraction that that produced and applied it to worldwide profits.

According to the Supreme Court, deciding whether one mechanism was better than the other was like trying to slice a shadow. And the Court concluded that absent extraordinary abuse in selecting or applying the apportionment factors, there was nothing in the due process clause that made the apportionment approach on a worldwide basis inherently unfair or unreasonable. The Court also considered the argument that there is an international practice reflected in what essentially all the major trading nations do and the US itself does at the federal level. That practice is using separate arm's-length accounting. The Court considered that that international practice had crystallised into a rule of US constitutional law and had to be followed by the individual states of the US in order to prevent undue local interference with national foreign affairs powers.

Although it was a closely run race in the Supreme Court, the Court ultimately rejected that argument as applied to domestic corporations. The Court said that if Congress really thought that this was that much of a problem it would have enacted legislation to avoid the interference with US foreign policy and tax policy that the disparate approach of the states would have caused. Rather than doing that, Congress rejected art. 9(4) of the UK–US tax treaty so there really was not much of an argument based on US notions of federalism and foreign policy. However, in a footnote, which is where most of the important bits of Supreme Court decisions in the US are, the Court said that it might reach an entirely different result if this were a foreign-owned corporation. That immediately produced another firestorm of litigation which is not over yet.

From 1983 to the present, a variety of things happened to try to persuade California to give up their worldwide apportionment system. In 1985 the UK enacted legislation which permitted retaliation against foreign jurisdiction which applied improper methods of taxation. The legislation was specifically targeted against California. From the time the legislation was enacted, the UK increasingly turned up the pressure on the California taxing authority saying essentially we will invoke this retaliatory tax regulation and increase the tax rates on California-based companies unless you change your unitary tax system. The UK never actually went forward with the retaliation, but, with increasing vigour and sincerity, indicated that it would retaliate against private companies based in California by increasing their UK taxes. The US federal government, along the same lines, put increasing pressure on California to abandon its worldwide unitary tax system. In 1986, I believe, California abandoned substantially the unitary tax approach that it hitherto had. It permitted companies to elect what was called a 'water edge approach' permitting a unitary tax to their US operations but not to non-US operations. This election was, in theory, designed to avoid the objection to worldwide unitary taxation by giving companies an option of selecting what amounted to arm's-length separate accounting. They can move into the water edge system, have their US income taxed at a particular rate . . .

Andreas F. Lowenfeld:

But not just California.

Gary Born:

That is right. All the states. In the *Container Corp* decision it was pretty clear that that would be permissible in the US. A number of states other than California had had a unitary tax approach. Idaho, Montana and some others. It really didn't matter much, they were small and empty. In any event, those states completely got rid of their unitary tax system. California was the only significant player. They moved to this water edge election system. But they attached three conditions to the water edge election which created a variety of resentments. One was that a fee had to be paid to make the election. The fee brought the state of California approximately $70m a year. It cost taxpayers that much as well and that created the argument that the election was being improperly conditioned. In addition, the state required a variety of information to be reported which could be used to test the legitimacy of the election which accordingly was the third condition: that the state retain the authority unilaterally to revoke or overrule an election in certain cases. It was not clear what cases, but presumably it applied in cases where it really mattered because the taxpayer's bill was substantially reduced.

Andreas F. Lowenfeld:

You mean that the election was a waiver to the objection to jurisdiction?

Gary Born:

I think the election would have been a waiver.

Andreas F. Lowenfeld:

If the third condition is what you say, I have not seen it.

Gary Born:

The third condition, as we will see, is moot. The UK and others were not happy with this California proposal and they continued to apply pressure. The federal government continued to apply pressure and, but for a hastily thought out Clinton campaign promise, things would have probably culminated pretty quickly, but President Clinton indicated that he would support California in a dramatic change of policy in its effort to preserve unitary taxation. Then, in the space of the last two or three months, two significant occurrences happened. Firstly, California has now repealed the three conditions attached to the waters edge tax election. Companies are now free to elect waters edge taxation and I think that will substantially answer most of the future complaints against the California system. California continues to permit companies, should they so choose, to accept worldwide unitary taxation. Interestingly, a number of companies like it for administrative reasons and for bottom line reasons. The California legislature, Governor Pete Wilson signed the legislation, I believe, yesterday or the day before, repealed the three conditions to the election of the waters edge taxation. Meanwhile, the second important occurrence happened: the US Solicitor General filed an *amicus curiae* brief in the so-called *Barclays* case.

The *Barclays* case involves that footnote that I mentioned in *Container Corp*. What does the US constitution say about California's unitary taxation as applied to foreign owned companies? At stake is approximately $4bn in back taxes from the period in which California imposed its unitary tax system with full vigour. This is liability going back into the mid and early seventies. There has been litigation in the California courts. The California Supreme Court has rejected the argument that either the due process clause or the foreign commerce clause prohibits unitary taxation on a worldwide basis as applied to foreign corporations. That decision was taken to the US Supreme Court on what we call a petition for *certiorari*, asking for discretionary review. The Supreme Court is holding that petition and has not yet acted on it and requested the views of the Solicitor General. The Solicitor General, in a brief filed the day after the California legislature amended its statute, said that the Court should not review the case. That will no doubt displease the UK as well as other trading partners of the US.

Andreas F. Lowenfeld:

That may not be conclusive, however.

Gary Born:

It may not be conclusive. Although given the character of the challenge which is a foreign policy, foreign commerce challenge, and given that the Solicitor General says not only that this is an unimportant case because it is moot now, but rather goes on to say that taking this case would have affirmatively disturbed US foreign policy, which is an extraordinary statement. I would guess that the Court will not review the *Barclays* case. One tries to predict these things at one's peril. But for the Solicitor General to not only not urge review but to say that review would affirmatively frustrate the very purposes of the foreign commerce clause that the appellants are relying on, I think, decreases the chance of further review.

Andreas F. Lowenfeld:

Would it be disturbed if the Court affirmed California? In other words, he thinks it is better not to take it than to lose. It is a funny way to put it.

Gary Born:

The argument is essentially that a political accommodation has been reached and the Court should not disturb it. That is a disingenuous position because from the European perspective an accommodation has been reached as to what is to go on in the future. But the Europeans also say that there is a case pending and we think as a matter of principle that it ought to be decided in a proper way, and also as a matter of $4bn. I think California will continue to have abandoned its particular approach towards worldwide unitary taxation and that ought to largely meet this issue. It will become an interesting historical episode. But it seems to me that there were several important points of principle, aside from the money, worth thinking about.

First, the US and every other country for that matter retained the power in applying separate arm's-length accounting methods to look at the companies' accounting and to look at their internal transfer prices, which is essentially what the whole fight is about. If California and other entities cannot apply apportionment formulas then they will look at transfer prices in a very aggressive way. The US IRS is doing that on a federal level. The first wave of criticism was directed at the Japanese companies which are going through audits right now. The next wave of inquiry is going to be in the other direction across the Atlantic and I think that the potential for double taxation and extraterritorial application is just as great under a separate accounting principle as it is under an apportionment principle, because when a taxing authority is able to look through the company's prices and say 'no' that is not what you should have charged, i.e. you should have charged some other amount, it can effectively attribute income to itself as opposed to some other place and it will be much more difficult to identify that as a point of principle. So I think that there will be debates about extraterritorial taxation but in an even more arcane way, even more the reserve of tax lawyers and transfer pricing specialists.

The second point that I think is interesting is the manner in which this particular dispute was resolved. When you cut through it all, essentially, you have the UK holding private US companies hostage and saying to California unless you abandon this unitary tax system we will punish your California-based companies. You cannot argue with success. The UK's approach got California to abandon a widely criticised approach. But the method ought to give private taxpayers pause. The US, of course, made clear that its reaction would not be to sit back. It in return has a retaliatory tax provision in the Internal Revenue Code and could have doubled the tax rates on companies based in any jurisdiction which applied discriminatory taxation. If the end-game were played out, private parties on both sides of the Atlantic would be caught in a governmental crossfire. It may be that the only way to resolve these disputes between sovereignty is to go after the private parties. But at least as a private lawyer and a private taxpayer that gives me pause and I wonder whether one ought to think very hard about invoking such methods and one ought to try to find alternatives to that. It may be that nothing else works. Then so be it. But one ought to hesitate before using private parties in that sense. Finally, I have just one comment on the principal speech.

The argument is often made that the way to resolve extraterritoriality disputes is by treaty and not in national courts. Under this view, national courts are not competent or capable of settling extraterritoriality disputes. I think that is right, but only as far as it goes. It seems to me that even though a national court cannot finally settle an extraterritoriality dispute, that does not mean that it should not try. It does not mean that positive results cannot come from national courts moderating, in the light of international law and practice, some of the implicit and explicit excesses of its legislature. I think decisions like the *Aerospatiale* decision and the footnote in *Container Corp*, for that matter, are useful tools in moderating national assertions of jurisdiction; they include affirmatively a good thing for national courts to take into account.

Finally, it seems to me that the proposition that treaties are the way to resolve extraterritoriality disputes is wonderful in theory but that actually making it work in practice is highly difficult. The tax that we are looking at today is about $4bn. You can divide it up and given one part to one country and another part to another country. Competitive practices, anti-competitive practices and the like are a far different thing. Dividing regulatory responsibilities between two countries in this context is a much more difficult prospect.

Sir Ian Sinclair:

Thank you very much, Gary. Are there any other comments that people would like to make?

Andreas F. Lowenfeld:

Yes. I know less about taxation than Gary. But I got interested in the subject because when we were drafting the Restatement we got a lot of pressure, including pressure from the national government, from the US Treasury, to come out and say that this unitary taxation was contrary to international law. We wrote a long reporters' note more or less up to 1987. I came to the conclusion that there was a lot to be said for the California view. Think about what they were really saying. That is really worth talking about. It is different from transfer pricing. They said: we have companies, whether they are American-owned or foreign owned, that have their research in Silicon Valley or on the outskirts of Stanford University or in Los Angeles. We have highly paid scientists, engineers and designers. They are making all kinds of computer chips and boards and so on, and then, when the designs are all done, it may well be that the sales in the US or in California are no greater than the payroll. Then they go to Honduras or Belize or El Salvador or Thailand and the things are assembled according to the designs and then there is a huge mark-up from there which avoids taxation in California. In other words, they were saying the real value added, the mental value, the design value, came from California. It seems to me there was a lot to be said for that. I do not think the formula, as such, was challenged as unfair. In an individual case you could play with it a little bit but the notion that you take the overall payroll as a measure, and then it turns out that one guy in Menlow Park earns what 20 guys in Belize earn. And that is where the profit is located. It seems to me that California had a lot going for it.

You started out saying that the basic jurisdiction is national, but, in fact, we really tax on sources, putting aside some worldwide nationality. When Pavarotti comes to give a concert he gets taxed only on the percentage of concert revenue or the record sales whatever and, if you think about the source in terms of value added, it seems to me that California has a good thing. Now I do not think that California should make foreign policy or frustrate a treaty with the UK because that is a quite different issue.

Karl M. Meessen:

If I may ask you, Andy, you said it is not a matter of transfer pricing. But isn't it in your example, that the California company somehow transferred know-how to Belize without receiving any payment for this transfer?

Andreas F. Lowenfeld:

Well, that's one way to look at it.

Karl M. Meessen:

And if you consider it under an arm's-length clause, there should be some income for the transfer of the know-how in California which is taxable.

Andreas F. Lowenfeld:

Well, there is probably some, but if you have the design in one place and the assembly in another. You can talk about it in terms of dresses but with computer chips it really becomes more dramatic. But you are right and I think Gary is right. One could talk about it as transfer pricing but then you have to attach value to the design and is very difficult to do as we have seen with the *Toyota* case and cases like that.

Harold G. Maier:

I just want to add one piece of information related to this material. If I remember correctly, there is another footnote in *Container Corp* that refers to the *Chicago Bridge and Iron Co* case. In that case the Solicitor General's Office, in fact, had filed a brief in which they challenged the unitary tax. The court wondered why the Solicitor General's Office did not appear. What meaning should be attached to their failure to appear?

Andreas F. Lowenfeld:

You mean, *Container?*

Harold G. Maier:

Yes, in *Container Corp.* There the Court said: 'We assume that the Solicitor General's office has changed its mind'. The reason it changed its mind was because the Reagan Administration, when it came into office, had informed the states that they would have to pay for many of the services for which the federal government had been paying. There was a great deal of pressure on the administration not to take steps which would inhibit individual states' ability to tax. And so, the administration was between this position (which I think had been taken earlier by the Carter Administration) and the new position. Therefore, they began to waffle on the questions of how far they would go in order to fight these efforts by the states to assess a unitary tax. There was a case in which Royal Dutch Shell was being subjected to a unitary tax via one of its US subsidiaries. An effort was made to attribute the entire income to Royal Dutch Shell to the subsidiary and then to divide it up basically the same way as in *Container Corp.*

Andreas F. Lowenfeld:

That subsidiary is a very big company.

Harold G. Maier:

It certainly is. What happened was that the Netherlands threatened to take the US before the International Court of Justice if the tax was imposed because the Friendship, Commerce and Navigation Treaty between the US and the Netherlands contained a clause, which is not in most of these treaties, that suggested national treatment for corporations owned and controlled by corporations of one country, operating in the other. That threat, of course, caused a big brouhaha at that point. The international issue was ultimately settled. I am not quite sure how it was settled but the administration was very loathe to go to the state of California to ask it to rescind its tax.

Andreas F. Lowenfeld:

Is the US, or states of the US, the only country that does this? Nobody else has thought of this?

Rutsel S. J. Martha:

In the beginning of this century the German Reich employed a similar technique. Basically the same result was achieved by the German legislature, which in fact considered the domestic subsidiary of a foreign corporation not to be a separate corporation, but as a branch. So it's not only the US, and probably the issue is basically sharing the income among states. The reason why I mentioned treaty as an outcome is because when the countries involved do not agree on sharing the money, one of them will not get the revenue.

Sir Ian Sinclair:

Well, I think I'm going to have to bring this discussion to a close. It's been very interesting. We could, I'm sure, carry on until eight o'clock. But we have one more topic to cover. So perhaps this is the point at which we should close this particular discussion and move on to the next and final topic for this evening, which is extraterritorial orders affecting bank deposits.

Chapter III

Extraterritorial Orders Affecting Bank Deposits

Campbell McLachlan

1. Introduction: The 'Mareva' in the Comparative Context

The names of the Republic of Haiti and 'Baby Doc' Duvalier are inextricably linked, not just because the Duvalier regime in Haiti became synonymous with corruption on a gargantuan scale, but also because they gave their names to a ground-breaking decision in this field of the extraterritorial scope of court orders affecting bank deposits.[104]

In *Republic of Haiti v Duvalier*, the all too short-lived new government of the Republic pursued 'Baby Doc' to France where he was taking refuge with his family and sued him for US$120m. Duvalier denied liability in France, claiming that it had been a tradition in Haiti for over 180 years for a new government to sue the previous regime. As Staughton L.J. observed:[105]

> One is reminded of the Roman historian who noticed that it was the practice of the later emperors to bring to justice the murderers of the previous emperor but one.

Evidence emerged that Duvalier's lawyer in France had written a book on how to use the secrecy provisions of the Swiss banking system in order to secrete funds and that this lawyer had been consulted by the Duvaliers, and received Haiti government funds. It was, more than anything, an acknowledgement of the limitations of discovery provisions in France which led the Republic's lawyers

---

[104] [1990] 1 QB 202.
[105] *Ibid.*, 206.

to come to England and apply for a worldwide injunction over 'Baby Doc's' assets with supporting disclosure orders. Their application was successful.

This paper concentrates on the particular English court order restraining a defendant from dealing with his assets prior to trial, known (after an early case of that name) as the Mareva injunction. [106] But this is not because England is unique in having a form of pre-trial court order which claims an extraterritorial effect. In America the grant of such orders is well known. One of the most celebrated cases involved another equally notorious former ruler being pursued by his successors: *Republic of the Philippines v Marcos*. [107] In civil law countries, the grant of interim relief of an extraterritorial character is widely recognised, despite doctrinal comment to the contrary. [108] In fact, the two leading European Court decisions on the enforceability under the Brussels Convention of interim court orders were both cases in which French courts had rendered interim orders in relation to assets in Germany. [109] There are examples in German jurisprudence (albeit not in the banking context) of orders being made relating to acts to be done abroad. Why, then, concentrate on the Mareva?

First, because of its novelty. It must be a matter of surprise, if not chagrin, to civil lawyers, who have had a well developed attachment remedy for centuries to find that English law – having long had nothing comparable – has developed in a mere 20 years a remedy which in a number of respects outstrips its civilian counterparts. Secondly, London's position as an international financial centre – and an international litigation centre – has meant that the practical effect of such orders, particularly on banks, has been farreaching. Thirdly, the extraterritorial Mareva has had a particular interest for public international lawyers – especially those from continental Europe and the US – as at least an aspect of UK practice which might invite a critical response in light of the UK's strict approach to the extraterritorial claims of other states.

This paper will examine the Mareva injunction and its effects on banks and in particular its extraterritorial aspect. Its purpose is to examine the relationship between the court's exercise of enforcement powers in the civil process and public international law. The paper's thesis is twofold:

(1) The so-called extraterritorial Mareva is really no more extraterritorial than much else in the civil process, not just in England but in most countries.

(2) The traditional territorial conceptions of jurisdiction, allied as they are to the shibboleth of sovereignty, may not be so easily applied to the civil

---

[106] *Mareva Compania Naviera SA v International Bulkcarriers SA* (1975) 2 Lloyd's Rep 509; see generally: Gee, *Mareva Injunctions and Anton Piller Relief* (2nd edn, 1990).

[107] 862 F.2d 1355 (9th cir, 1988); *cert. denied* 490 US 1035.

[108] See the discussion of the civil law approach in Schlosser, 'Extraterritoriale Rechtsdurchsetzung im Zivilprozeß', in Pfister und Will (eds.), *Festschrift für Werner Lorenz*.

[109] *De Cavel v De Cavel (No. 1)* (1979) ECR 1055; *Denilauler v Couchet Freres* (1980) ECR 1553.

process as some public international lawyers would have it. [110] An internationalist approach to the civil process must balance jurisdictional concerns with the common objective of courts not to allow territorial boundaries to defeat the efficacy of the civil justice process.

2. The Mareva Injunction and its Effect on Banks

Before 1975, the rule in England was that 'you cannot get an injunction to restrain a man who is alleged to be a debtor from parting with his property'. [111] In this respect the English courts lacked any procedure akin to the effective civil law remedy of attachment (which had survived in Scotland and in the US). The lacuna was all the more notable, since in other respects, the English courts had very effective procedures for preserving the status quo pending trial, through use of the equitable interim injunction. [112]

The historic anomaly was at any rate removed in 1975 when, in a series of cases, the courts sanctioned pre-trial personal injunctions to restrain defendants from removing their assets from the jurisdiction or dissipating them. The original mischief which the new remedy was developed to redress was the problem of the unscrupulous foreign defendant (often a one-ship company) which would remove its only asset in England (say, a sum on deposit in a London bank account) prior to trial. The plaintiff would then find that his judgment was a pyrrhic victory – the debtor having in the meantime rendered himself judgment proof. But the new remedy was quickly extended to embrace equally unscrupulous English defendants as well, and to prevent dissipation as well as removal of assets. [113]

The key characteristics of such an order are that it is granted *ex parte* and often just prior to the issue of originating process – so that the first the defendant will know of the matter will be on service of the order. Its effect, however, is *in personam*. It does not operate *in rem* as an attachment might on the property itself, and is not designed to create a security interest in the property. Rather, it creates a personal obligation on the defendant to obey its terms. That obligation is made good by the sanction of contempt of court for breach. This can result in the committal to prison of an individual and the sequestration of a company's assets. [114] The effect of such an injunction on a third party – such as a bank – with notice of its terms requires careful treatment. Before that is addressed it is necessary to say something about the basic conditions for the grant of such an order.

---

[110] See generally: McLachlan, 'The Influence of International Law on Civil Jurisdiction', (1993) *Hague YBIL* 125.

[111] *Robinson v Pickering* [1881] 16 ChD 660, 661 (CA) per James I.J.

[112] See generally: *Kerr on Injunctions* (6th edn, 1927).

[113] Section 37(3) of the Supreme Court Act 1981.

[114] Pursuant to Order 52 of the Rules of the Supreme Court.

The plaintiff must show three things:

(1) that he has a cause of action in England;[115]
(2) that he has a good arguable case on that cause of action; and
(3) that there is a real risk that, if the injunction is not granted, the defendant will either remove his assets from the jurisdiction or dissipate them so as to frustrate the final judgment.

For present purposes, the first of these conditions requires some qualification. It does not require the plaintiff actually to sue in England. If there was ever any doubt about that,[116] it has been dispelled by the House of Lords in *Channel Tunnel Group Ltd v Balfour Beatty Construction Ltd.*[117] Moreover, the restriction no longer applies where the plaintiff is suing in another European country, party to the Brussels/Lugano Conventions.[118] But in all other cases, the plaintiff must still show that the English court has jurisdiction over the defendant and that the plaintiff has a cause of action under English law.

So much for preliminaries, what of the effect of such order on a bank? The banker typically has two concerns on receiving notice of such an order, which names one of its customers as a defendant:

(1) What is my personal exposure if I do not ensure compliance with the order?
(2) If I do comply, what is the effect on the bank's other rights and obligations?

For present purposes,[119] suffice to say that banks, in common with all third parties with notice of a court order, are potentially liable themselves in contempt, if they aid its breach or fail to take steps to prevent it. What this may mean in a cross-border context will be explained in a moment. However, the bank which does act to prevent breach of a Mareva injunction will find that its own rights and obligations remain largely unaffected. Thus, its right of set-off is generally preserved,[120] and it is free both to pay and receive funds under documentary credits.

The occasions on which a bank itself can be made the object of a Mareva injunction will be rare. The purpose of such injunctions is not to interfere with a defendant's ordinary business or to prevent him from paying his ordinary debts

---

[115] *The Siskina* (1979) AC 210, see: McLachlan, 'Transnational Applications of Mareva Injunctions and Anton Piller Orders', (1987) 36 *ICLQ* 669, 670–74.

[116] *House of Spring Gardens v Waite* (1984) FSR 277 expressly sanctions the use of an injunction in support of foreign substantive proceedings – the plaintiff putting his English action to sleep in the meantime. See McLachlan note 115 above, at 673 note 12.

[117] [1993] AC 334.

[118] Section 25 of the Civil Jurisdiction and Judgments Act 1982, the route used in *Republic of Haiti v Duvalier op. cit.*, note 104 above.

[119] For more detail see: McLachlan, 'Remedies Affecting Bank Deposits', in Cranston (ed.), *Legal Issues of Cross-Border Banking* (1989).

[120] *Oceanica v Mineralimportexport* [1983] 1 WLR 1294.

as they fall due. In a case involving a central bank, this has been applied to discharge an injunction which would have inhibited the bank's ability to repay depositors and invest their funds.[121]

3. Extraterritorial Orders and their Effect on Banks

Courts commonly enjoin defendants from committing acts abroad. As the US Court of Appeals pithily put it in *Marcos*:[122] 'Because the injunction operates *in personam*, not *in rem*, there is no reason to be concerned about its territorial reach'.

This is not a phenomenon restricted to common law courts. But in English jurisprudence one need look no further than the power to restrain a person from pursuing vexatious and oppressive litigation abroad.[123] As one nineteenth century judge put it:[124]

> In truth, nothing can be more unfounded than the doubts of the jurisdiction. That is grounded, like all other jurisdiction of the court, not on any pretension to the exercise of judicial and administrative rights abroad, but on the circumstances of the person of the party on whom this order is made being within the power of the court. If the court can command him to bring home goods from abroad, or to assign chattel interests, or to convey real property locally situate abroad; − if, for instance, as in *Penn v Lord Baltimore* (1750) 1 Ves Sen 444 it can decree the performance of an agreement touching the boundary of a province in North America; or, as in the case of *Toller v Carteret* (1705) 2 Vern 494 can foreclose a mortgage in the Isle of Sark, one of the Channel Islands; in precisely the like manner, it can restrain the party being within the limits of its jurisdiction from doing anything abroad . . .

But the English courts were, at least initially, more than usually coy about extending the effect of the new Mareva injunction to foreign assets.[125] That was all reversed in a dramatic series of three cases in the summer of 1988,[126] in which the Court of Appeal both sanctioned the grant of orders over worldwide assets and mapped out the metes and bounds of their scope.

What prompted this volte-face? The reason is simple: All three cases involved allegations of massive frauds, conducted on an international scale and involving a sophisticated misuse of the international banking system to secrete assets. The

---

[121] *Polly Peck v Central Bank of the Northern Republic of Cyprus* [1992] 4 All ER 769.
[122] *Op. cit.*, note 107 above, at 1363.
[123] *SNI Aerospatiale v Lee kui Jak* [1987] AC 871; *Barclays Bank plc v Homan* [1993] BCLC 680.
[124] *Lord Portalington v Soulby* [1834] 3 My à K 104, 8.
[125] *Ashtiani v Kashi* [1987] QB 888. For the development of the law on this aspect, see: McLachlan, *op. cit.*, notes 115 and 119 above.
[126] *Babanaft International Co SA v Bassatne* [1990] Ch 13; *Derby & Co Ltd v Weldon (No. 1)* [1990] Ch 48; *Republic of Haiti v Duvalier* [1990] 1 QB 202. The Court of Appeal refined the new jurisdiction in two further applications in the *Derby v Weldon* affair: (*Nos. 3 and 4*) [1990] Ch 65 and (*No. 6*) [1990] 1 WLR 1139.

English courts simply refused to stand idly by in the face of that kind of problem.

The modern form of order is now set out in a Practice Direction.[127] The order is explicit as to the reach over the worldwide assets of the defendant, but contains some important provisos:

> (2) *Effect of this Order outside England and Wales.* The terms of this Order do not affect or concern anyone outside the jurisdiction of this court until it is declared enforceable or is enforced by a Court in the relevant country and they are to affect him only to the extent they have been declared enforceable or have been enforced UNLESS such person is:
>
> (a) a person to whom this Order is addressed or an officer of or an agent appointed by power of attorney of such a person; or
>
> (b) a person who is subject to the jurisdiction of this Court and (i) has been given written notice of this Order at his residence or place of business within the jurisdiction of this Court, and (ii) is able to prevent acts or omissions outside the jurisdiction of this Court which constitute or assist in a breach of terms of this Order.

An undertaking in the standard form of order also requires the plaintiff to obtain the leave of the English court before seeking either to enforce the extraterritorial part of the injunction or to obtain orders of a similar nature against the defendants in any other country, it not being a breach of the undertaking merely to notify persons believed to hold or control the assets of the terms of the order. These provisions give an apparent comfort in relation to their impact on foreign third parties, and prompt the question: are such orders really extraterritorial?

4. Are Such Orders Really Extraterritorial?

A. *Effect on the Defendant*

So far as defendants themselves are concerned, the effect of such an injunction is undoubtedly extraterritorial in the subject-matter sense: it commands application irrespective of the location of the defendant's assets. The English courts' remedies for disobedience in contempt of court would exist irrespective of where the acts were in fact done.[128] The defendant is also at risk of the potentially more effective sanction (from the plaintiff's point of view, at any rate) of having his defence struck out and judgment entered against him.[129]

---

[127] *Ex P Mareva Injunctions and Anton Piller Orders* 28 July 1994 (*The Times*, 2 August 1994).
[128] Collins, 'The Territorial Reach of Mareva Injunctions', 105 *LQR* 262, 283 (1989).
[129] See, Gee, *op. cit.*, note 106 at 180–82, and the closely analogous case of an illusory compliance with a disclosure order: *ISC Technologies Ltd v Guerin* [1992] 2 Lloyd's Rep 430. The default judgment was subsequently held enforceable in the US: (*unrep.*, Finesilver J., 15 July 1993, US District Court, Florida; *upheld on appeal* 16 February 1995).

The reason the courts give for their claim that such orders give rise to no extraterritoriality issues is that the defendant is subject to the *in personam* jurisdiction of the court. Therefore, it is said, it matters not how and where he is ordered to comply. Valuable though it may be as a justification, the *in personam* label hides a multitude of long-arm effects. As Lowenfeld has commented: [130]

> All I really know is that slogans like 'Equity acts in personam' . . . do not begin to address the conflicting values of security, sovereignty, reliance and fairness that emerge in a kaleidoscope of variations.

The use of the personal character of such orders as a justification for their extraterritorial operation carries some force where the defendant is physically present within the jurisdiction. However, that will frequently not be the case in the types of matters in which Mareva injunctions are sought and granted. Indeed, the original justification for such orders was precisely to ensure that *foreign* defendants could not frustrate the English judicial process.

Where the defendant is not physically present in England, the exercise of the court's power to act *in personam* will be by virtue of a 'long-arm' head of jurisdiction. The exercise of jurisdiction on such a basis is not always, despite the suggestions of some English judges, [131] contrary to international law or exorbitant. [132] In many contexts in which Order 11 of the English Rules of the Supreme Court recognises a legitimate ground for English jurisdiction, the case will have a very close connection with England because, for example, it involves a breach of a contract or a tort committed there. [133] (Similar subject-matter bases for jurisdiction over European defendants are allowed under art. 5 of the Brussels/Lugano Conventions.) Moreover, the Order 11 procedure involves substantial safeguards designed to ensure that jurisdiction is only taken over foreign defendants in cases where it is proper. [134] These include requirements that the plaintiff shows:

(1) a good arguable case that his claim falls within one of the specific heads of Order 11;
(2) a serious issue to be tried; and
(3) that England is a convenient forum for trial of the action. [135]

However, these extensive safeguards do not mean that in every case in which the English court exercises long-arm jurisdiction it does so on a basis which demands international acceptance. There has, for example, long been objection taken to

---

[130] Lowenfeld, 'Injunctions Across National Frontiers: A Tale of Two Cities', 2 *Amer. Rev. of Intl Arbitration* 3, 15 (1992).
[131] Per Lord Diplock in *The Siskina* [1979] AC 210, 254.
[132] See, McLachlan, 'The Influence of International Law on Civil Jurisdiction', [1993] *Hague YBIL* 125.
[133] RSC Order 11, rules 1(1)(d) and (f).
[134] RSC Order 11, rule 4.
[135] *Seaconsar Far East Ltd v Bank Markazi* [1993] 3 WLR 756 (HL).

the English court exercising jurisdiction simply on the basis that the proceedings relate to a contract governed by English law[136] – a head of jurisdiction which can lead to cases with no other connection between the facts of the parties and England being litigated in England.[137]

Secondly, a Mareva injunction will typically be obtained *ex parte* before the defendant has had an opportunity to challenge the jurisdiction of the English court. It has been held that: 'The moment a person is properly served under . . . [Order 11] that person, so far as the jurisdiction of this court is concerned, is precisely in the same position as a person who is in this country'.[138] However, it is essential to the Mareva jurisdiction that the English court has personal jurisdiction over the defendant under Order 11 and that the plaintiff has a cause of action under English law.[139] If it is subsequently held that the English court has no jurisdiction, the effect will be that an injunction has been granted, possibly over worldwide assets, in circumstances where the English court had no jurisdiction to deal with the matter at all.

In a recent decision[140] the Court of Appeal declined to regard a defendant's challenge to the English court's jurisdiction as sufficient reason for refraining to make a worldwide disclosure order in support of an injunction. The Court held that the ability of a defendant to raise jurisdiction issues which may be appealed to the Court of Appeal and the House of Lords and referred to the European Court of Justice might result in lengthy delays. In the meantime, it would be impossible to police the Mareva injunction which is the main purpose of a disclosure order. Steyn LJ considered that an acceptance of the defendant's arguments in the case would be a 'drastic emasculation of the utility of this exceptional but useful remedy'.

The *in personam* justification for the extraterritorial Mareva injunction must be qualified in a third respect in relation to proceedings involving European defendants. This is because, by virtue of art. 24 of the Brussels and Lugano Conventions (which apply to jurisdiction matters between European Union and European Free Trade Association states), the English court has jurisdiction to grant an injunction in support of substantive proceedings taking place in another contracting state. In *Republic of Haiti v Duvalier*,[141] the Court of Appeal held that the statutory jurisdiction to order an injunction in support of proceedings in another contracting state did not require the English court to have any other basis for jurisdiction. On the contrary, since it was anticipated that the English court would be acting in support of proceedings elsewhere, the English court

---

[136] RSC Order 11, rule 1(1)(d)(iii); see e.g. Mann, 'The Doctrine of Jurisdiction in International Law', reprinted in *Stud. in Intl L.* 1, 66 (1973).

[137] *Amin Rasheed Shipping Corp v Kuwait Insurance Co* [1984] AC 50.

[138] *Re Liddell's Settlement Trusts* [1936] CH 365, 374.

[139] *The Siskina* [1979] AC 210; *Channel Tunnel Group Ltd v Balfour Beatty Construction Ltd* [1993] AC 334.

[140] *Grupo Torras SA v Sheikh Fahad Mohammed Al-Sabah* (*unrep.*, 16 Feb. 1944, CA).

[141] *Op. cit.*, note 104 above.

would not be contemplating jurisdiction on the merits. Rather, it would be exercising a jurisdiction specifically conferred on the court to act in aid of foreign contracting states. It is doubtful whether it was seriously contemplated under the Convention's scheme that the court would proceed to do what the English court then did, which was to grant a worldwide injunction and an ancillary disclosure order where neither the defendants, nor any of their assets were present in England, and where the substantive proceedings were taking place in a French court (which had no similar powers of disclosure).

The salient point of all this, however, is that this extraterritorial effect on the defendant is not so much a novel feature of Mareva injunctions. Rather it is the natural consequence of the exercise of the court's enforcement powers within the framework of the civil process. We should be slow to regard the exercise of such powers as contrary to an international law of jurisdiction — since they are so much a part of many states' existing law.

B. *Effect on Third Parties Including Banks*

If the courts have been somewhat sanguine about potential extraterritorial effects on defendants, they have been rather more careful about third parties. In fact, the foreigner acting wholly abroad from a foreign place of business ought to have had little to fear from an extraterritorial Mareva injunction. This is because the sanction on a third party who, with notice of such injunction, persists in its breach, is the quasi-criminal sanction of contempt. The strict territoriality of the criminal jurisdiction ought to have applied to ensure that a foreign third party acting wholly abroad could not be liable for contempt in England.[142] Third parties, and in particular banks, who will most commonly find themselves on the receiving end of such injunctions, will, however, take comfort from the proviso which seeks to put to rest any doubt that may have existed as to the scope of that principle.

However, the proviso does not resolve what has always been the most difficult potential application of such orders to third parties, namely where the assets are held abroad but by a party who also has a presence within the jurisdiction. This very commonly arises, for example, with banks which are generally organised as single entities with branches in many parts of the world. The issue is particularly acute in London, where a majority of the world's trading banks maintain branches. Such banks are persons who are subject to the jurisdiction of the English court and may be given written notice of the order at their place of business within the jurisdiction. The question is whether they are to be regarded as being able to prevent acts or omissions outside the jurisdiction of the court which constitute or assist in the breach of the terms of the order, as contemplated by the exception to the proviso.

This problem was discussed in two English decisions with conflicting results.

---

[142] Collins, note 128 above, at 282–3.

Both cases involved applications for injunctions by public regulatory authorities. In *Securities and Investments Board v Pantell SA*,[143] the SIB, a regulatory body established, under the Financial Services Act 1986, in the UK, sought an *ex parte* injunction against Pantell SA, a Swiss company, to restrain it from dealing with its assets in both England and Guernsey. Guernsey, being one of the Channel Islands, is outside the jurisdiction of the English courts. The order relating to the Guernsey assets contained the *Babanaft* proviso. The Vice-Chancellor explained its effect on Barclays Bank as follows:[144]

> The result of that proviso in the present case is to ensure that my order has no operation within the Channel Islands and does not trespass upon the jurisdiction of the Guernsey court. However, if the branch of Barclays Bank in Guernsey is holding moneys belonging to either of the defendants, the bank (being a bank locally resident in England) will, after service of the order, be required not to part with such moneys from the accounts held with the bank with their Guernsey branch.

The Vice-Chancellor thus treated Barclays Bank as a single entity and regarded service on the head office in London as sufficient to oblige it to ensure compliance with the order in Guernsey.

In *The Matter of M*,[145] the court granted an injunction for the benefit of the UK Customs and Excise affecting bank accounts maintained by the defendant at a branch of the Bank of Ireland within the Republic of Ireland. The bank was incorporated in Ireland and had its head office there. But it also had a number of branches in England and the order was served on the Southampton branch. The bank came to the English court to clarify the extent of its obligation to comply with the order. Ognall J approached the matter on the basis that the proviso, when it referred to a person being 'able to prevent acts or omissions' meant '*lawfully* able, under the relevant domestic law, to prevent acts or omissions'. He rejected a wider form of proviso which would have explicitly provided as follows:

> PROVIDED that nothing in this Order shall, in respect of assets located outside of England and Wales and in particular in Eire, prevent the Governor and Company of the Bank of Ireland ... from complying with:
>
> (i) What [the Bank] reasonably believes to be its obligation, contractual or otherwise, under the laws and regulations of the Country or State in which those assets are situated or under the proper law of the account in question.

He moreover expressed the view that insofar as a foreign bank established a branch in England 'it should be treated as implicitly undertaking to do all that is necessary to co-operate to the fullest extent with the courts and law enforcement agencies of this country'.

However, it is submitted that the formulation of the order which the judge

---

[143] [1990] 1 Ch 426.
[144] *Ibid.* 432–3.
[145] (*Unrep.*, Ognall J, 9 July 1993) and see, Malek & Lewis, 'Worldwide Mareva Injunctions: The Position of International Bank', [1990] *LMCLQ* 88.

did sanction, empties the proviso of much of its practical effect. Whether or not the law of the foreign country in question makes it an offence to comply with the foreign court order in such circumstances (as in Switzerland),[146] it is hard to imagine a state whose legal system would not, in the absence of a particular local law or order to the contrary, require a bank to act on its customer's instructions. Thus, the bank will be faced with the stark conflict between local law at the place of the account and the extraterritorial order.

The simplistic solution may be to extend the principle which applies in many other contexts of distinguishing branch from head office for the purpose of the court's enforcement powers.[147] That was not the approach taken in *SIB v Pantell*, and it does have the effect of absolving what is after all a single entity from responsibility for foreign branches. It may be that Ognall J was really exhorting the bank to seek directions from the Irish court (which may in fact have been able to recognise the English order under the Brussels Convention).

It is difficult to reconcile the two decisions as a matter of principle, unless (which may well be a fair basis of decision) the test comes down to the practical ability of officers of the bank to control acts abroad. In that context, the head office of Barclays may be in a more powerful position than the English branch of the Bank of Ireland. Despite the comments of Lord Donaldson MR to the contrary,[148] there may be a real distinction between the London branch which merely takes no steps and either:

(1) the local branch official who actively abets a foreign branch; or
(2) the head office director who has it in his power to prevent a foreign branch.

Perhaps the Vice-Chancellor felt more able to impose obligations on Barclays Bank in relation to their branch in Guernsey since that would not raise international law implications of the same character as the unrestricted enforcement of the English court's order on accounts of the Bank of Ireland in Ireland would have done.

The challenge of the potential for conflicts between jurisdictions, should not blind one to the very limited contexts in which the extraterritorial Mareva will be granted and can usefully operate.[149]

In almost all cases the plaintiff is better advised to pursue his interim remedies locally – where they will bite directly on the defendant's property. The apparently all-powerful Mareva may well prove of limited practical effect in relation to foreign assets. The order itself will rarely be enforceable abroad. Its main utility

---

[146] Article 271, Swiss Penal Code.
[147] *Mackinnon v Donaldson Lufkin & Jenrette* [1986] Ch 482.
[148] *Derby & Co Ltd v Weldon (Nos. 3 & 4)* [1990] Ch 65, 83–4.
[149] For more discussion of the practical limits and uses of the extraterritorial Mareva, see McLachlan, 'Transnational Interlocutory Measures for the Preservation of Assets, in *Singapore Conferences on International Business Law: Proceedings of Conference VII: Current Legal Issues in the Internationalization of Business Enterprises* (at press).

will often be in the ancillary disclosure orders and in the powers of court appointed receivers to supervise the defendant's assets.[150]

In the long run, in the field of transnational fraud (which is where the extraterritorial Mareva has arisen), banks may have more to fear from the widening scope for direct claims against them in the fraud context, proprietary tracing claims (where the rules are being liberalised)[151] and restitutionary remedies. But what lessons does the developing practice in this area of international civil procedure have for the international law of jurisdiction?

5.   Implications for the International Law of Jurisdiction

Civil jurisdiction (both original and enforcement) is a field traditionally claimed by public international law as a subset of the international law of jurisdiction, itself an attribute of sovereignty. But (for reasons developed more fully elsewhere)[152] this proposition must be treated with considerable caution. The civil process is as much (if not more) about the determination of a private dispute as it is about the exercise of state power. Of course private parties resort to the courts partly to obtain the benefits of state enforcement and the Mareva is an example of that. But the courts themselves have a strong interest in making their process effective.

These factors militate in policy terms against narrow conceptions of territorial jurisdiction. The rules at stake rarely engaged the attention of states. The important considerations are the balance of equities between the private parties (including affected third parties) and the international efficacy of the civil justice process itself – a matter of common international interest.

So far as defendants are concerned, it has been argued here that the real issue is not so much about the territorial scope of the enforcement order. It is about the width of the court's personal jurisdiction. So far as that is concerned, it is internationally accepted that courts may exercise civil jurisdiction over foreigners. The battle ground is: in what cases? As the author has shown elsewhere, this is not a matter on which international law is, or should be, silent. The determination of which disputes are sufficiently connected with a particular legal system to justify subjecting a foreigner to its courts, is (contrary to the reductionists[153]) something on which an international consensus may be discerned. Provided a defendant is properly personally subject to a court's jurisdiction, it does seem right that he should play the game according to the

---

[150] *Id.*
[151] See e.g. *El Ajou v Dollar Land Holdings plc* [1993] 3 All ER 717; [1994] All ER 685 (CA).
[152] McLachlan, *op. cit.*, note 110 above.
[153] Notably: Akehurst, 'Jurisdiction in International Law', (1972/3) 46 *BYIL* 145; Mayer, 'Droit International Privé et Droit International Public sous l'angle de la notion de Compétence', 68 *Rev. Crit. d.i.p* 1 349, 537 (1979).

local rules.[154] In saying this, one must accept that there are real limits on the court's ability to *execute* where it is minded to enforce.[155]

The English courts have, however, derived false comfort from the scheme of the Brussels/Lugano Conventions. In *Babanaft*,[156] Lord Justice Kerr thought that the Mareva should be extended extraterritorially because the Conventions would provide for its enforcement. Of course the Conventions did not inhibit at least an *inter partes* interim order from being enforceable abroad.[157] But the scheme of the Conventions contemplate that interim orders will be granted where the assets are situated in support of substantive proceedings elsewhere in Europe.[158] If anything, the extraterritorial Mareva rides roughshod over that.

Secondly, the English courts have misguidedly piggy-backed on their new-found ability to act in support of substantive proceedings elsewhere in Europe, by granting in *Duvalier* worldwide remedies against a foreigner in support of French proceedings.

So far as third parties are concerned, the jurisdictional issues present themselves much more directly. No question of original jurisdiction arises. The third party (such as a bank) is only involved by the operation of a state's enforcement jurisdiction.

The courts have rightly foreborne from regulating foreigners, and have also shown themselves mindful of the advice of Dr Mann:[159]

> The mere fact that a State's judicial or administrative agencies are internationally entitled to subject a person to their personal or curial jurisdiction does not by any means permit them to regulate by their orders such person's conduct abroad. This they may do only if the State of the forum also has substantive jurisdiction to regulate conduct in the manner defined in the order.

In the present state of the law, it is simply unclear in what circumstances the bank with single corporate personality but many branches may pray such a doctrine in aid. It is respectfully submitted that the court should look in addition for some element of actual control, direction or collusion on the part of the local officials.

To some extent the old jurisdictional certainties will have to give way to the larger international objective – reflecting the modern character of the international payments system – which puts the efficacy of the civil justice process first.

---

[154] *South Carolina Insurance Co v Assurantie Maatschappij De 'Zeven Provincien' NV* [1987] AC 24.

[155] See e.g. *Larkins v National Union of Mineworkers* [1985] ILR 671, on the unenforceability abroad of a sequestration order, because of its penal character.

[156] *Op. cit.*, note 126 above.

[157] *Op. cit.*, note 109 above.

[158] Article 24.

[159] Mann, 'The Doctrine of Jurisdiction in International Law', (1964) 111 *Hague Recueil* 146, cited with approval by Hoffmann J. in *Mackinnon v Donaldson Lufkin & Jenrette* [1986] ChD 482, 493.

Andreas F. Lowenfeld:

You don't do *ex parte*? I'm wondering about that.

Campbell McLachlan:

Well, yes, but in practice it is difficult because this order would have been denied. I'll come on in a moment to the practical considerations. The practical considerations often militate against asking for an order of this kind actually. The very important proviso, now called the *Babanaft* proviso, is the qualification set out on p. 4 which says that insofar as this order purports to have any extraterritorial effect no person shall be affected thereby or concerned with its terms unless (1) the order has been declared enforceable by a foreign court and then only to the extent so enforced; (2) the defendant (i.e. A), or a person who is subject to the jurisdiction of this court, has been given written notice of the order, and importantly (3) this is really where the problems arise, the defendant is able to prevent acts or omissions outside the jurisdiction of this court which assist in the breach of the terms of this order. So people who are in England but can do something about foreign branches are still not off the hook, but purely foreign third parties have nothing to fear from this order. So are such orders really extraterritorial?

So far as their effect on the defendant is concerned, the answer is undoubtedly 'yes' in the sense that the order relates to acts and property abroad. It requires defendants to go off and ensure that money is not removed from its Swiss bank account or its Panamanian bank account or whatever it might be, and in fact, affirmatively to give instructions to the bank as ordered to insure that that does not happen. And the contempt sanction is relevant. This is not totally clear but in my view contempt sanctions as against defendants bite irrespective of where the particular act may be concerned namely if the defendant in breach of this order gives instructions to the Swiss bank to pay the money away, he can be held in contempt of court in England.

Andreas F. Lowenfeld:

If he is there, can the court seize the assets in implementation of the contempt?

Campbell McLachlan:

There are two remedies in contempt. One is that a man who spends most of his time sleeping under the stairs in the Royal Court of Justice comes and drags you off to prison, this after a hearing, of course, The second remedy is the sequestration of assets, but effectively that would be sequestration of English assets.

Andreas F. Lowenfeld:

If they take the money that was subject to the freeze under the Mareva then the debtor-plaintiff loses something he might eventually go on, so it is not in his incentive to do that?

Campbell McLachlan:

That is correct and that is why you never apply for contempt unless in extraordinary circumstances because procedurally the safeguards are such that it is very difficult to obtain relief.

Andreas F. Lowenfeld:

I've been seeking such a case. I've been looking. Maybe that's the reason.

Campbell McLachlan:

Anyway, the other relief, as you are very well aware having worked with me on the case on this point (to Professor Lowenfeld) is that you can strike out the defendant's defence if you can show he is in breach. Now it may be said with a foreign defendant that is an illusory, pyrrhic victory. But in fact, as we show it in a case we recently did, it need not be because there is no reason, in principle, why a judgment given on that basis should not be enforced elsewhere in the world. In fact, although otherwise an unknown decision, the decision of Justice Feinsilber in Florida enforcing the court judgment against the head of the key perpetrator of the fraud supports the proposition that you can enforce abroad a judgment given as a result of a strikeout for contempt for breach of an order.

Andreas F. Lowenfeld:

It was not a Mareva order, but a summary order which is similar.

Campbell McLachlan:

All of this, most of which is waiting for a court to come to a decision on this extraterritorial effect as against the defendant, is justified as a part of the court's unlimited power to act *in personam* in relation to defendants subject to its jurisdiction, to act personally against the defendants and not to distinguish, or to use what I call judicial jurisdiction, in the same way against a foreigner as it would against a local defendant. But, of course, this *in personam* tag is a bit of a fiction. Sometimes the defendant is actually physically present in the jurisdiction but equally often he may be subject to the court's *in personam* jurisdiction because of long-arm jurisdiction. Under Rule 11, it says that the case has sufficient connection with England to justify the taking of jurisdiction over a foreigner. Although the heads are rather different, that is no different under the Brussels Convention where you have heads of special jurisdiction which allow the taking of jurisdiction based on the connection of the case with the country concerned over a foreigner.

Philip Bovey:

. . . except for summary order 11 head jurisdiction at least one is cut out.

Campbell McLachlan:

Well yes, as I said the definition of the heads may differ but the principle is the same.

Andreas F. Lowenfeld:

I just recently had a case where a maintenance creditor, a wife, who gets summary injunction against a husband in Spain. Do you know the case I mean? I just wrote a piece about it on venue. She doesn't even have to serve.

Campbell McLachlan:

That's not fair! The fourth respect in which the tag *in personam* jurisdiction may be a bit illusory is also the result of the Brussels Convention, art. 24 which enables an injunction to be given in support of proceedings elsewhere which does not seem to carry with it any original judicial jurisdictional basis necessary between the person concerned and the court granting the order and, in fact, quite the contrary, the idea is that you get your measure where there is some point in getting it, where there are assets or whatever although your original judicial jurisdiction may point elsewhere to the substance.

So far as the parties are concerned, in my view, these orders are not extraterritorial and I do not think that they would have been extraterritorial even without the *Babanaft* proviso or at least it is arguable that they were not. Because as against a foreign third party, who has no credit's name, acting wholly outside the jurisdiction, the English courts can take the power, which is, after all, the teeth behind the order, is clearly recognized as being quasi-criminal in nature, and would be, by all operation ordering principles of territoriality so far as the criminal law is concerned, not capable of dealing with breaches by third parties abroad. But if there are those who are squeamish about relying on simply such a robust view they will be no doubt comforted by the *Babanaft* proviso which, in my view, simply makes explicit what the general rule would have achieved anyway.

But all of this leaves two rather tricky problems. First, what do you do about National Westminster Bank or Barclays which has its head office in London but has branches all over the world, one juridical entity. In a decision taken after all of these Court of Appeal developments, the Court had to rule in the extraterritorial Mareva in relation to the defendant's assets, some of which were believed to be held by Barclays Bank in Guernsey, which is a matter of long standing national scandal. It is not part of England or Wales and not subject to the English courts. It is our nearest monetary haven. The Court expressly held that Barclays would be in breach of the order if it failed to prevent its branch in Guernsey from paying out the money.

Philip Bovey:

What is more, the provision that they enforced, the right that they enforced, was a public right, a securities act offence too.

Campbell McLachlan:

Correct. So that it was doubly settled.

Andreas F. Lowenfeld:

Does that make it stronger or weaker? The British view has been that you don't look at public law.

Campbell McLachlan:

Exactly. The American view would have been that it makes it stronger, that is, the state has a greater interest than some guy who got defrauded. But that is not the English view.

Philip Bovey:

But the bit of the English law, which they were acting on, was copied out from the American law.

Andreas F. Lowenfeld:

Yes, you do occasionally learn from us.

Campbell McLachlan:

Well both of these cases, *SIB v Pantell*, and also the very well known decision of *In the Matter of M*, which has only very recently been handed down, both actually concern the use of the Mareva procedure by public bodies for public ends, which places an interesting wrinkle on the whole debate. So Barclays would have been in breach if it had failed to make payment out of its Guernsey branch. This leaves the bank with a very real problem. There are some countries, and Switzerland is an obvious example, where it may be putting itself in positive breach of express mandatory stipulations of local law if it did take action which in any way interfered with the customer's right to withdraw. But you don't need that dramatic conflict situation to see that an obvious conflict arises. Because it is difficult to think of any jurisdiction in the world which does not provide that in the absence of a local court order the customer is free and the law obliges the bank to pay the customer on demand at the branch where the account is kept. So in every case, therefore, the bank is, in that sense, going to be acting contrary to local law unless the English order is recognised in any way in the foreign country and that situation . . .

Andreas F. Lowenfeld:

Think of Bankers Trust in London.

Campbell McLachlan:

Well that is right. That situation was thrown out in the second case which concerned the Bank of Ireland, a foreign bank with a branch in England, they had been served in England with the order, and the customer held his funds in Ireland. The bank came in and asked the court what they should do, were they obliged to stop withdrawals from Ireland or not? The decision regrettably is something of a fudge because what the court says is that the phrase in the proviso that you are able to prevent acts or omissions outside the jurisdiction means that you are lawfully able to prevent them, which completely begs the question. He left the bank to go off to Ireland and find out the answer. The answer is that they are not as a matter of Irish law lawfully permitted to prevent it at all unless the English injunction has some effect in Ireland, because the law in Ireland, as in England, says that you must pay the customer if he demands to be paid.

Andreas F. Lowenfeld:

Why is that not a recognition of judgments? Why should not the Irish court, recognise the English judgment?

Campbell McLachlan:

Because it is an *ex parte* injunction.

Andreas F. Lowenfeld:

But it does not have to be *ex parte*. If the depositor wants his money let him contest it in either London or Dublin.

Campbell McLachlan:

Well going into *partes* is a way around this, which I will deal with in the practical considerations.

Ulrich Bosch:

Generally when you have international treaties on the recognition of judgments or when you have domestic rules on the recognition of judgments that is judgments on the merits, but not . . .

Andreas F. Lowenfeld:

They do not exclude it. They do not say you cannot recognise the judgment they just say it is without reference . . .

Campbell McLachlan:

Generally they do. Although the US is very liberal on this, more so than anywhere else, to its credit, but most schemes both domestic law on enforcement of foreign judgments and various conventions are concerned with final money judgments.

Andreas F. Lowenfeld:

That is certainly true.

Campbell McLachlan:

So in the end, *In the Matter of M* is a fudge. It leaves this terribly difficult question. There is one legal entity, the Bank of Ireland, it is undoubtedly present in England. The Bank of Ireland, factually, could have prevented payment out but is there a distinction to be drawn between the branch in England and the head office? Does it make a difference which is where? Plainly there is in *Pantell*. The court thought the fact that the head office was in London and it obviously could control its branches made a difference but the judge was very uncomfortable about that, I think this is also understandable, that a foreign bank with a branch in England should be any less subject as it were to English jurisdiction than an English bank that may have branches abroad.

So, practical implications. The first practical implication is that as a matter of practice if you can, you should always forget about extraterritorial Marevas and go for local remedies. And the reason for that is obvious. Provided you know where the assets are, your local remedy will always be more effective and art. 24 of the Brussels Convention positively facilitates you rushing off and getting your attachments wherever assets are.

Andreas F. Lowenfeld:

But you can also use the Mareva to find out where the assets are.

Campbell McLachlan:

So the real reason why everyone asks for the extraterritorial Mareva is not for injunctive relief but for disclosure, which is, of course, where we got Mr Garen in the high technologies case and in *Republic of Haiti v Duvalier*, on which there has not been enough time to get into full detail on the facts but in other ways perhaps is the most doubtful of all the decisions from a public international law point of view. The real reason they came to England was because the Duvaliers' English lawyers had information about their worldwide assets which they were able to get by virtue of serving the ancillary disclosure order, and getting the extraterritorial injunction itself was just the icing on the cake, because, apart from everything else, even if you wanted to, your prospects of actually enforcing your extraterritorial Mareva abroad are very limited because it is an *ex parte* order. Now, it is possible to convert *ex parte* orders into *inter partes* orders by having a subsequent hearing and, in fact, this order is drafted very much on that basis. But it is still an undecided and open question whether at that point under the Brussels Convention scheme it is enforceable or not. But what is clear, and I have cited the *MI* case there, is that an *ex parte* order – in this case it is one from Germany – is not enforceable under the Convention.

Andreas F. Lowenfeld:

If my client is a defendant and the assets in England are not so great as compared to others, you say do not come in? The defendant can convert it into *inter partes* by appearing?

Philip Bovey:

Correct.

Andreas F. Lowenfeld:

But you say that's a mistake because that may make it more enforceable?

Philip Bovey:

Well, yes. I hate to tell people don't appear but it doesn't matter whether you do or not . . .

Campbell McLachlan:

So, the other reason why you may want such an injunction is the sort of reason that was given in a very much earlier case on this, trying to preserve the status quo. Get the information, and then rush around and get your attachments. But in practice that is rarely a good idea because all you do is give the defendant notice that you are after him and it will be too late to make the attachment bite. The final practical point I want to make before discussing the real point of this seminar was that all of these big cases, the ones that change the rule, were really fraud claims where the plaintiffs probably had proprietary remedies. They probably had a proprietary claim to these assets if they could have proved that they were their assets and the most recent developments in English law have not actually been to push Mareva so much further but to reform the rules of tracing to enable you to trace your assets much more easily and effectively and the new, dare I say, practical threat to banks, and the recent case is *Ostdeutsche Landesbank*, may be that it is much easier, and much more effective, to establish a proprietary remedy. Of course, if you have a proprietary remedy you sue the bank directly as the current holder of the assets.

Anyway, there's not time to go into the potential of all of that. Coming back to the relevance of all of this to our discussion on the international law of jurisdiction, I am not one of those people who believe that international law has no application at all on civil jurisdiction. You may be shocked to hear there is in fact, a respectable coterie of private international lawyers who think just that, but I am not one of them. But I do believe that the sovereignty framework is not sufficient to resolve problems in this area. I am talking, here, I should say, specifically about private civil law disputes and excluding areas like securities and antitrust where plainly different considerations apply.

It seems to me, and I could demonstrate it but I do not have time, that there is very wide acceptance, comparatively, of the idea that national courts may exercise original judicial jurisdiction over foreigners in appropriate cases. The arguments are about what are the appropriate cases, and secondly, what the courts can ask or compel foreigners to do and the third parties who may be put out once they take original judicial jurisdiction. So far as the plaintiffs are concerned, the general rule of state practice, if I can be permitted to use that expression, seems to be that once a court has taken original jurisdiction it does have an unlimited power to make personal orders against the defendant. That rule is very widely accepted. But as I have shown the *in personam* label is something of a myth because it can lead to taking of jurisdiction across a very wide range of foreign defendants. My submission, at any rate, is that there is a core of cases where the *situs* of the dispute, if you like, the connection of the dispute itself with a particular country, amply justifies taking original jurisdiction which is not, despite what some English judges have commented in House of Lords decisions, exorbitant at all. It simply recognises the fact that some cases have a very strong connection with a particular country even if the defendant happens not to be there.

So far as third parties are concerned, the rule seems to be much narrower and it does seem to depend on the actual physical presence of the third party in the jurisdiction. But what does that mean for multinational parties such as banks? Physical presence may be no more than a branch and yet the bank may have operations all over the world. Well, the cases have tried to grasp at the Brussels Convention as a means of developing some principles in relation to extraterritorial enforcement rules of the kind we have been discussing this evening, but I'm not sure how far that takes you. Lord Justice Carr tried to rely on the Convention as justifying the extraterritorial Mareva by saying that because such orders could, in principle, be enforceable provided they were given *intra partes*, etc. That showed that the Convention sanctioned them. Well, the fact that the Convention doesn't outlaw them does not seem to me to suggest that it positively promotes them and the scheme of art. 24 is that you go to the local place where the assets are and get a locally focused order in support of the substantive proceeding where the substance of the dispute is to be litigated.

The other fallacy, I think, in these cases so far as the Convention is concerned, is the idea that you can get an extraterritorial order in support of proceedings in another convention country where there is actually no personal jurisdiction over the defendant at all. That was the real problem with the *Republic of Haiti v Duvalier*. It would have been fine if the English court gave an order relating to

. . .

Andreas F. Lowenfeld:

But the Swiss have done that for years.

Campbell McLachlan:

But the idea that you could go to ... Let's get to the substance in France. That there happens not to be a local French extraterritorial remedy so you come to England and get that remedy even though the defendant has no connection to England at all I find a bit egregious.

Well, does the Restatement and the concept of balancing interest and the like help us in this field? In my humble opinion, this is not an area where the balancing of interest is either appropriate or useful. Civil litigation is not, after all, just an exercise of state power, not just an attribute of sovereignty, it is also the resolution of a private dispute. This seems to me to have the consequence that in the exercise of original jurisdiction there are many cases where states have no real interest in which court exercises original jurisdiction. And also, extraterritorial jurisdiction at the originating stage is very very widely practised and sanctioned as I've said. So it seems to me that to try and balance state interests in asking yourself, trying to find a basis for a rule for extraterritoriality in civil disputes, is really asking the wrong question and it may be positively injurious in entrenching attitudes of sovereignty in an area where the real consideration should be as to the equity of the civil justice process and fairness to the defendant. So, at the very least, narrow conceptions of territoriality must be much enlarged and it does seem to me and here is where I would rely on the Brussels and Lugano Conventions that there is some common ground developed on the notion of exercise of original jurisdiction based on the *situs* of the dispute. And I think the traditional idea of saying once you take personal jurisdiction, even if that were reasonable, you can do anything, is not enough. Rather, it is important to distinguish between personal and subject-matter jurisdiction in asking yourself what orders courts can make in the civil process.

Sir Ian Sinclair:

Thank you very much, Mr McLachlan.

I think we could go on discussing this all night, but I wanted to close this meeting tonight at 8 o'clock. Therefore, I will immediately call upon Professor Drobnig, to say a few words.

Ulrich Drobnig:

I should perhaps first state my disqualifications. I am not a public international lawyer. I am not a practitioner so I am not at all conversant with the details of injunctions or Mareva injunctions. But I have come from private law and I have especially some experience with respect to international civil procedure.

Let me try to start matters from a somewhat different angle, or theoretical approach: what are the typical questions which arise? I think, one should distinguish between three stages. First, of course, the exercise of extraterritorial jurisdiction by a country and its possible effects. The second stage arises in the country abroad, I will call it 'local jurisdiction' where the order or decision made in the first country purports to have effects, and then there is a third stage and that is, if in stage number two, there are effects abroad, counter-measures. To what degree should the first country take those effects into account?

I think the paper on taxation has alluded to all of these three stages but I think that for a theoretical approach it helps to clarify the issue and make a distinction along these lines. If I come to the question of orders affecting bank deposits, I should wish to say that banks more than other commercial enterprises are subject to be affected by extraterritorial actions. Why is this so? I think that this is due to the way banks structure their international business. Normal commercial enterprises would incorporate foreign business of some substance in separate subsidiaries and therefore to some degree, in civil law countries more than in the US of course, insulate themselves from effects which could be caused by acts in their own country. Banks, due to reasons which are probably known to you, do not do so in general. They operate with the help of branches and branches are not legally independent but part of the whole enterprise, and therefore are much more put to the risk of being affected by commands both from the home state to judicial decisions and effects, as well as acts by the local state.

Having said this, I should try to very briefly summarise the German practice in this field. In fact, there are to my knowledge practically no cases which deal directly with bank deposits. But I think that German writers in the general field of international civil procedure and German courts in other related fields have established principles which can be applied easily.

So I start with the first stage. What would German courts do if the issue arises with respect to bank deposits held in a foreign branch of a German bank? The answer to this is, generally speaking, the following: German courts, as I said in other areas, have without any reservation issued decisions and orders which oblige the defendant to carry out acts in the foreign country, let's say in Spain in a vacation home, but to give information which can only be obtained abroad or to produce documents which are held abroad. So the courts have no hesitation and certainly no public international law restrictions before them. They issue such orders and decisions. Of course, the execution of such an order, if the defendant is not willing to comply, depends on the foreign country if enforcement must be sought abroad, but if enforcement can be sought in Germany of course it will be sought, even if it relates to those foreign parts.

The same general and very broad scope of jurisdiction always provided that the ordinary sources of jurisdiction exist either by international law or by treaty. The same challenge on a broad scope is used if orders for the gathering or acquisition of evidence are issued by the courts. We have had one case in the Federal Supreme Court in which an Italian man was ordered to come before a German court as an alleged father. He was tried. He was asked to take blood tests in order to prove or disprove his paternity. He did not do so, he did not follow the order and the court held that the non-willingness to undergo this blood test would be held against him, that is the negative consequences would be the same as if the blood test result had been against him. So that is the situation on the first stage. If bank deposits are concerned, I think a German court would act in the same way as the US Supreme Court acted in the case *United Case v First National City Bank* decided in 1964, where the issue was an order against dispositions with respect to the deposit held in the Uruguay branch of First National City. I think they would do the same. And please if I may remind you that in that case the courts especially underlined the fact that it was only a branch, not a subsidiary, and that apparently there was no issue of any Uruguay law against the compliance with that order.

Second stage: an order or decision is issued in the home country which assumes extraterritorial effect, how does the local jurisdiction react? I will now assume that the order or decision has been issued abroad and that Germany is the local jurisdiction. And of course, whether that order will be enforced in Germany depends on German law, on the general rules of recognition and enforcement, which I do not want to expose here. I will refer you to one German case which has a certain relevance. It is a case decided by a district court in Kiel in 1982 which refused to recognise a subpoena which had been issued by an American Grand Jury and which had subpoenaed a German bank with respect to deposits of its German client. That client was under investigation in the US and the subpoena had demanded information from the bank about the client's background and his holdings in the bank. The reason for declining to enforce the subpoena was that German bank secrecy was held up and it was said by the court that only important reasons would stand up, and would prevent an objection against a foreign order of this kind. The priority of the German procedure was derived by the court by giving German bank secrecy the value of a constitutional rule. It was derived from the constitutional right of freedom of action. I think that reason is a rather doubtful one. If, by contrast, there is a freeze order issued in the home country against other branches of the bank, I refer to the famous *Bankers Trust* case, which was just mentioned, I think the German court would decide exactly like the English court, the reason being that this is a temporary expropriation of a sovereign nature which in general would not be given effect in Germany. An exception would only be accepted, I think, if that order was qualified as being also of the German interest.

Andreas F. Lowenfeld:

For instance, suppose that an American bank with a German branch holds assets belonging to Saddam Hussein, and the American order identifies him. I think the Germans would enforce it because there is a UN Resolution.

Ulrich Drobnig:

Yes, that would be the only valid ground.

Andreas F. Lowenfeld:

And if you remember in the Iranian cases they never decided it.

Campbell McLachlan:

I know but if they entered into a UN mandatory resolution, that creates quite a different situation.

Ulrich Drobnig:

We have had an order to substantiate the exception which I mentioned, two cases in which contracts relating to transportation and deliveries which were against the COCOM rules which at that time were not binding on us, were still recognised on the ground that the violation of those rules was also injurious to Germany in the common fight against communism.

Now very briefly to the third stage as a home state. Germany again issues orders or decisions but which are met by countervailing or contradictory decisions or are contrary to law of any kind in the local jurisdiction. The question arises, to what degree will the German court take that foreign legislation into account. Again, there is no direct authority in the case of bank deposits, but we have case law in other areas, which shows that the courts are willing to protect interests, not state interests but rather interests of the private parties involved. One case is rather strong in that respect. It dealt with a German-English sales contract concluded before the outbreak of the First World War, but then frustrated by the war, the German buyer sued the English party. The complaint was denied on the ground that the English party was justified in relying on the English Trading with the Enemy Act. I think that is really remarkable. It really is not state interests which were involved because clearly the Act was directed against Germany. But still the German court was willing to regard it. It looked at the situation of the party involved. There may, of course, be extreme cases where one would say that goes so much against our state interests and would be contrary to all German public policy that we cannot accept it. If only private parties are involved, then German courts are, in general, quite liberal in protecting interests.

Sir Ian Sinclair:

Thank you very much, Mr Drobnig. It has been very very helpful. I am sure we could go discussing this particular topic, until 11 o'clock tonight, but I am sure, you all are, as I am, anxious to get something perhaps to eat. So I would propose to draw our proceedings today to a conclusion.

Chapter IV

Jurisdictional Rules in Customary International Law

Harold G. Maier

1. Introduction

I have divided this topic into three segments. The first addresses the relationship between the principle of territorial sovereignty in customary international law and international legal limitations on the exercise of extraterritorial jurisdiction. The second reviews the origins and role of the principle called 'international comity' as it places self-imposed limitations on the scope of extraterritorial assertions of authority. The third segment describes the blending of these two concepts in the Restatement (Third) of Foreign Relations Law of the United States.[160]

2. Customary International Law

Modern customary international legal limitations on a nation's exercise of extraterritorial authority have their roots in those fundamental principles of territorial sovereignty that still inform much of modern international law. Traditionally, lawyers, scholars, judges and statespersons describe the international community as a community of independent sovereign states.

The term 'sovereign state' echoes a time when dealing with a nation or tribe meant dealing with a specific individual whose decisions were recognised as

---

[160] This paper was originally commissioned as a general introduction to the Conference. It should be read in that light although scheduling considerations caused it to be delivered during the Conference's second day.

authoritative by his or her people, a time when trade and travel were, for most people, confined by territorial borders. That term, 'sovereign state' describes nothing more – and nothing less – than a group of people with a general commonality of interests living in an artificially bounded geographical area. That commonality of interests is largely defined by that common territorial bond and by the population's acceptance of the proposition that some few of their number may legitimately make and enforce rules about relationships among the members of the group, between the group and individuals, both members and non-members, and between the group and other such groups.[161] Today, improvements in means of communication and transportation both facilitate international economic and social intercourse and support the proposition that the effects of governmental encroachments upon human liberty often transcend territorial boundaries, thus creating community interests in limiting or preventing such entanglements. In this same vein, interests in the effects of commercial activities, and the resulting need to regulate them can no longer be localised within national boundaries. These increasingly complex inter-relationships between national, social and economic interests foster a recognition by the world community that there are occasions when both national and community interests are served by permitting a nation to address, under its laws, activities carried on outside its national borders.[162]

On the other hand, the idea that sovereign authority is limited by territorial boundaries is far from dead. The corollary of sovereign power is sovereign responsibility. The recognition of territorial sovereignty fixes responsibility for compliance or non-compliance with community norms upon designated institutions who can speak for, and listen on behalf of, the people living within a designated geographical area. Considered in this way, the concept of territorial sovereignty has become a useful metaphor for a system of communication. Without such a system, one could not even begin to attempt to harmonise and co-ordinate the efforts of the groups of people who make up the world community while both serving localised interests and a general interest in community stability and predictability that is essential for social and commercial security.[163]

Although the presumed limitation of governmental authority to a nation's territorial boundaries flows from the historic concept of the modern nation state, the proposition that a state may on occasion exercise authority over events beyond its borders also flows, paradoxically, from the principle that the interests of the people that make up the state's population are territorially defined. This

---

[161] Harold G. Maier, 'The Principles of Sovereignty, Sovereign Equality, and National Self-Determination', in Paul B. Stephan III, and Boris M. Klimenko, (eds.), *International Law and International Security: Military and Political Dimensions* 241–43 (1991).

[162] See statement by John R. Stevenson, Dept. of State Bulletin 12 Oct. 1970, at 429, to the effect that the activities of the modern multinational corporation cannot be regulated solely by territorially bounded national laws.

[163] Maier, *op. cit.*, note 161 above, at 242.

conclusion is made clear in the opinions in the case of the *SS Lotus*, decided by the Permanent Court of International Justice in 1927.[164]

The *Lotus* case represents one of the best and most rational expositions of why the concept of territorial sovereignty may justify a nation in applying its legal norms to both nationals and non-nationals beyond its borders. In *Lotus*, Lieutenant Demon was officer of the deck on a French ship on the high seas when that ship struck the Turkish ship *Bozkort*, sinking it and killing several members of its crew. The *Lotus* entered the harbour at Istanbul where the Turkish government asked Demons to come ashore to describe what had happened. When he complied, the Turks arrested him and sought to try him for manslaughter under Turkish criminal negligence law. The French government objected on the grounds that Demons' acts were confined to the French ship on the high seas, and that therefore Turkish law could not apply to determine his guilt. France and Turkey took the case to the Permanent Court.

The Court ruled that Turkish law could govern, even though all of Demon's acts were carried out in French territory. In doing so, the Court adopted the proposition that the independence of sovereign states implied that, as a rule, territorial sovereigns were free to do what they wished, as long as such action did not violate a prohibitory rule of customary or conventional international law. With respect to the assertion of jurisdiction, the Court wrote:

> Far from laying down a general prohibition to the effect that States may not extend the application of their law and the jurisdiction of their courts to persons, property and acts outside their territory, it leaves them in this respect a wide measure of discretion which is only limited in certain cases by prohibitive rules. As regards other cases, every state remains free to adopt the principles which it regards as best and most suitable.[165]

And the *Lotus* Court went on to articulate what has come to be known in some domestic circles as the effects doctrine of international law — that a nation has jurisdiction over outside events that have effects within its borders. The Court's conclusion is not, of course, binding on states other than those actually before it. Its broader effect flows from its ultimate good sense. A consensual legal system could not, in logic or practice, contain a rule prohibiting a sovereign state from prescribing rules against activities outside its borders that have harmful effects within the state's territory. Any other conclusion would legally place each sovereign and, more importantly, the people whom that sovereignty protects, at the mercy of the internal acts and politics of every other. Although it is perhaps conceivable that a nation state might, by explicit agreement, commit its people and its territory to this form of international subservience, without such an agreement there is insufficient evidence of community consent to a rule that would legitimise such external interference. The *Lotus* Court, therefore, correctly

---

[164] *SS 'Lotus'* (France v Turkey), 1927 P.C.I.J., Ser. A, No. 10 (Judgment of 7 Sept. (hereinafter, *Lotus* case)).

[165] *Lotus* case, note 164 above, at 19.

refused to infer such a prohibition from the general principle of territorial sovereignty.

The absence of such a general prohibition does not, of course, mean that nation states are free to interfere with each other's internal affairs whenever harmful local effects might justify such interference. Rather, this recognition of the legal possibility of concurrent jurisdiction of two or more states over the same acts and the persons committing them necessarily suggests that community members are required to accommodate their conflicting interests in good faith on a case-by-case basis when each has legitimate authority to prescribe.[166]

The principles of the international law of jurisdiction were outlined in the Harvard Research of International Law,[167] which was carried out by the members of the Harvard Law School faculty in the 1920s and 1930s as part of an effort to codify the international rules of jurisdiction. That work was the intellectual, if not the institutional, forerunner of the American Law Institute's Restatements (Second)[168] and (Third) of the Foreign Relations Law of the United States. Four of the five jurisdictional principles described in those three documents recognise circumstances under which a state's authority is not constrained by its territorial boundaries. A short review of these principles may be helpful to put the remainder of this discussion in context.

The first principle is the territorial principle. It is the most universally recognised because control over defined territory is not only a legal prerequisite for statehood but is also essential to permit a state's government to be responsible to other nations for internal compliance with its external community commitments. In order to answer for the conduct of persons living within its territory a state's government must be able to communicate and listen on their behalf. Consequently, control over territory is essential to the exercise of such authority. In fact, the entire concept of consent of nations as a basis for international law requires that some institution be able to speak for a population in order to give such consent.

The *Lotus* case added the proposition that control over territory necessarily included control over events that affected that territory. These two territorial theories are generally referred to as the subjective and objective theories of territorial jurisdiction. Both are found in at least two international conventions, the Convention for the Suppression of Counterfeited Currency (1929)[169] and

---

[166] See s. 403(3), Restatement (Third) of the Foreign Relations Law of the United States 1987 (hereinafter Restatement (Third)).

[167] Harvard Research on International Law: 'Jurisdiction with Respect to Crime', 29 *American J. of Intl L.*, Supplement 1, 435, 445 (1935).

[168] American Law Institute, Restatement (Second) of the Foreign Relations Law of the US 1965.

[169] Article 9, International Convention for the Suppression of Counterfeiting Currency and Protocol, 112 League of Nations Treaty Series No. 2624, 20 April 1929 (hereinafter Counterfeiting Convention).

the Convention for the Suppression of Illicit Traffic in Dangerous Drugs (1936).[170]

The second generally accepted jurisdictional principle identified in the Harvard Research project and the Restatements is that a state has jurisdiction over its nationals (and, perhaps over permanent resident aliens) no matter where these persons are located. Since people travel across national boundaries, this principle, taken together with the territoriality principle, necessarily recognised the legal possibility for legitimate and concurrent jurisdiction by more than one nation over the same act when perpetrated by the nationals of one country within the territory of another.

In addition to the territorial and nationality principles, the Harvard Research project and the Restatements identify three others: The protective principle that recognises a state's extraterritorial jurisdiction over acts designed to injure its process of government,[171] and the universality principle, recognising a state's jurisdiction to punish universally recognised crimes,[172] were found to be generally accepted by the world community. The Harvard Research project noted, but rejected, the so-called passive personality principle, recognising a state's right to punish offences against its own citizens no matter where such offences may have occurred.[173]

Each of these principles, including the objective territorial principle, recognises that in some circumstances a state is legally free to act outside its territory to reprehend and punish activities that threaten it or its people. The resolution of claims of authority based on the various combinations of

---

[170] Articles 2 and 3, Convention of 1936 for the Suppression of the Illicit Traffic in Dangerous Drugs, 198 League of Nations Treaty Series No. 4648, 26 June 1936 (hereinafter Illicit Drugs Convention).

The purpose of both conventions is to permit states to act against both internal and external events designed to further the criminal activities that the conventions address. Each treaty contains, however, the following identical provision:

The Participation of a High Contracting Party in the present Convention shall not be interpreted as affecting that party's attitude on the general questions of criminal jurisdiction as a question of international law.

Article 17, Counterfeiting Convention, note 169 above; art. 14, Illicit Drug Convention.
[171] No effect on the territory of the state seeking to regulate this foreign-based activity is required because once an effect is felt, it may be too late for the state that is the object of the activity to save itself.
[172] This principle is generally accepted as the basis for punishing pirates and is accepted by many nations as the grounds for exercising jurisdiction over genocide, aircraft hijacking and other forms of international terrorism. It is the nature of the crime, not the effect of the criminal act, that makes a crime universally punishable.
[173] Accord: s. 402, Comment g Restatement (Third). In the *Lotus* case, note 164 above, the Turks argued they had jurisdiction over Demon's acts because those acts had injured Turkish nationals, a proposition that the Permanent Court of International Justice did not adopt. The US has been one of the greatest opponents of the passive personality principle. However, the US Congress, somewhat to the discomfort of the US Department of State, has asserted the passive personality principle with respect to injuries to US citizens by international hijackers and terrorists. Section 1202, Omnibus Diplomatic Security and Antiterrorism Act of 1986, 18 U.S.C. s. 2231.

concurrent jurisdiction to which these principles give rise is found in an accommodation process operating outside the limits of formal international law. That process of accommodation is described by the principle of international comity.

The proposition that a state is free to act against events or persons outside its territory unless restrained by a prohibitory rule of international law is informed by a recognition that a state is justified by its interest in protecting its society when its self-interest is engaged by acts outside its territory that have an effect within its territory. The pragmatic basis for this legal conclusion is clear. A nation is hardly likely to have consented to a prohibition that would prevent it from acting to protect itself, i.e. its economy and society, from injury caused by acts outside its borders. To conclude otherwise would put every state at the mercy of every person acting in every other state when the government at the *situs* of the acts has no self-interest in preventing those acts. The nation that is the *situs* of the acts necessarily has a similar self-interest in determining whether the acts in question should be reprehended. That self-interest is defined by the *situs* state's freedom as an independent sovereign to govern its own society within its territory. If each state is legally free to act under the principle of territorial sovereignty, the resolution of these legitimate assertions of concurrent jurisdiction must be found outside international law. [174] The resolution of such conflicts is addressed under the principle of international comity.

3. International Comity

Today's international comity principle had its origins in the writings of the Dutch scholar Ulricus Huber, who used the principle to answer the question 'How can a nation that is absolutely sovereign within its own territory nonetheless make use of the laws and policies of another nation in deciding a case before the forum sovereign's courts?' Huber's answer was simple. Since it was a sovereign's forum that chose to make use of another sovereign's legal rules, that choice was itself an

---

[174] An early version of the Restatement (Third) appeared to adopt a contrary view. It provided that when concurrent assertions of otherwise legally valid authority resulted in conflicting commands to persons subject to those concurrent jurisdictions, the state with the lesser interest lost its legal right to exercise its jurisdiction. See American Law Institute, Restatement (Revised) Foreign Relations Law of the United States, Tent. Draft No. 2, s. 403(3) (hereinafter Restatement (Revised)). This provision was changed by vote of the ALI in May 1986, to make relinquishment of jurisdiction in interest balancing situations a matter for each nation's choice, not an international legal requirement. See ALI, Restatement (Third) s. 403(3), 1987. For an informative discussion of the implications of the earlier draft, see letter from Judge Malcolm R. Wilkey to Professor Louis Henkin, reprinted as an appendix to Harold Maier, 'Resolving Extraterritorial Conflicts or "There and Back Again"', 25 *Virginia J. of Intl L.* 7, 43–48 (1984) (hereinafter 'Resolving Conflicts'). See also, *Laker Airways Ltd v Sabena, Belgian World Airlines* 731 F.2d 909, 948–51 (D.C. Cir. 1984). Professor Lowenfeld's letter, objecting to Judge Wilkey's conclusions about the meaning of s. 403(3), Tentative Draft No. 2, Restatement (Revised), is excerpted in Maier, 'Resolving Conflicts', above, 36–37.

exercise of forum sovereignty. This comports with the conclusion, reached centuries later in the *Lotus* case, that there is no compulsion external to the forum to give effect to the laws or decisions of the foreign state.[175]

Rather, under Huber's comity analysis, the informing principle is the forum's self-interest in avoiding inconvenience to the 'commerce and general intercourse of nations' by not casting into doubt foreign-created rights and duties, unless to give them effect would be clearly repugnant to the forum's interests.[176]

In the early nineteenth century, US Supreme Court Justice Joseph Story, author of what was at the time the world's most widely translated and used treatise on private international law, provided the best statement of the role of the self-interest principle in informing decisions based on the principle of comity. He wrote:

> The true foundation on which the administration of international law must rest is that the rules which are to govern are those which arise from mutual interest and utility from a sense of the inconvenience which would result from a contrary doctrine and from a sort of moral necessity to do justice in order that justice may be done to us in return.[177]

With reference to the extraterritorial application of domestic regulatory legislation, the principle of comity counsels judicial or governmental restraint in applying such legislation to foreign-based persons or events.[178] Under this usage, the term 'comity' describes a kind of international golden rule, a principle of conduct: Each nation should give that respect to the laws, policies, and interests of others that it would have others give to its own in the same or similar circumstances.[179] As the US Supreme Court wrote in *Hilton v Guyot*:[180]

> 'Comity' in the legal sense, is neither a matter of absolute obligation, on the one hand, nor of mere courtesy and good will, upon the other. But it is the recognition which one nation allows within its territory to the legislative, executive, or judicial acts of another nation, having due regard both to international comity and convenience, and to the rights of its own citizens, or of other persons who are under the protection of its laws.[181]

Considered in this light, the concept of comity is a pragmatic principle of

---

[175] See text at note 165 above.

[176] Davies, *The Influence of Huber's de Conflictu Legum on English Private International Law*, 18 Brit. *YBIL* 49, 59 (1937).

[177] J. Story, 'Commentaries on the Conflict of Laws' 33, Bigelow (ed.) (1883). This view did not match that of contemporary continental writers who believed that the rules of private international law were dictated by a *jus gentium* whose content could be derived by analysis of first principles. See generally Yntema, 'The Comity Doctrine', 65 *Mich. L. Rev.* 9 (1960).

[178] See Gary B. Born and David Westin, *International Civil Litigation in United States Courts*, 24–25 (2d edn, 1992).

[179] Maier, 'Resolving Conflicts', note 175 above, at 15; Harold Maier, 'Remarks, Panel Discussion, International Comity and US Federal Common Law', 1990 Proceedings, *American Society of International Law*, 326, 340.

[180] 159 US 113 (1895).

[181] 159 US 113.

reciprocal expectations. It is informed by a perception of a fundamental attribute of human nature – that if one treats other human beings fairly, he or she is likely to be treated fairly in return. In this context, the comity principle does not answer Huber's question, 'how' can one sovereign use another's law. Rather, it addresses the question 'Which law', domestic or foreign, shall be applied to determine the rights of the parties in the case at hand. [182]

4. Comity, the Restatement and Interest Balancing

The Restatement (Third) of Foreign Relations Law of the United States, published in 1987, is the most recent thorough scholarship treating international legal limitations on the exercise of sovereign authority. Section 403 of that work effectively combines the principles of customary international law with the principle of comity to establish a comprehensive framework for analysing extraterritoriality cases. [183]

The development of the Restatement (Third) was not without controversy

---

[182] The Court in *Hilton* went on to misapply the concept of natural reciprocity reflected in the comity principle by turning reciprocity into a sword of retortion, rather than a reflection of probable mutually beneficial conduct. The Court ruled that US courts would refuse conclusive effect to a foreign country's judgment, absent a showing that the foreign country's courts would give similar conclusive effect to judgments from the US. Few, if any, modern US courts have followed this portion of the *Hilton* case, a perfectly permissible result since *Hilton* was decided under a body of private law specially applicable in US federal courts, not binding on the states. This law, erroneously called 'federal common law' since the early decision in *Swift v Tyson* 41 US (16 Pet.) 1 (1842), required that federal courts apply their own version of the common law in diversity jurisdiction cases. That sort of 'federal common law' (better described as 'federal courts law' because it applied only when a case was in a federal court) did not create precedent binding upon the states. See e.g. *Cowans v Ticonderoga Pulp and Paper Co* 219 App. Div. 120, 219 N.Y.S. 284, *aff'd* 246 N.Y. 603, 159 N.E. 669 (1927). For a discussion of this distinction, see Harold Maier, 'The Three Faces of Zapata: Maritime Law, Federal Common Law, Federal Courts Law', 6 *Vanderbilt J. of Transnat. L.* 387–88 (1973); Elliott Cheatham and Harold Maier, 'Private International Law and Its Sources', 22 *Vanderbilt Law Review* 27, 58 (1968). See generally Hill, 'The Law-Making Power of the Federal Courts: Constitutional Preemption', 67 *Columbia L. Rev.* 1024 (1967). Neither the *Hilton* court, nor any other US court, has challenged the fundamental proposition that the principle of comity, as properly applied in these situations, presumes that reciprocal conduct will result from efforts by decision makers to take the interests and concerns of other nations into account when arriving at decisions about the applicability of domestic or foreign rules and judgments. See generally Gary B. Born and David Westin (eds.), *International Civil Litigation in United States Courts* 22–26 (2nd edn, 1992).

[183] My good friend Professor Andreas Lowenfeld of NYU was an Associate Reporter for the Restatement (Third) and is the intellectual father of its sections dealing with limitations on the exercise of national jurisdiction. See Andreas Lowenfeld, 'Public Law in the International Arena: Conflict of Laws, International Law, and Some Suggestions for Their Interaction', 163 *Recueil Des Cours* 315 (1979 II). In addition, Professor Karl Meessen who organised this conference, was Special Consultant on International Economic Law to the ALI for the Restatement (Third).

and some of that controversy focused on the theoretical premises that informed the sections dealing with extraterritorial jurisdiction. [184]

Despite its nationalistic title, much of the Restatement does not necessarily describe the views of the US government concerning the content of international legal norms. Rather it

> represents the opinion of the American Law Institute as to the rules that an impartial tribunal would apply if charged with deciding a controversy in accordance with international law. [185]

With respect to the Restatement sections dealing with limitations on the exercise of state authority, [186] those sections are in fact a blend of international law and the principle of comity. The Restatement correctly argues that the exercise of state authority is, as in all international law, conditioned by the requirement that one state may not act in an unreasonable manner toward another. [187]

This conclusion is, in fact, a truism but a useful one. The consensual legal system could not exist if it included legal consent to unreasonable actions even though, in most circumstances, such actions would be deemed legally permissible. Whether an act is 'reasonable' can be determined only in the context in which that act occurs. The Restatement (Third) therefore concludes that, even though a state's assertion of authority satisfies one of the four generally accepted jurisdictional principles, that assertive act may nontheless be illegal if it is unreasonable in the context in which it is performed.

This reasonableness requirement reflects the reciprocal interest of all nations in the world community in dealing reasonably with each other. It is in this respect that the Restatement's requirement closely resembles the principle of international comity. The difference between the two is that the principle of comity reflects the state's freedom under the law to choose the path most likely to encourage reciprocal action by other states in later situations. That freedom was identified in the *Lotus* case. [188] Section 403(1) of the Restatement (Third) reflects the limitations of international law; international law reprehends unreasonable acts.

Considerable controversy arose during the development of the Restatement (Third) over whether a nation having jurisdiction to apply its law but with lesser interests in doing so than another nation having concurrent jurisdiction to apply its law was required by some rule of international law to renounce its title to that decision. In other words, did international law require that states asserting

---

[184] For a more complete discussion of the nature of this controversy, see generally Panel Discussion, 'The Restatement (Third) of Foreign Relations Law of the United States (Revised): How Were the Controversies Resolved?' 1987 Proceedings; *Amer. Soc. of Intl L.* 180.

[185] Preface, ALI Restatement (Third).

[186] See especially, ss. 401–403, Restatement (Third).

[187] Section 403(1), Restatement (Third).

[188] See text at note 165 above.

concurrent jurisdiction balance their respective interests and tip the scales in favour of the one whose interest was greatest.

The American Law Institute did not endorse such a requirement but did conclude that wise policy would encourage deference by the state with the lesser interest to the one with the greater interest at stake in the result.[189] This conclusion reflects the principle of comity: that a state should recognise the greater interests of a sister state so that, in the future, when the weights of interests might be reversed, that other state would be likely to grant it the same reasonable result. Evidence of an international legal rule requiring this result is sparse. At best one can argue that the courts of several nations do in fact employ this interest balancing technique, but there is little evidence that they do so because they believe that this approach is required as a customary practice accepted as law.

5. Conclusion

I hope that this excursion through this conceptual maze is helpful. At least it may get us talking about the same things. If we are to make preparation to suggest a resolution at the general meeting in Buenos Aires next summer, I would like to add a caveat.

When the law ceases to reflect the realities of life it is the law, not life, that will change. This is just as true of a treaty as it is of customary law. One of the realities of modern life is that most states have interest in events that occur in other states; and sometimes those interests rise to a level that calls for local attention to those foreign-based activities. The state of the *situs* of those activities often has at least as great an interest as the affected state, often a conflicting one.

The International Law Association is to consider a resolution on this issue, such a resolution should not begin by playing linguistic games with legal labels. Characterisations like 'territorial' v 'extraterritorial' or 'rule of law' v 'principle of comity' describe results already achieved; they do not direct decision makers to the relevant policies and, therefore, to the appropriate result in the next situation or case. At best, they tell us what to argue about, but not the result of that argument.

The question for the decision maker is always, 'What are the appropriate policies that should inform the result in this case?' The decision maker looks to rules of law and sometimes other evidences to find those policies. The principal question in every extraterritoriality case is, 'In the light of the policies reflected in the competing characterisations and rules of law that are being urged upon the decision maker, what decision in this case makes objective good sense?'

---

[189] For a discussion of the ALI floor debates leading up to this conclusion, see Harold G. Maier, Review of Lange and Born (eds.), 'The Extraterritorial Application of the Antitrust Laws' (1987), 83 *AJIL* 676, 678–79 (1989).

Rules of law based on objective good sense will necessarily achieve a greater acceptance among both the private persons and government officials who make the actual decisions in these situations. Such rules will also affect the human beings in whose interests these competing policies are weighed and in whose interests rules of law should, and must, ultimately function if they are to have any meaning at all in what is, in actual practice, still a consensual legal system.

Sir Ian Sinclair:

Thank you very much, Harold. That was a very useful introduction that will generate a certain amount of comment around the table, but before we open the discussion more generally, I will call upon Andrea Bianchi from the University of Siena to comment.

Andrea Bianchi:

Thank you, Sir Ian. When I was invited by Professor Meessen to act as a discussant on this topic, I started wondering what the proper role of a discussant should be. I thought that it would not be proper to present my own views and that I should confine myself to highlighting the most relevant issues inherent in the principal speaker's contribution. On second thoughts I realised that even the latter would not be an objective exercise. Therefore, I set aside any theoretical preoccupation with the propriety of the role and decided to submit my own arguments for the purpose of stimulating the ensuing debate. After all, as Ronald Dworkin has expounded in his writings, legal argumentation is but an 'interpretative enterprise' and, as such, highly subjective.

1.   Introductory Remarks

At a time of increasing perplexity about the actual content of the rule of state sovereignty in contemporary international law, the scientific debate on the customary law of jurisdiction seems to be gaining momentum again.[190] The complexity of economic relations and financial transactions in the world market makes it difficult at times to determine which jurisdiction controls what activities. The issue of what legal basis may be legitimately used by states to justify their

---

[190] See C. Schreuer, 'The Waning of the Sovereign State: Towards a New Paradigm for International Law?', 4 *Eur. J. Intl L.* 447–471 (1993) and N. MacCormick, 'Beyond the Sovereign State', 56 *Mod. L. Rev.* 1–18 (1993). For a critical approach to the concept of sovereignty as elaborated by international legal scholarship see M. Koskenniemi, *From Apology to Utopia* 192–263 (1989). Current attempts to revise the traditional tenets of the concept of sovereignty have also affected the debate on the cognate question of jurisdiction. In this respect, an interesting contribution can be read in: Note, 'Constructing the State Extraterritorially: Jurisdictional Discourse, the National Interest and Transnational Norms', 103 *Harvard L. Rev.* 1273–1305 (1990).

claims then becomes crucial. Although a certain consensus can be traced in state practice as to what criteria may be adduced *in abstracto* as an appropriate legal foundation for the exercise of jurisdiction,[191] little agreement exists on the application of such criteria in practice.[192] Further, what international law prescribes in case of concurring jurisdictional claims is still a matter of great controversy.[193]

The widely accepted use of the expression 'extraterritorial jurisdiction' to refer to the issue of the lawfulness of jurisdictional claims is quite telling of the traditional approach under international law. As a corollary of the principle of

---

[191] Commonly accepted principles of jurisdiction include territoriality, nationality, effects doctrine, passive personality, universality and protective principles. The above principles, mainly evaluated with reference to the exercise of criminal jurisdiction (see 'Harvard Research on International Law: Jurisdiction With Respect to Crime', 29 *AJIL*, Supplement 1, 445 (1934)), have subsequently come to be accepted as principles of general applicability. Even among different schools of thought, they are now generally admitted as a proper legal basis for a state to lay a jurisdictional claim. For a more recent presentation of admissible legal bases of jurisdiction in international law see R. Higgins, 'The Legal Bases of Jurisdiction', in C. Olmstead (ed.), *Extraterritorial Application of Laws and Responses Thereto* 3–14 (1984).

[192] It is worth noting that jurisdictional principles are all expressive of a connection between the regulating state and the matter to be regulated. Their application to concrete cases, however, is controversial especially when two or more states claim jurisdiction over the same matter on the basis of different principles. In such instances the issue arises as to whether a hierarchy among the principles can be established under international law. This problem is given different solutions in legal scholarship. While some authors argue that all jurisdictional principles have equal standing in international law (see Stern, 'Quelques observations sur les règles internationales relatives à l'application extraterritoriale du droit', 32 *AFDI* 7, at 43 (1986)), others maintain that territoriality ought to be given priority (see *Oppenheim's International Law* 458 *et seq.* (9th edn, edited by Sir Robert Jennings and Sir Arthur Watts) (London, 1992, Vol. I). The view taken by the American Law Institute in the revised Restatement, is that a legitimate basis of jurisdiction notwithstanding, the exercise of jurisdiction has to be 'reasonable'. Such an additional requisite of 'reasonableness' would be imposed by international law (Restatement (Third) of the Foreign Relations Law of the United States, s. 403, Comment a) (St Paul, Minnesota, 1987).

[193] The Restatement, note 192 above, provides that in case of a jurisdictional conflict, each state should assess its own interest and eventually defer to the competence of the state that has a stronger interest in regulation (s. 403(3)). Similarly, K. Meessen in his writings maintains the existence of a rule which would impose on the states involved the balancing of their respective sovereign interests and the consequent deferral to the state having an 'Enlightened self-interest' in the regulation of the matter (K. Meessen, *Völkerrechtliche Grundsätze des internationalen Kartellrechts* (Baden-Baden, 1975); 'Antitrust Jurisdiction Under Customary International Law', 78 *AJIL* 783 *et seq.*; 'Conflicts of Jurisdiction Under the New Restatement', 50 *Law & Contemporary Problems* 47 (1987); 'Competition of Competition Laws', 10 *Northwestern J. of Intl L.* 17 (1989)). Other authors maintain that international law has no substantive rule which may solve jurisdictional conflicts among equally legitimate claims. Therefore, conflicts should be solved either by reference to general principles of peaceful settlement of disputes (see P. Picone, 'L'applicazione extraterritoriale delle regole sulla concorrenza e il diritto internazionale', in *Il fenomeno delle concentrazioni tra imprese nel diritto interno e internazionale* 81–206 at 166 *et seq.* (Padua, 1989) *accord* M. Benedettelli, 'Sull'applicazione extraterritoriale delle misure di embargo degli Stati Uniti relative al "gasdotto siberiano"', 73 *Rivista di diritto internazionale* 529–574 at 565 *et seq.* (1984)) or by recourse to the 'comity of nations' as a principle of judicial self-restraint, according to H. Maier, 'Extraterritorial Jurisdiction at a Crossroads: an Intersection Between Public and Private International Law', 76 *AJIL* 280 (1982); 'Interest Balancing and Extraterritorial Jurisdiction', 31 *Amer. J. Com. L.* 583 (1983); 'Extraterritorial Jurisdiction', 31 *Amer. J. Com. L.* 583 (1983); 'Extraterritorial Conflicts, or "There and Back Again"', 25 *Va. J. Intl L.* 7 (1984).

sovereignty, states are deemed to have jurisdiction over their own territory.[194] Therefore, any issue concerning the lawfulness of the exercise of such authoritative power can only arise in connection with claims reaching out to persons and activities which are beyond the physical limits of the regulating state. The recent emergence of alternative methods to traditional analysis, which rather focus on the concept of a state's interests in order to assess the lawfulness of jurisdictional claims, does not seem to have had any major impact on the use of the term.[195] In fact, extraterritoriality has come to be accepted as a standard term in approaching the issue of the lawfulness of jurisdictional claims.[196] Ultimately, the basic question to be tackled remains to what extent, in the absence of an international agreement, a state may regulate matters not exclusively of domestic concern or, in other words, matters which present more or less significant links with other legal orders.

Given the complexity of a highly heterogeneous practice, the re-opening of the debate on the international law of jurisdiction is no easy task. As is clearly shown in sectoral studies, jurisdictional issues deeply diverge from one another depending on the particular field in which they arise. Unfortunately, divergencies

---

[194] On the relationship between territorial sovereignty and jurisdiction see F.A. Mann, 'The Doctrine of Jurisdiction in International Law', 111 *RdC* 9–159 at 10 *et seq.* (1964); 'The Doctrine of International Jurisdiction Revisited After 20 Years', 186 *RdC* 9–98 (1984), reproduced in *Further Studies in International Law* 4 *et seq.* (Oxford, 1990); I. Brownlie, *Principles of Public International Law* 289 (4th edn, 1990). See also the ruling by the Permanent Court of International Justice in the *Legal Status of Greenland* case (Series A-B, 1933) where jurisdiction is defined as 'one of the most obvious forms of State sovereignty' (at 48). One of the most often cited domestic cases on the exclusive jurisdiction of the territorial state over its own territory is *The Schooner Exchange v MacFaddon* (1812 Cranch's Reports 116, 136):

> The jurisdiction of the nation within its own territory is necessarily exclusive and absolute. It is susceptible of no limitation not imposed by itself . . . All exceptions, therefore, must be traced up to the consent of the nation itself.

[195] On the origin of the balance of interests rule see G. Born/D. Westin, *International Civil Litigation in United States Courts* 603 *et seq.* (2nd edn, Deventer/Boston, 1992). However, the main credit for the introduction of interest analysis, as developed in US conflict of laws theory, in public international law doctrine has to be given to the writings of A. Lowenfeld. See, in particular, A. Lowenfeld, 'Public Law in the International Arena: Conflict of Laws, International Law, and Some Suggestions for their Interaction', 163 *RdC* 315–445 (1979). See also H. Maier, 'Extraterritorial Jurisdiction at a Crossroads: an Intersection Between Public and Private International Law', note 193 above. None of the authors who have adopted such an approach to jurisdictional conflicts seems to question the propriety of the term extraterritoriality. For the early application of the 'balance of interests rule' in US case law see the well known cases *Timberlane Lumber v Bank of America*, 459 F.2d 497 (9th Cir. 1976), reconsidered in 1984 (749 F.2d 1378 (9th Cir. 1984)); and *Mannington Mills v Congoleum Corp*, 595 F.2d 1287 (3rd Cir. 1979).

[196] For a tentative definition of extraterritoriality see K. Meessen, 'General Report on Extraterritorial Jurisdiction in Export Control Law', in K. Meessen (ed.), *The International Law of Export Control* 3–14, at 9 (London/Dordrecht/Boston, 1992). For a recent effort to provide an accurate definition of different kinds of extraterritoriality see B. Stern, 'L'extraterritorialité revisitée (1). Où il est question des affaires Alvarez-Machain, Pâte de bois et de quelques autres (2)', 38 *AFDI* 239–313, esp. 239–262 (1992).

do not occur only in state practice. The wide spectrum of doctrinal stances attests to the difficulty of providing a common denominator to the theoretical framing of jurisdictional issues in international legal scholarship. Problems of terminology and methodology further contribute to hampering the process of mutual understanding between scholars belonging to different legal traditions.

After a preliminary attempt to clarify some of the theoretical premises underlying the paper, a cursory review of current trends in legal scholarship will be made with a view to highlighting the shortcomings that seem to prevent the achievement of consensus on the state of the customary law of jurisdiction in contemporary international law. Secondly, a tentative analytical approach will be suggested in the light of state practice. Ultimately, the question of whether a unitary international law regime of jurisdiction can be deemed to have survived the emergence of the many innovations that international practice has brought about in recent times will be briefly addressed.

2. Extraterritoriality and Jurisdiction: A Matter of Degree

The international law of jurisdiction is mainly regarded in both state practice and international legal scholarship as a single concept concerning the exercise of authoritative power by states.[197] This power can be exercised at different stages and to varying degrees. It can relate to the prescription of rules or to the capacity to subject entities to adjudicatory or enforcement mechanisms. The recent attempt made by the Restatement (Third) of the Foreign Relations Law of the United States to split the concept of jurisdiction into several categories, in principle subject to different regimes, reveals an effort to provide the otherwise difficult notion of jurisdiction with some form of systemic classification.[198] One should be aware, however, that such a rigid categorisation, however acceptable as a matter of pure logic, does not accurately reflect the state of international practice on the matter.[199]

---

[197] See, among others, D. Carreau, *Droit international* 1, 317 *et seq.* (3rd edn, Paris, 1991); P.M. Dupuy, *Droit international public* 56 *et seq.* (Paris, 1992); I. Brownlie, *Principles of Public International Law*, note 194 above, at 309–310.

[198] See Restatement, note 192 above, s. 401, distinguishing between jurisdiction to prescribe, jurisdiction to adjudicate and jurisdiction to enforce. Sections 402 to 433 further specify the content of the legal regime applicable to any of the three categories of jurisdiction. For a presentation of the treatment of extraterritoriality issues under the Restatement see: K. Hixson, 'Extraterritorial Jurisdiction Under the Third Restatement of the Foreign Relations Law of the United States', 12 *Fordham Int 1 L. J.* 127–152 (1988).

[199] Accurate criticism of the classification of jurisdictional categories proposed in the Restatement has been advanced by K. Meessen, 'Conflicts of Jurisdiction Under the New Restatement', note 193 above. As known, autonomous sections on jurisdiction are devoted in the Restatement to subjects such as tax law, activities of foreign branches and subsidiaries, securities regulations and criminal law, whereas other areas remain subject to the general regime of jurisdiction. Meessen would have rather opted for the adoption of specific substantive rules in each particular area.

In fact, a careful scrutiny of relevant practice reveals that states accept a less articulate theoretical distinction based on the different intensity of the authoritative power actually exercised by the regulating state(s). A distinction seems to be made only between legislative jurisdiction (i.e. the competence under international law which a state has to impose commands by the enactment of norms) and the actual enforcement of rules by way of more or less coercive means.[200]

As rightly pointed out in legal scholarship,[201] the practical relevance of the distinction is arguable, since the enactment of rules by a state carries with it a presumption of future enforcement. This explains why many states, potentially affected by the extraterritorial effects of foreign laws and regulations, decide to object to the lawfulness of the enacting state's conduct at the time of drafting or adoption of the relevant measures. Although alleged violations of the international law of jurisdiction are usually invoked at the stage of enforcement, i.e. when the enacting state attempts to execute its commands in a manner not deemed consistent with international law prescriptions, many instances can be traced to state practice in which diplomatic protests have preceded any enforcement attempt.

Jurisdiction is therefore a matter of degree.[202] A state's authority to subject people and things to its legal order varies in intensity. This is why jurisdiction ought to be regarded as a unitary phenomenon characterised by different stages of exercise of authoritative power.

As a corollary of the concept of jurisdiction, extraterritoriality can be framed in similar terms. Phenomena of extraterritorial jurisdiction also escape strict categorisations and vary a great deal in intensity, depending on the potential of collision with other states' commands and on how intrusive into other legal orders the attempt to exercise authority turns out to be. The retroactive

---

[200] Some authors go even further and deny any significant distinction between legislative and enforcement jurisdiction. See, for instance, Brownlie:

> There is again no essential distinction between the legal bases for and limits upon substantive (or legislative) jurisdiction, on the one hand, and, on the other, enforcement (or personal, or prerogative) jurisdiction. The one is the function of the other. If the substantive jurisdiction is beyond lawful limits, then any consequent enforcement jurisdiction is unlawful.

Principles of Public International Law, note 194 above, at 309. See also R. Quadri, *Diritto internazionale pubblico* 636 (5th edn., Naples, 1968).

[201] See F.A. Mann, 'The Doctrine of Jurisdiction in International Law', note 194, at 14:

> ... The mere exercise of prescriptive jurisdiction, without any attempt at enforcement, will not have normally to pass the test of international law, for so long as a State merely introduces a legal rule without taking or threatening steps to enforce it, foreign States and their nationals are not necessarily affected. But this depends on the facts and it is not difficult to visualize circumstances in which the exercise of legislative jurisdiction so plainly implies the likelihood of enforcement that foreign States are entitled to challenge its presence in the statute book.

[202] See A. Lowenfeld, 'Public Law in the International Arena: Conflict of Laws, International Law and Some Suggestions for Their Interaction', note 195 above, at 423.

imposition of sanctions directly upon foreign companies is different from ordering one's own nationals not to trade with such companies. Also, an order of discovery issued by a domestic court to require a national parent company to produce the documents of a foreign subsidiary is different from suing the domestic subsidiary of a foreign parent company for the sale of defective products in the forum state.[203] All of the above instances contain elements of extraterritoriality. Nobody would deny, however, that each of them is different from the others, in terms of the intensity of the authoritative power exercised by the regulating state.

The above remarks inevitably lead to the conclusion that extraterritoriality is also a matter of degree. What may sound like a truism is actually not deprived of important implications. It calls for the need to focus upon forms of regulation which are shaped by and can adjust to the complexities of cases. Different cases cannot be treated alike: it would run counter to elementary notions of fairness and justice common to all jurisdictions.

3. A Question of Methodology: Public International Law or Conflicts Rules?

Among the preliminary questions which ought to be addressed before approaching the topic of extraterritorial jurisdiction, perhaps the most compelling one is whether such an issue should be dealt with at the level of national conflict of laws systems or, rather, be analysed as a matter of public international law.[204] The issue is one of normative perspective and the choice is between the internal perspective of the particular norms of one state and the external perspective of some neutral or, at least, less subjective standpoint.

The main difficulty in leaving the solution of such cases to domestic systems of conflict of laws is that like cases would not be treated alike in different

---

[203] A fairly exhaustive illustration of phenomena of extraterritoriality in international practice is given in the 'Preliminary Report on the Extraterritorial Jurisdiction of States', presented by Rapporteur M. Bos to the Institut de Droit International and published in 65 *Annuaire de l'Institut de Droit International* 14 *et seq.* (Paris, 1993).

[204] The first attempt seriously to question the public international law perspective in the treatment of jurisdictional issues has to be traced to the much celebrated writing of A. Lowenfeld, 'Public Law in the International Arena: Conflict of Laws, International Law and Some Suggestions on their Interaction', note 195 above. Lowenfeld maintains that 'public international law has been too rigid, too rule-oriented, and therefore too abstract, in part because it has been insulated from the more flexible, approach-oriented developments of private international law' (321). More recently by the same author see *International Litigation and Arbitration* (St Paul, Minnesota, 1993). Other authors such as Maier argue instead that '... both the public and the private international systems coordinate human behaviour, and ... thus the values that inform both systems must necessarily be the same'. ('Extraterritorial Jurisdiction at a Crossroads: an Intersection Between Public and Private International Law', note 193 above, at 281.)

jurisdictions.[205] For instance, the Anglo-Saxon approach is such that in a contract case the political character of foreign embargo laws might not be an issue if it is part of the applicable law,[206] whereas it would be a bar to enforcement in other European jurisdictions.[207] Similarly, balance of interests or policy analysis techniques, alien to most European jurisdictions, would probably lead to a varying case law. Similar considerations apply to doctrines such as the act of state and foreign compulsion defence, which have developed differently in different countries.[208] Traditional European approaches to the conflict of laws, otherwise known as single-aspect methods for their giving priority to one connecting factor in order to determine the applicable law,[209] would fall short of doing justice in many cases even if they could provide some certainty and predictability in terms of solutions of like cases. This lack of uniformity causes one to look elsewhere to find some common standards.

Such standards can be found in the public international law of jurisdiction as it stems from the contemporary practice of states. Before turning to the application of domestic techniques of conflict resolution, a preliminary test should be passed by foreign laws whose application is relevant to a case. In this respect the approach taken by a Dutch court in a case concerning the applicability of extraterritorial export controls enacted by the US is illustrative. In the *Sensor* case the court refused to take US regulations into account as an exonerating circumstance for breach of contract, since they violated international

---

[205] For a good description of the private international law approach used by domestic courts, although with a limited focus on export controls, see J. Basedow, 'Private Law Effects of Foreign Export Controls – An International Case Report', 27 *GYIL* 109–141 (1984) and R. Prioux, 'Les lois applicables aux contrats internationaux de vente d'armes', *RBDI* 217 (1993).

[206] See, for instance, *Libyan Arab Republic v Banker's Trust Co* (1988), 1 Lloyds Rep. 259. See also F.A. Mann, 'L'exécution internationale des droits publics', 77 *RCDIP* 1–27 (1988).

[207] Although European scholars have come to accept a limited application of foreign public and political laws when they are part of the governing law of the contract, they traditionally remain opposed to their application (see Y. Loussouarn/P. Bourel, *Droit international privé* at 201 *et seq.* (3rd edn, Paris, 1987); F. Rigaux, *Droit international privé. Tome I: Théorie générale* at 125 *et seq.* (Bruxelles, 1977); G. Balladore Pallieri, *Diritto internazionale privato italiano* at 105 *et seq.* (Milan, 1974); K. Zweigert, 'Droit international privé et droit public', 54 *RCDIP* 645–666 (1965); G. Badiali, *Ordine pubblico e diritto straniero* at 102 *et seq.* (Milan, 1963); B. Conforti, *L'esecuzione delle obbligazioni contrattuali nel diritto internazionale privato* at 114 *et seq.* (Naples, 1962); R. Quadri, *Lezioni di diritto internazionale privato* at 374 *et seq.* (Naples, 1962); *id.*, 'Leggi politiche e diritto internazionale privato', in *Giurisprudenza comparata di diritto internazionale privato*, 1941, reproduced in R. Quadri, *Scritti giuridici* at 365 *et seq.* (Vol. II, Milan, 1988); G. Barile, *Appunti sul valore del diritto pubblico straniero nell'ordinamento nazionale* at 35 *et seq.* and 42 *et seq.* (Milan, 1948)).

[208] For an up to date and comprehensive review of the act of state and foreign compulsion defence doctrines see G. Born/D. Westin, *International Civil Litigation in United States Courts*, note 195 above, respectively at 647 *et seq.* and 623 *et seq.*

[209] See D. Trautman/A. von Mehren, *The Law of Multistate and Multinational Problems* (Cambridge, MA, temporary edn 1990–1991), defining internal legal systems of conflict of laws using a single connecting factor to relate a multistate or multinational case to a single legal community as 'single-aspect methods'.

jurisdictional rules.[210] As to the objection that not all domestic courts may directly enforce international law, this could be overcome by interpretative techniques such as the presumption of consistency of domestic law with international norms. Such a principle is common to civil law and common law jurisdictions as well.[211]

Obviously, there are many analogies with domestic conflict of laws systems. Some of the issues involved in a domestic conflict case are similar to the ones which a conflict of jurisdiction between states presents. After all, our problem concerns jurisdiction and applicable law. Internal techniques of conflict of laws resolution can be used occasionally as an interpretive paradigm for discerning the pros and cons of some of the viable options. Their being transposed lock, stock and barrel to the level of public international law, however, besides being incorrect as a matter of methodology, might turn out to be misleading, given the different normative perspective from which they originate.

4. International Agreements

Several authors maintain that the resolution of conflicts of jurisdiction should be pursued by means of international agreements.[212] This view fails to account for all those instances in which an agreement cannot be reached. Indeed, such a situation seems to be the rule rather than the exception. Provided that they do not violate peremptory norms of *jus cogens*, states may agree on anything they like and it is a well accepted principle that consent by the injured state is an

---

[210] *Compagnie Européenne des Pétroles v Sensor Nederland*, President District Court The Hague, 17 Sept. 1982 (22 ILM 66 (1982)). The Dutch court, in the course of the Siberian pipeline affair, granted relief to the plaintiff, a French corporation which had sued the Dutch subsidiary of an American corporation for breach of contract, ordering the Dutch subsidiary to deliver the goods according to the agreed contractual terms. The Dutch corporation *Sensor* raised *force majeure* as a defence for contractual non-performance, on the grounds that the goods had been subjected to the embargo issued by the US Department of Commerce against the Soviet Union, which would have been the final consignee of the goods via France, and that *Sensor* as the foreign subsidiary of an American corporation was to abide by them. The court dismissed the argument, stating that relevant US regulations were contrary to admitted principles of jurisdiction under international law and refused to take them into account as exonerating circumstances for the company's failure to perform the contract.

[211] On the application of the rule, generally, see B. Conforti, 'Cours général de droit international public', 212 *RdC* 56–57 (1988), to which we refer for further bibliographical references. On the application of the rule in common law countries see F.A. Mann, *Foreign Affairs in English Courts* 130 (Oxford, 1986); Restatement, note 192 above, s. 140. In the US this rule of statutory construction dates back to last century: see *The Charming Betsy*, 6 US (2 Cranch) 132, 143 (1804).

[212] See J.G. Castel, *Extraterritoriality in International Trade* 289 (Toronto/Vancouver, 1988); J. Griffin/M. Calabrese, 'Coping With Extraterritoriality Disputes', 22 *J. of World Trade* 5–25 (1988); K.W. Abbott, 'Collective Goods, Mobile Resources and Extraterritorial Export Controls', 50 *Law and Contemporary Problems* 117–152 (1987); J. Brown, 'Extraterritoriality: Current Policy of the United States', 12 *Syracuse J. of Intl L.* 493–519 (1986).

exonerating circumstance for the wrongdoer.[213] If the regulating state can get the 'target' state to accept the extraterritorial reach of its domestic law, extraterritoriality is no longer an issue.[214] This solution is not free of risks, however. In order to attract investments or pushed by other policy reasons, weaker states may be forced to accept the impositions of more powerful states. Once again general international law becomes important in providing the standards for negotiation. The bargaining position of weaker states might be stronger if it is perceived as conforming with accepted principles and rules of international law.

Other difficulties with international agreements can be envisaged. Practice shows that it is quite extraordinary that states reach agreement on the matter of extraterritorial jurisdiction. More often international agreements can be useful to channel disputes into institutionalised mechanisms of dispute settlement agreed on by treaty.[215] Understandings or other non-binding instruments are a different matter.[216] These may provide a framework for co-operation among states, which can be instrumental in preventing controversies. The US-EC understanding on antitrust, which favours co-operation and transparency, is a good example of this.[217] But if such instruments fail, the need to rely on legal rules to ascertain reciprocal rights and liabilities comes to the surface again.

---

[213] See art. 29 of the International Law Commission Draft Articles on State Responsibility (1980 Yearbook ILC, II/2, 30 *et seq.*):

> Chapter V: Circumstances Precluding Wrongfulness. Art. 29. Consent. 1. The consent validly given by a State to the commission by another State of a specified act not in conformity with an obligation of the latter State towards the former State precludes the wrongfulness of the act in relation to that State to the extent that the act remains within the limits of that consent....

[214] This has often occurred in Canadian practice with reference to US extraterritorial claims, especially as far as sanctions imposed by the US against China, Cuba, Libya, Poland, Afghanistan, USSR, Uganda and Nicaragua were concerned. On this matter see the recent study of A.L.C. de Mestral/T. Gruchalla Wesierski, *Extraterritorial Application of Export Control Legislation: Canada and the United States, passim* (Dordrecht/London/Boston, 1990).

[215] See, for instance, the recently adopted NAFTA (North America Free Trade Agreement) Treaty (32 ILM 605 (1993)), whose general provisions on dispute settlement procedures (Ch. 20) could be applied generally also to extraterritoriality disputes. On the application of the 1985 US-Canada Treaty on Mutual Legal Assistance in Criminal Matters (24 ILM 1092 (1985)) to litigation concerning the extraterritorial reach of the US embargo against Nicaragua see de Mestral/Gruchalla Wesierski, note 214 above, 117.

[216] In the field of international trade of strategic goods many non-binding understandings exist to the effect of co-ordinating exporting states' policies. For a comprehensive review of such instruments see A. Bianchi, *L'applicazione extraterritoriale dei controlli all'esportazione. Contributo allo studio dei fenomeni di extraterritorialità nel diritto internazionale,* esp. Ch. X, at 411 *et seq.* (Padua, 1995) and L. Migliorino, *Le restrizioni all'esportazione nel diritto internazionale* 177 *et seq.* (Padua, 1993).

[217] See Decision 145/95/CE of the Council and Commission of 10 April 1995, in OJEC L/95 of 27 April 1995. The previous agreement on the same matter, signed by the Commission in 1992, had been held invalid by the Court of Justice (Case C-327/91, *France v Commission*) on the ground that the treaty making power as regards the subject at hand was vested in the Council. For a short comment on the 1992 Agreement see 86 *AJIL* 119 (1992).

5.   Current Trends in Legal Scholarship: The Alleged Antinomy Between Traditional Approaches to the International Law of Jurisdiction and Recent Methods of Interest Analysis

One of the major hindrances to achieving some form of codification of this subject is the lack of constructive communication and interaction between the approaches, respectively used by US and European scholars.[218] The former approach focuses on interest analysis, whereas the latter rather hinges upon the operation of traditional jurisdictional principles under classical international law theory. In particular, 'the rule of reasonableness' and the 'principle of territoriality' are perceived as the two distant poles of a legal analysis spectrum in which common grounds for discussion can hardly be discerned.[219]

Inevitably, the search for a breakthrough has to be made by smoothing rather than highlighting the numerous discrepancies which divide the two doctrines. Otherwise, any effort effectively to contribute to the development of the subject risks being seriously undermined. The intention is to bridge the difficulties in order to overcome the present impasse. After all, the alleged discrepancies are often more apparent than real and both approaches present shortcomings which need to be overcome.

A.   Criticism of the Classical International Law Doctrine

As is generally known, in classical international law theory jurisdiction is mainly regarded as a corollary of state sovereignty. States are free to assert jurisdiction in their own territory unless a prohibitory rule of international law prevents them from doing so; whereas outside their territory their jurisdictional claim must be supported by an international legal rule that allows them to exercise jurisdiction. In any event their claims must be grounded on accepted jurisdictional principles such as territoriality, nationality and so on. Often the debate hinges upon too great a theoretical preoccupation with the lawfulness *in abstracto* of these broad jurisdictional principles to the detriment of a realistic approach to the complexities of actual cases. The above doctrinal framework, largely based on the ruling of the Permanent Court of International Justice in the *Lotus* case,[220]

---

[218] See A. Bianchi, 'Extraterritoriality and Export Controls: Some Remarks on the Alleged Antinomy Between European and U.S. Approaches', 35 *GYIL* 366–434 (1992).

[219] In fact, such a firm mutual opposition should be regarded as entirely unfruitful. The two rival visions of the state of the law will thrive on mutual contradictions, until some supervening dialectical synthesis reconciles all those elements from works of both schools which any sound theory on the law of jurisdiction has to embrace.

[220] *Lotus* case (1927), PCIJ, Ser. A, No. 10. The *Lotus* case has been interpreted differently in international legal scholarship. Its basic tenets, however, seem to be that while a state may not 'exercise its power in any form in the territory of another State ... except by virtue of a permissive rule derived from international custom or from a convention', states enjoy 'a wide

has long represented the prevailing approach to jurisdictional issues in international law.

The issue of how to deal with the possible overlapping of concurrent jurisdictional claims, equally legitimate for being grounded on accepted principles of jurisdiction, has been tentatively solved in legal scholarship either by establishing a hierarchy of jurisdictional principles, in which territoriality and/or nationality enjoy the highest ranking, or by denying the existence of substantive international rules regulating jurisdictional conflicts. In the latter case, resort to ordinary international law rules of peaceful dispute settlement is suggested.[221]

Basically, the main criticism of this doctrine stems from the need to reassess an obsolescent and no longer viable notion of state sovereignty. Without denying that territorial sovereignty still has a major role to play in this area (after all the term extraterritoriality itself is quite suggestive of the origin of the issue), traditional precepts of sovereignty as enshrined in classical international law theory can no longer be held as the guiding principles in the field. All the more so when one realises that the presumption of state sovereignty, underlying the *Lotus* case,[222] implies the logical impossibility of setting priorities among conflicting sovereign prerogatives.[223] If one assumes that states, as independent and equal entities, are entitled to exercise their jurisdiction freely in the absence of prohibitory norms of international law, then jurisdictional conflicts can only be resolved by resorting to an equitable balance of equally legitimate claims.[224]

Moreover, the notion of domestic jurisdiction, so closely intertwined with the concept of sovereignty, has undergone major changes.[225] Parallel to this development, what can be called 'transnational solidarities' have emerged

---

cont.
  measure of discretion' as to the extension of the application of their laws and of the jurisdiction of their courts to persons, property and acts outside their territory (at 19).
[221] See note 193 above.
[222] See *Lotus*, note 220 above, at 18:

  International law governs relations between independent States. The rules of law binding upon States therefore emanate from their own free will as expressed in conventions or by usages generally accepted as expressing principles of law and established in order to regulate the relations between co-existing independent communities or with a view to the achievement of common aims. Restrictions upon the independence of States cannot therefore be presumed.

[223] This issue is highlighted by M. Koskenniemi, *From Apology to Utopia. The Structure of International Legal Argument* 220 *et seq.* (Helsinki, 1989). See also, by the same author, 'The Politics of International Law', 1 *European J. Intl Law* 14 *et seq.* (1990).
[224] See, for instance, the case law of the International Court of Justice in the field of delimitation of maritime boundaries between opposite or adjacent states, extensively reviewed, among others, by I. Brownlie, *Principles of Public International Law*, note 194 above, at 225 *et seq.*
[225] On the notion of domestic jurisdiction as embodied in art. 2(7) of the UN Charter see: Cançado Trindade, 'The Domestic Jurisdiction of States in the Practice of the UN and Regional Organizations', 25 *ICLQ* 715 (1976); Cot/Pellet, *La Charte des Nations Unies* at 141 *et seq.* (1985); B. Simma (ed.), *Charta des Vereinten Nationen* at 110 *et seq.* (1991).

recently.[226] By the latter expression we intend to refer to a set of values and interests, common to each and every state, which are perceived as shared concerns by the international community as a whole. Less theoretically and more pragmatically, the same internationalisation of commercial and financial markets has enormously complicated factual matrices so that the strict application of fairly simple and general rules such as those of the traditional international law of jurisdiction would fall short of doing justice in many cases. Retention of the fairly simplistic formula 'chacun chez soi' seems therefore very inappropriate nowadays.[227]

B. Criticism of the Balance of Interests Rule

The balance of interests approach is roughly meant to address the question of who has a stronger interest in regulating a certain case. The uneasiness with that approach can be expressed by another question: *who is to balance what and how?* As to the *who* part of the question the options are generally two: either the executive or the judiciary. As to the former, a great deal of scepticism can be expressed. The outcome of relevant controversies will be in the hands of diplomats or government officials. Respect for the rights of private parties will be meaningless if they do not coincide with the overall political interests of their national states. Further, ordinarily, people who lay claim to legal rights go to court. Should domestic courts stay the proceedings and defer the matter to the executive? The legitimate expectations of the parties as well as the predictability of the law would almost certainly be compromised. Moreover, this would prove to be difficult in legal systems in which the separation of powers principle is one of the founding pillars. If it is the judiciary which is to decide (which practice seems to confirm as the prevailing trend) then the poor record, in terms of fairness and objectivity, attained by the application of the rule in the US and the many protests of foreign countries against its judicial application, do not encourage support for its adoption as a solution.[228] Further, to most jurists trained in civil law jurisdictions, reasonableness or interest balancing sound as a fairly 'unhelpfully vague' concept, whose real content is but the vast discretionary power left with the judges.[229] The reality that most of the time jurisdictional controversies are decided by domestic courts and not by a distinguished group of

---

[226] See: Note, 'Constructing the State Extraterritorially: Jurisdictional Discourse, the National Interest, and Transnational Norms', note 190 above.

[227] H. Batiffol, *Aspects philosophiques de droit international privé* 260 (1956):

> chacun Etat légifère sur les relations juridiques se déroulant sur son territoire, et l'ordre international sera satisfait en vertu de la maxime de bon sens 'chacun chez soi'.

[228] See the extensive study by I. Jalles, *Extraterridorialidade e Comércio Internacional. Um Exercício de Direito Americano* (Bertrand Editora, 1988).

[229] It is of note that the expression 'unhelpfully vague' is Professor Brownlie's: see *Principles of Public International Law*, note 194 above, at 308.

eminent scholars familiar with the balance of interests technique should not be overlooked.

Some authors maintain that interest balancing should be a major concern for legislative bodies as well. Experience shows, however, that this rarely occurs in practice. Most of the time this is due to a lack of sensitivity about extraterritoriality issues in national parliaments. On other occasions it is difficult to reconstruct the legislator's intent and judges have to venture into interpretive exercises which do not necessarily produce consistent results.[230]

As to the *what* part of the initial question, the issue becomes, if possible, even murkier. To say that interests should be balanced does not facilitate the task of the interpreter very much. Plenty of the more or less exhaustive lists of factors which should be weighed in the process have been elaborated.[231] Private as well as governmental interests are weighed on the same footing with the demands of the international legal system. But how can one weigh interests of such a different nature? This intriguing question paves the way to address the final problem of the modalities of interest balancing.

How judges assess the policies and interests underlying foreign states' conduct or legislation should be a source of major concern. Preoccupation with the integrity of the principle of separation of powers may lead courts almost automatically to defer the matter to the executive. Interventions by the executive would then become the rule in such cases. Even when the judges ventured into the uncertain realm of speculation about foreign states' interests, independently of any guidelines issued by the executive, one wonders, not without irony, whether satisfactory results in terms of fairness and predictability of the law can be reasonably expected.[232]

C.   *More on the Concept of Interest*

As an appendix to the above remarks an additional comment on the concept of interest is required. A preliminary concern with interest balancing techniques should be the evaluation of which interests international law recognises and protects and subject to what conditions. In fact, not all national interests are deemed worthy of protection by the international legal system.

---

[230] See for instance the US Court of Appeals for the District of Columbia Circuit opinion in *Environmental Defense Fund v Massey*, concerning the extraterritorial application of the National Environmental Policy Act to Antarctica, and, *contra*, the US Supreme Court opinion in *Smith v US*, related to the application of the Federal Tort Claims Act to Antarctica. Both cases are reproduced in 32 ILM, respectively at 505 *et seq.* and 516 *et seq.* (1993).

[231] See A. Lowenfeld, 'Public Law in the International Arena: Conflict of Laws, International Law and Some Suggestions for their Interaction', note 195 above at 328–329 and the Restatement, note 192 above, s. 403(2).

[232] See the interesting *dictum* of the court in *Laker Airways v Sabena and KLM* 731 F.2d 909 (DC Cir. 1984), reproduced also in 23 ILM 519 (1984). The court stated that at the time of the decision it knew of just one case 'where United States jurisdiction was denied when there was more than a *de minimis* United States interest' (at 558–559). See also Rosic, 'The Use of Interest Analysis in the Extraterritorial Application of United States Antitrust Law', 16 *Cornell Intl L. J.* 170 (1983).

For instance, subject to a few limitations imposed by international law, the unimpeded exercise of authority over one's territory, otherwise known as territorial sovereignty, has long been an undisputed principle.[233] Although it still remains a fundamental interest protected by international law, recently it has been tempered by international human rights law and possibly environmental law as well.[234] Such new limitations now stand beside the customary law limits on the treatment of aliens. As mentioned earlier both the concept of domestic jurisdiction and the notion of sovereignty have undergone major changes. Although there is a strong presumption in favour of jurisdiction for the territorial sovereign – after all common law countries also indulge the principle in case of conflicting commands[235] – it is nevertheless necessary to prove the existence of an effective and significant link between the regulating state and the relevant facts or conducts. For instance, the mere presence of individuals in the territory cannot in itself be sufficient ground to exercise jurisdiction.[236] The more we depart from the territorial sphere of state sovereignty the less the presumption of the existence of sufficient links to exercise jurisdiction will hold. The same happens with regard to the law of the sea. The closer one comes to other states the more mitigated the jurisdictional powers of the flag state become.[237]

At times states insist on national interest as a legitimising factor for their extraterritorial claims. Indeed, even in the field of export controls where state interests are supposed to be more compelling than in other fields, it does not seem that in international practice an entirely different treatment is conceded to claims based on such strong interests as national security or foreign policy. This should not come as a surprise. After all, as appears from the works of the ILC on state responsibility, national interests cannot be pleaded as a defence to wrongfulness, except for the controversial case of the state of necessity, where

---

[233] J.L. Brierly, *The Law of Nations* at 162 (6th edn, Oxford, 1963):

> At the basis of international law lies the notion that a state occupies a definite part of the surface of the earth, within which it normally exercises, subject to the limitations imposed by international law, jurisdiction over persons and things to the exclusion of the jurisdiction of other states.

[234] On these recent developments see O. Schachter, *International Law in Theory and Practice* at 330 *et seq.* and 362 *et seq.* (Dordrecht/Boston/London, 1991). On restrictions upon territorial authority see also *Oppenheim's International Law*, note 192 above, at 391–392.

[235] See Restatement, note 192 above, s. 441 (foreign state compulsion).

[236] See F.A. Mann, 'The Doctrine of International Jurisdiction Revisited After 20 Years', note 194 above, at 6 *et seq.* It is of note that the Restatement (Third), contrary to the Restatement (Second) of the Foreign Relations Law of the United States, no longer regards merely transitory presence as a reasonable ground for the exercise of jurisdiction to adjudicate (s. 421, Comment e, RN 4). For a critical view on the application of 'tag jurisdiction' even in an interstate conflict within a federal state *see:* A. Ehrenzweig, 'The Transient Rule of Personal Jurisdiction: the "Power" Myth and Forum Conveniens', 65 *Yale L. J.* 289 (1959). *Contra* the recent decision by the US Supreme Court in *Burnham v Superior Court of California* 110 S. Ct. 2105 (1990), commented in G. Born/D. Westin, *International Civil Litigation in United States Courts*, note 195 above, 54 *et seq.*

[237] A concise review of jurisdictional issues in the law of the sea is given in L.B. Sohn/K. Gustafson, *The Law of the Sea* 15 *et seq.* (St Paul, Minnesota, 1984).

vital interest may become relevant under particular circumstances and subject to strict conditions (see art. 33 of the ILC Draft Articles on state responsibility).[238]

Different is the case for the protection of obligations *erga omnes*, i.e. for obligations whose fulfilment is in the interest of the whole international community.[239] Provided that they are not disguised measures which aim to protect mere national interests, unilateral embargo measures of an extraterritorial character enacted to sanction systematic and massive violation of human rights, to protect the environment or to prevent the spread of arms of mass destruction have not been the object of strong opposition by other states.[240] This trend can be easily explained if one looks at the particular interests pursued by the above measures, namely *interests that have been indicated by the same states in international practice as common to the whole international community*. Unilateral enforcement of *erga omnes* obligations by means of the extraterritorial application of municipal law might be a novel method of enforcement of international law, but certainly one worth exploring.

6. The Search for a Common Denominator

An unconditional deference to either of the two doctrines cursorily presented above, cannot lead legal scholarship very far in the elaboration of commonly agreed rules and reliable international standards. The above doctrinal disaccords, however, should not be an absolute barrier to the interpreter. Rather than

---

[238] See (1980) Yearbook ILC, II/2, 27 *et seq.*

[239] As known, the existence of *erga omnes* obligations was acknowledged by the International Court of Justice in the case of *Barcelona Traction Light and Power Co Ltd* (1970 ICJ Reports 32). See P. Picone, 'Obblighi reciproci ed obblighi erga omnes degli Stati nel campo della protezione internazionale dell'ambiente marino dall'inquinamento', in V. Starace (ed.), *Diritto internazionale e protezione dell'ambiente marino 77 et seq.*, (Milano, 1983) providing a profound theoretical insight on the nature and character of obligations *erga omnes*.

[240] It is of note that the far-reaching extraterritorial effects of the US Uganda Embargo Act (92 Stat. 1051, codified at 22 USC 287–7 (Supp. V, 1981)), enacted in 1978 to sanction systematic and massive violations of human rights by the former leader of Uganda, Idi Amin, were not protested against by other states. Although the sanctions were lifted relatively shortly thereafter, the lack of reaction by other states might be due to the universal condemnation of systematic and massive violations of human rights. Nor have the fairly sweeping extraterritorial provisions of the recent US legislation on the control of chemical and biological weapons (see The Chemical and Biological Weapons Control and Warfare Elimination Act, Pub. L. No. 102–82, 105 Stat. 1245–1258, codified at 22 U.S.C. ss. 5601–5606 and at 50 U.S.C. App. ss. 2401–2410) been opposed by other states. This trend to broaden the jurisdictional powers of states with regard to the enforcement of such a common interest as the prevention of the spread of arms of mass destruction is confirmed also by treaty practice (see, for instance, the Convention on the Physical Protection of Nuclear Material, Legal Series No. 12, Vienna, IAEA, 1982 (art. 8(3)(4)), and the 1993 Convention on the Prohibition of the Development, Production, Stockpiling and Use of Chemical Weapons and on their Destruction, 32 ILM 800 (1993) (art. 7(1)(a)(b)). Finally, for a recent case of extraterritorial application of an environmental domestic statute see: *Environmental Defense Fund v Massey*, note 230 above. Generally, on this issue see A. Bianchi, *L'applicazione extraterritoriale dei controlli all'esportazione*, note 217 above, at 467 *et seq.*

pondering over their theoretical premises, one should inquire whether a common starting point can be traced in such different legal analyses.

Such a common point of departure can no longer be identified in the *Lotus* case, decided in 1927 by the casting vote of the President of the Permanent Court of International Justice over an equally split court.[241] Further, the Court's judgment concerned a very specific matter, namely the exercise of criminal jurisdiction over cases concerning collisions of ships at sea. The *Lotus* case is too anachronistic and specific to be a starting point for analysis. One may reach the same conclusion as the Permanent Court but only after a reassessment of contemporary practice.

An alternative point of departure could be a careful scrutiny of contemporary international practice, which can be easily accepted as a common denominator. After all, international lawyers try to explain and frame international practice so as to derive legal rules from patterns of conduct or from certain standards. No one seems to deny that state practice can provide the necessary means to evaluate the state of international law on the subject.[242] Nor does there seem to be any fundamental objection to the relevance of general international law to the subject. On the contrary, a general consensus exists on the proposition that international law provides legal parameters against which the lawfulness of jurisdictional claims can be assessed. No recent attempts at codification seem seriously to question this statement.[243] It is also a widely shared belief that these criteria can be evaluated by looking at state practice. To inquire afresh how international law regulates the exercise of jurisdiction by states requires the relinquishing of any *a priori* theoretical construction to the benefit of an inductive approach which takes into account the complexities of current practice in the various sectors in which extraterritoriality issues arise.

Such a pragmatic approach, based on inductive analysis, should secure a satisfactory degree of certainty and predictability as well as the flexibility required to make the evaluation of complex cases a relative exercise that also depends on the facts and relevant circumstances.

---

[241] See note 220 above.

[242] See Permanent Court of International Justice, *Nationality Decrees in Tunis and Morocco*, 1921, Series B., No. 4, 23–24: 'jurisdiction, which in principle, belongs solely to the state, is limited by rules of international law'. See also *Lotus*, note 220 above, at 19 and Restatement, note 192 above, s. 401. The theoretical controversy, which originated in the aftermath of the *Lotus* case, rather concerns the existence of a general principle which leaves states free to act unless the existence of a prohibitory rule of international law can be shown. Or, whether states may act only pursuant to a principle or rule of international law conferring such a power (see O. Schachter, *International Law in Theory and Practice*, note 234 above at 250 *et seq.*). But, even if it is widely accepted that international law regulates the exercise of jurisdiction by states, the problem remains to evaluate how this is done, whether the rules have a substantive or procedural character and whether they are general rules or, rather, specific rules which have emerged in particular areas.

[243] See the Draft Resolution of the Institut de droit international, published in 65 *Annuaire de l'Institut de Droit International*, at 174 *et seq.* (1993) and Restatement, note 192 above, s. 401.

7. The Customary Regime of Jurisdiction in Contemporary International Law

The author's personal inference from a survey of sectoral studies, which pervasively reviews contemporary practice, is that international customary law makes the legality of extraterritorial jurisdictional claims dependent on the existence of an *effective and significant connection* between the regulating state and the activity or fact to be regulated. A connection can be held to be significant when it is *perceived* as such by the same states in international practice.[244]

Contrary to previous theories that focus on factual links or similar criteria,[245] the application of the proposed principle is not subject to the operation of other principles, nor is it amenable to the jurisdictional principles of extraterritoriality highlighted by the classical doctrine of the international law of jurisdiction. The novelty of this approach is that the effectiveness and significance of a connection are entirely determined in the light of state practice in a given area. Only those claims that are founded on connections which have been accepted by the majority of states as sufficiently effective and significant for jurisdictional purposes will be regarded as lawful under international law.

Claims that are not based on such an effective and significant connection between the regulating state and the factual matrix to be regulated amount to an international wrong.[246] On the contrary, if a claim is founded upon an effective connection which is held to be significant in the practice of states, international law recognises its validity and opposability *vis-à-vis* other states. What amounts to an effective and significant connection appears from the specific content of the substantive standards which emerge from state practice and which are peculiar to different subject matters. Once it is acknowledged that states may have legitimate and concurrent jurisdictional claims, the focus should be shifted to analyse in each particular area the specific substantive standards which have emerged. The complexity of international relations and the intricacy of most international economic transactions call for an empirical analysis of state practice which at the

---

[244] See A. Bianchi, *L'applicazione extraterritoriale dei controlli all'esportazione*, note 216 above, at 445 *et seq.*.

[245] See F.A. Mann, 'The Doctrine of Jurisdiction in International Law', note 194 above, at 49; F.A. Mann, 'The Doctrine of International Jurisdiction Revisited After 20 Years', note 195 above, at 12; I. Brownlie, *Principles of Public International Law*, note 194 above at 309ff.; *Oppenheim's International Law*, note 192 above, at 457–458; B. Stern, 'L'extraterritorialité revisitée', note 196 above, at 250 *et seq.* Similarly, E. Jimenéz de Aréchaga in 159 *RdC* 182 (1978) states the existence of an international obligation for states not to exercise jurisdiction over matters, persons or things with which they have absolutely no concern.

[246] As to the fact that the consequences of an international wrong in this area have not yet developed into a unitary regime, this should not come as a surprise given the precarious existence of the law of state responsibility in a decentralised system of interstate relations (see I. Brownlie, *Principles of Public International Law*, note 194 above, at 509). Sometimes states merely exercise a *droit de regard*, by pointing to the unlawful character of the jurisdictional claim and asking for its repeal; only rarely do they resort to countermeasures.

present stage of development already contains sufficient elements to assess the content of these standards. This effort to trace substantive standards applicable in concrete cases is instrumental to give content in each particular instance to the above mentioned general principle.

The significant connection that needs be established in order to lay a legitimate jurisdictional claim does not exclude the existence of concurrent claims. The substantive standards derived from state practice will determine which one is perceived to be stronger and therefore prevail over the others. The main difference with balance of interests techniques is that judges ruling on concurrent jurisdictional claims, rather than weighing the interests involved themselves or deferring the matter to the government, would be forced to look at state practice, which is a far more reliable and objective source, in order to evaluate relevant connections. The normative perspective would then change and would be an external and more objective one with respect to the internal perspective of national conflict of laws systems. Digests, scholarly works, codification by institutions of a private nature or affiliated with international organisations, already provide guidance. With a view to further codification one could consider the opportunity of writing a Restatement of sorts, spelling out specific standards for all relevant subject matters.

Similar regimes have developed in other areas of international law. One may think of the case of nationality, in which the international validity and opposability of national claims is subject to their being in conformity with international law standards. It is widely believed that states may freely choose their domestic rules on the attribution of nationality.[247] Practice shows that some criteria are generally accepted as expressive of some bonds between the state and its nationals and therefore as fit to confer nationality.[248] Arguably, these principles belong to the category of those 'general principles of law' mentioned in art. 38 of the ICJ Statute. Be that as it may, international law intervenes only when such rules become relevant for the international legal order, namely when a contrast originates between different nationality claims either for diplomatic protection or for other purposes.[249] At that stage international law provides a substantive standard in determining the most effective and genuine link of the individual with any of the claiming states and makes it prevail over the others.[250]

---

[247] See *Nationality Decrees in Tunis and Morocco* case, note 242 above, at 24; art. I of the 1930 Hague Convention Concerning Certain Questions Relating to the Conflict of Nationality Laws, 179 League of Nations Treaty Series, Vol. 179, at 89.

[248] See 'Laws Concerning Nationality', UN Legislative Series ST/LEG/SER.B/4, July 1954; and, more recently, D. Campbell (gen. ed.) and J. Fisher (ed.), *International Immigration and Nationality Law*, Vols 1 and 2, (Dordrecht/London/Boston, 1993).

[249] On different international law aspects of nationality *see Oppenheim's International Law*, note 192 above, II, 851 *et seq.*

[250] See the much celebrated *Nottebohm* case, (1955) ICJ Reports 4 *et seq.* For a comment see I. Brownlie, *Principles of Public International Law*, note 194 above, at 407 *et seq.* The principle of the effective link has been applied to several cases before the Iran-US Arbitral Tribunal: see B. Leurent, 'Problèmes soulevés par les demandes des double nationaux devant le Tribunal des différends irano-américain', 74 *RCDIP* 273–299(1); 471–503 *et seq.* (1985).

To reason in terms of a general principle whose specific content is determined by substantive standards to be traced in specific areas, would fulfil the need to have a generally applicable set of legal prescriptions which are specific enough to meet the challenge of the regulation of complex cases.

8.   Export Control: A Case Study

The case of the extraterritorial reach of national export control laws and regulations is an illustrative example of the suggested approach to the analysis of the contemporary international law of jurisdiction. In the area of export controls enacted for national security and foreign policy purposes, some substantive standards seem to have emerged in state practice.[251]

First of all, it should be noted that forms of direct enforcement in foreign territory are in principle considered as infringements of the principle of state sovereignty and as such deemed unlawful under international law. Although the principle of territorial sovereignty has to be given a restrictive interpretation in times of economic interdependence, states still appear to consider it an absolute bar to foreign states' enforcement measures.[252] Instead, other techniques of extraterritoriality are tolerated to the extent that they tend to regulate or sanction a course of conduct that presents an effective and significant connection with the forum state.[253]

With a view to assessing which substantive standards can meet the above-mentioned requirements of effectiveness and significance, some trends can be evaluated in state practice. With regard to the factual matrices which most often give rise to extraterritoriality disputes, the following examples could provide some guidance.

In principle, non-resident citizens can be subjected to the jurisdiction of their national state. However, when the state of residence imposes upon them

---

[251] The findings presented below are largely based on A. Bianchi, *L'applicazione extraterritoriale dei controlli all'esportazione*, note 216 above, and *id.*, 'Extraterritoriality and Export Controls: Some Remarks on the Alleged Antinomy Between European and U.S. Approaches', note 218 above.

[252] The principle has been reasserted recently in A.L.C. de Mestral/T. Gruchalla Wesierski, *Extraterritorial Application of Export Control Legislation: Canada and the United States*, note 214 above, at 269.

[253] See also the interesting distinction between direct and indirect extraterritoriality techniques, which appears, among others, in P. Juillard, 'Le contrôle des exportations et l'application extraterritoriale des lois économiques en droit international', in B. Chantebout/B. Warusfel (eds.), *Le contrôle des exportations de haute technologie vers les pays de l'Est* 110–113 (Paris, 1988). The two techniques are accurately described by K. Meessen, 'General Report on Extraterritorial Jurisdiction in Export Control Law', note 196 above, at 8 *et seq.* A different classification of extraterritoriality issues is propounded by B. Stern, 'L'extraterritorialité revisitée', note 196 above.

conflicting commands, these are deemed to prevail.[254] The *ratio* for giving priority to the state of residence's claim has to be traced in the attempt to ensure a better protection for individuals (be they physical or juridical persons) and their interests. Ordinarily, the state of residence will have actual control over the persons concerned and their activities. Thus, there is a presumption that enforcement action is more likely to be taken by the state of residence. Compliance with its commands can be ensured by coercive means and may result in a greater detriment to the interests of the affected individuals. Therefore, it is widely accepted that the national state's power to exercise jurisdiction over its non-resident citizens has to yield to the concurrent power of their state of residence.

The imposition of sanctions against the foreign subsidiaries of domestic parent companies has also raised an issue of extraterritoriality.[255] In principle, foreign subsidiaries doing business abroad are considered separate legal entities and as such are entitled to be qualified as foreign companies provided that they are incorporated in the foreign state in which they operate or have their registered offices. In general, therefore, the conduct of companies can be controlled by the state where they are incorporated and where they do business. No significance is attached to such other criteria as ownership or economic and/or political control. Although they still predominate in state practice, the rather formalistic criteria of the place of incorporation and the seat of the registered offices, indicated by the International Court of Justice in the *Barcelona Traction* case as the only admissible legal bases for the attribution of nationality to corporations for diplomatic protection purposes,[256] are not particularly well suited to discern and evaluate the complex structure of corporate entities. Undoubtedly, in domestic legal systems the evaluation of corporate affiliation and agency relationship for jurisdictional purposes is currently carried out by means of more sophisticated techniques which adopt different criteria.[257] It is reasonable to

---

[254] See F.A. Mann, 'The Doctrine of International Jurisdiction Revisited After 20 Years', note 194 above, at 30 *et seq.*; see also Restatement, note 192 above, s. 441.

[255] A good illustration of the problem is given by the well known affair of the Siberian pipeline, too well known to be recounted in detail. For a full account of factual and legal aspects of the dispute see the contributions of D. Vagts, K. Meessen, P. Kuyper and J. Basedow in 27 *GYIL* (1984); see also P. Merciai, 'Multinational Enterprises, International Transfer of Technology and Unilateral Export Controls', 22 *Diritto comunitario e degli scambi internazionali* 567–607 (1983); R. Ergec, *La compétence extraterritoriale à la lumière du contentieux sur le gazoduc Euro-Sibérien* (Bruxelles, 1984). In general, on extraterritoriality issues arising in the context of the parent-subsidiary affiliation see F.A. Mann, 'The Doctrine of International Jurisdiction Revisited After 20 Years', note 194 above, at 40 *et seq.*; Restatement, note 192 above, s. 414.

[256] *Barcelona Traction*, note 239 above. For a critical view of the formalistic solution supported by the court's holding see F. Francioni, *Imprese multinazionali, protezione diplomatica e responsabilità internazionale* esp. 57 *et seq.* (Milano, 1979).

[257] Incidentally, one should note that, as far as personal jurisdiction is concerned, US courts have traditionally asserted it over foreign companies only when the domestic subsidiary can be proved to be merely the 'alter ego' of the foreign parent. That is, when the separate entity of the subsidiary is so much disregarded by the parent that the subsidiary appears almost as a fictitious entity. See *Cannon Manufacturing Co v Cudahy Packing Co* 267 US 33 (1925),

speculate that in the future, such newly developed criteria might be applied as 'generally recognized principles of law'.[258] Yet, for the time being, state practice indicates that there is a strong presumption in favour of the separate entity of foreign subsidiaries.[259] In principle this would exempt them from the jurisdiction of the parent company's state, unless it could be proved that they have actively participated in a conspiracy to circumvent the latter's regulations on the export of goods.

In fact, an interesting peculiarity of the export controls area is that participation in a conspiracy to circumvent the original conditions for the export of goods from the regulating state seems to be regarded as a legitimate basis for the imposition of sanctions against foreign physical and juridical persons.[260] In such cases extraterritorial measures seem to be tolerated by states provided that the wilful intent of the addressees of sanctionary measures to take part in the illegal transaction can be adequately proved. There is no indication that the *locus delicti* is considered a decisive factor. Whether or not the conspiracy has taken place, wholly or partly, in the regulating state's territory does not appear to be a crucial issue.[261] In such hypotheses, however, it seems reasonable to require that

---

cont.

probably overruled by *International Shoe Co v Washington* 326 US 310 (1945). The *Cannon* strict test has been the object of a more lax interpretation in later judgments by lower courts: see *Hargrave v Fireboard Co* 710 F.2d 1154 (5th Cir. 1983). US courts have also asserted jurisdiction on grounds of 'agency relationship' over foreign corporations that have systematically and continuously conducted business in the US through the agency of a subsidiary (see *Frummer v Hilton International* 281 NYS 2d 41 (1967)). The above examples seem to attest that the US is cautious in 'piercing the veil' of corporate affiliation. This indirectly supports the proposition that the principle of 'separate entity' still represents a fairly strong presumption.

[258] The same International Court of Justice in the *Barcelona Traction* case acknowledged the possibility that also other criteria, derived from domestic legal systems, might gain general consensus so that 'sometimes links to one State have to be weighed against those of another' (1970) ICJ Reports 42.

[259] A.V. Lowe, 'International Law Issues Arising in the Pipeline Dispute: the British Position', 27 *GYIL* 55–71 (1984), has accurately noted that also the US has indirectly recognised the principle in *Sumitomo Shoji American v Avagliano* 457 US 176 (1982). The court's ruling, however, seems to be rather based on the interpretation of the Treaty of Commerce, Friendship and Navigation between Japan and the US.

[260] Similarly, a Canadian court has found jurisdiction in a charge of conspiracy (to traffic in drugs) over defendants who did not commit any act within the *forum*. The court held that the fact that the conspiracy with which they were related had been carried out by one or more other conspirators physically present in the jurisdiction justifies the exercise of jurisdiction over the defendants. See *Re Bin Hin Low and Others* (Canada, British Columbia Supreme Court, 16 July 1975), published in 69 *ILR* 99 (1985)).

[261] This is what one can infer from the recent practice of the US Office of Export Enforcement, in charge for the enforcement of the Export Administration Act and the Regulations adopted thereunder (15 CFR, s. 770.2). Such practice is reviewed in detail in A. Bianchi, *L'applicazione extraterritoriale dei controlli all'esportazione*, note 216 above, at 180 *et seq.* and *id.*, 'Extraterritoriality and Export Controls', note 218 above, at 399 *et seq.*, to which we refer for specific references. The earlier practice of the United States is expounded in A. Lowenfeld, *Trade Controls for Political Ends* (2nd edn, 1983).

the burden of proof be on the regulating state and that enforcement measures be subject to judicial review in any case.[262]

As far as the highly controversial topic of re-exports is concerned, international practice does not support unilateral claims of jurisdiction by the exporting state over goods and/or technical data on the basis of their origin. Such extraterritorial claims, often asserted by the US, have been firmly and constantly rejected by other states.[263] Once they have reached the dominion of another state such goods and technical data are assumed to have come under its jurisdiction.[264] The exporting state can no longer claim control over them as a matter of international law, unless the international responsibility of the importing state as the state of final destination of the goods has been engaged by treaty or other international pledge.[265] Therefore, re-exports can be controlled by the exporting state only with the consent of the importing state. The latter may occasionally tolerate extraterritorial claims in the framework of international understandings or other agreed upon policies.[266] There have been instances in state practice in which the importing state has agreed to share the policy aims of the exporting state by enacting identical or very similar laws.[267]

---

[262] In the US judicial review of export control administrative enforcement procedures is made possible before the US Court of Appeals for the District of Columbia (see s. 2428(a)(1) of the 1988 Omnibus Trade and Competitiveness Act (Pub. L. 100–418, 102 Stat. 1107), reproduced also in 28 ILM 399 (1989)).

[263] See the comments presented by the EC Commission together with a formal diplomatic note to the US Department of State on 12 August 1982 in the course of the *Siberian Pipeline* affair (21 ILM 891–904 (1982)), firmly rejecting the application of the nationality principle to goods and technologies.

[264] See *American President Lines Ltd v China Mutual Trading Co Ltd*, Supreme Court of Hong Kong, (1953) Am. Mar. Cas. 1510; *Moens v Mankiewicz and Hamburg-American Line* (sometimes cited as *Moens v Ahlers et al*), Commercial Tribunal of Antwerp, in: 30 *Rechtskundig Weekblad* 1966–67, kol. 360–363, reported and commented on also in: Comment, 'Western European Sovereignty and American Export and Trade Controls', 9 *Columbia J. of Transnat. L.* 109–139, at 115 (1970).

[265] One may wonder whether an 'end user certificate' or the IC/DV (Import Certificate/Delivery Verification) system, largely used for exports within CoCom countries, can trigger the international responsibility of the importing state, provided that such relevant documents certifying the importing state as the state of final destination have been signed by state officials. In this respect, one could argue that the grant of a licence by the exporting state and the signing of an 'end user certificate' or other similar documents by the importing state's authorities qualify as an agreement in simplified form. After all, it is a well accepted principle that international law does not set any substantive requirement of form as to the negotiation and conclusion of agreements. On the point see A. Bianchi, 'Esportazione e transito di materiali di armamento: profili di diritto internazionale', 75 *Rivista di diritto internazionale* 65–90, esp. 78–82 (1992).

[266] See K. Meessen, 'General Report on Extraterritorial Jurisdiction in Export Control Law', note 196 above, at 10–11.

[267] See note 214 above.

9.   The Relevance of Other Principles of International Law

Often extraterritoriality issues are embedded in a subtle texture of normative prescriptions in which jurisdictional rules are closely intertwined with other norms of the international legal order.[268] This is relevant because jurisdictional issues sometimes arise in connection with the application of primary substantive rules of international law. In such hypotheses, what has to be discerned is the precise scope of application of the relevant principle or rule of international law. Therefore, customary law rules of jurisdiction will apply *per se* only to cases not covered by other more specific rules. Much of the puzzling lack of uniformity in international practice and legal scholarship can be explained against this background. The residuary nature of the international legal regime of jurisdiction is hardly ever acknowledged and alleged breaches of customary jurisdictional rules are erroneously invoked when the violation of other international principles has occurred. To ascertain whether a certain jurisdictional rule emanates from the international law of jurisdiction or from other general principles might be relevant for interpretive purposes, to determine what remedies are available and, ultimately, to foresee further normative developments.

First, any enforcement action in foreign territory by a state's organ or private subjects acting on behalf of a foreign state is to be regarded as an infringement of the customary rule on territorial sovereignty, which protects the unimpeded exercise by the territorial state of enforcement jurisdiction within its territory. The territorial state in turn is subject to limitations concerning the treatment of aliens. As is well known, the treatment of aliens is one of the oldest regimes under international customary law.[269] Further, many bilateral treaties and other multilateral agreements set up precise standards for the treatment of aliens and their economic interests.[270] Some authors maintain that a general principle has emerged in state practice with the effect of preventing the territorial state from imposing duties and liabilities on the foreign national which are disproportionate to the social attachment or allegiance the alien owes to the territorial state.[271]

---

[268] On the relevance of other principles of international law to the law of jurisdiction see question No. 9 of the Questionnaire presented by Rapporteur M. Bos to the Members of the Nineteenth Commission of the Institut de droit international and their replies, in 65 *Annuaire de l'Institut de Droit International* 49 et seq. (1993).

[269] See R. Lillich (ed.), *International Law of State Responsibility for Injuries to Aliens*, (Charlottesville, 1983); I. Brownlie, *Principles of Public International Law*, note 194 above, at 518 et seq., D.J. Harris, *Cases and Materials on International Law* 493 et seq. (4th edn, London, 1991); P.M. Dupuy, *Droit international public* 82 et seq. (Paris, 1992).

[270] See L. Migliorino, *Gli accordi internazionali sugli investimenti* (Milano, 1989); T. Hefti, *La protection de la propriété étrangère en droit international* (Zurich, 1989); Asante, 'International Law and Foreign Investments: a Reappraisal', (1988) *ICLQ* 588 et seq.

[271] See B. Conforti, 'Diritto internazionale' 201 (1992); *id.*, 'Cours géneral de droit international public', 212 *RdC* 145 (1988); *id.*, *International Law and the Role of Domestic Legal Systems*, (Dordrecht/Boston/London, 1993) 133–134:

> ... aliens may be subjected to State territorial jurisdiction only if there exists, and only in

Rules on the treatment of aliens may be relevant to some forms of indirect extraterritoriality, for instance when the territorial state exercises jurisdiction over aliens in the absence of a significant connection, especially when the relevant conduct has taken place abroad. In some limited cases measures of embargo may amount to a discriminatory and arbitrary taking of property. Finally, in all those cases in which a judicial remedy is not available to the recipient of civil or administrative measures one might argue that there has been a denial of justice. Therefore, in certain instances, extraterritorial measures might violate customary or treaty rules on the treatment of aliens rather than the international law of jurisdiction.

In extreme cases the principle of non-intervention is likely to be violated by extraterritorial assertions of jurisdiction. Indeed, non-intervention is one of the most controversial principles of international law.[272] The difficulties arise from the evaluation of which state interests the international legal order recognises as worth protecting. Without venturing into ambitious theoretical definitions, a closer look at state practice might be necessary. In fact, unilateral measures aimed at forcing change in the form of government of foreign countries have been the object of different evaluations by states. It is of note that the fairly sweeping extraterritorial measures enacted by the US against Uganda for the systematic violation of fundamental human rights under the regime of Idi Amin, did not cause other countries to protest. The 1978 embargo laws marked a change in US legislation since they added the 'controlled in fact' subsidiaries of US parent companies to the usual spectrum of addressees.[273] Nevertheless they were not protested by others. The lack of reaction may be due to the universally accepted condemnation of genocide as a crime against humanity so that unilateral measures otherwise intolerable are tolerated by third states in the common belief that they are used to sanction an egregious violation of fundamental values, which are shared by the international community as a whole.[274]

Different considerations apply to the 1993 US Cuban Democracy Act and the Regulations adopted thereunder, where similarly stringent extraterritorial measures have been firmly condemned and protested by foreign states, even

---

cont.
    proportion to, a connection between them or their property and the territorial community ... [The] ... customary rule stated above is the *only rule* which applies to limitations on the territorial State's freedom as to economic matters, including the implementation of antitrust and international commerce regulation.

[272] On intervention, generally, see *Oppenheim's International Law*, note 192 above, at 427 *et seq.*, to which we refer for further bibliographical references. In addition, see B. Conforti, 'The Principle of Non Intervention', in M. Bedjaoui (ed.), *International Law: Achievements and Prospects* at 467 *et seq.* (Dordrecht, 1991) and R. Sapienza, *Il principio di non intervento negli affari interni* (Milano, 1990).

[273] See 43 Fed. Reg. 58, 571–573 (1978).

[274] See note 240 above. Occasionally, *prima facie* unlawfulness of unilateral extraterritorial measures can be reconsidered if it can be established that the latter have been enacted as countermeasures directed to sanction a prior violation of international law by other states.

such close allies as Canada and the UK.[275] The measures, whose rationale is to be traced to a deliberate effort to coerce the freedom of choice, by the citizens of the target state, of their political, economic and social system, have been judged as an unacceptable interference in Cuba's internal affairs.[276] In this hypothesis extraterritorial measures are meant to intensify the effects of the embargo in order to undermine the target country's economy and are an integral part of the international wrong represented by the violation of the non-intervention principle.

Another pertinent issue concerns the relationship between the exercise of personal jurisdiction and the international law of human rights. In particular, it is interesting to wonder whether a principle of international human rights law concerning 'due process' has emerged in state practice. Although the expression originates in US constitutional law,[277] due process has become a widely accepted term which, to some extent, allows for transposition to different legal orders. In particular, one may think of some principles such as 'fair hearing' and 'fairness of the proceedings' embodied in the notion of procedural due process, which are also contained in art. 6 of the European Human Rights Convention as well as in art. 14 of the UN Covenant on Civil and Political Rights and some constitutional charters of European states. Whether such a general principle exists under general international law is arguable. If it does, which remains to be demonstrated, its application might affect jurisdictional issues: for instance, jurisdiction based solely on nationality, jurisdiction of the courts where the assets of the defendant are located, or the accidental place of a tortious act might be seen as heads of jurisdiction which violate a basic principle of due process.[278] The practice of non-recognition of judgments stemming from such excessive exercise of jurisdiction could be equated to protests for the purpose of reconstructing states' *opinio juris* on the subject. It is of note that the 1968 Brussels Convention on Jurisdiction states that certain excessive grounds of jurisdiction

---

[275] See US Cuban Assets Control Regulations, 31 C.F.R. 515. As to the UK reaction, see the Order and General Directions issued on 14 Oct. 1992 by the Minister for Trade, pursuant to the Protection of Trading Interests Act (SI 1992/2449). US measures were also condemned by U.N.G.A. Res 47/19 of 24 Nov. 1992 and by a Resolution of the European Parliament, adopted on 17 Dec. 1992. Also the EC forwarded a diplomatic note of protest to the Department of State on 7 Oct. 1992. All relevant documents can be read in: M. Krinski/D. Golove (eds.), *United States Economic Measures against Cuba. Proceedings in the United Nations and International Law Issues* (Northampton, MA, 1993) and A. Bernardini/F. Lattanzi/M. Spinedi, *Riflessioni sulla conformità o meno al diritto internazionale dell'embargo economico commerciale e finanziario attuato dagli Stati Uniti nei confronti di Cuba* (Roma, 1993).

[276] On the incorporation of the non-interference principle in the international jurisdictional framework see D.J. Gerber, 'Beyond Balancing: International Law Restraints on the Reach of National Laws', 10 *Yale Intl L. J.* 185–221 (1984).

[277] See L. Tribe, *American Constitutional Law* 629–632; 663–768 (procedural due process); 553–586; 1302–1435 (substantive due process) (2nd edn, Mineola, N.Y., 1988).

[278] See the interesting study of P. Schlosser, 'Jurisdiction in International Litigation. The Issue of Human Rights in Relation to National Law and to the Brussels Convention', 74 *Rivista di diritto internazionale* 5–34 (1991).

cannot be invoked against domiciliaries of the Community.[279] Such exorbitant grounds include jurisdiction based solely on nationality, transient jurisdiction and jurisdiction based on the mere location of assets of the defendants within the state's territory.[280]

The above remarks by no means claim to be an exhaustive treatment of the relevance of other principles and/or rules of international law to extraterritoriality matters. An alleged principle of economic sovereignty as opposed to territorial sovereignty[281] and the controversial doctrine of abuse of right[282] have been occasionally invoked as well as a general principle of moderation and self-restraint in the assertion of extraterritorial claims.[283] However, the very existence of such principles in contemporary international law should be the object of careful analysis before considering their applicability to specific cases in which jurisdictional claims are involved.

---

[279] European Convention on Jurisdiction and the Enforcement of Judgments in Civil and Commercial Matters, art. 3(2).

[280] See art. 3(2), listing 'the most important and best known of the rules of exorbitant jurisdiction' (see the Official Report by Jenard in 1979 OJEC C 59/19, 5 Mar. 1979). The drafters of the Convention spotted the above-mentioned heads of jurisdiction by looking respectively in the domestic legal orders of France, England, and Germany.

[281] See S. Waller/A. Simon, 'Analyzing Claims of Sovereignty in International Economic Disputes', 7 *Northwestern J. of Intl L.* 1–4 (1985) and A.V. Lowe, '*The Problems of Extraterritorial Jurisdiction: Economic Sovereignty and the Search for a Solution*', 34 *ICLQ* 724 (1985).

[282] See para. 11 of the EC Comments, note 263 above. See also P. Kuyper, 'The European Community and the US Pipeline Embargo, 27 *GYIL* 71-96, 84 *et seq.* (1984). Some scholars maintain that the doctrine of the abuse of right would be applicable as a general principle of law, under art. 38 of the ICJ statute, given the *lacunae*, or the unclear character of applicable rules of the international law of jurisdiction (see G. Fitzmaurice, 'The General Principles of Law Considered from the Standpoint of the Rule of Law', 92 *RdC* 5 at 55–59 (1957/II)). This stance can be easily rebutted in the light of the existence of the substantive rules of international law highlighted above. Others maintain that the abuse of right doctrine is an integral part of an international rule that prescribes the existence of a significant link between the regulating state and the conduct or event to be regulated (see Dahm, *Völkerrecht*, Vol. II at 256 and 260 (3 Volumes, Stuttgart, 1958–1961) quoted in F.A. Mann, 'The Doctrine of Jurisdiction in International Law', note 194 above, at 49). The incongruity of this thesis is apparent. Either there is a rule that prescribes that in order to exercise jurisdiction a state must have a significant connection with the conduct or event and, therefore, in the absence of such a connection it has no entitlement to lay an extraterritorial claim of jurisdiction; or, such a rule does not exist and therefore there is no legal parameter against which an abuse can be assessed. The problem then is to determine the exact scope of the jurisdictional principle and not the existence of an abuse of right.

[283] See Judge Fitzmaurice's separate opinion in the *Barcelona Traction* case, note 239 above, at 105.

10.   The Fragmentation of the International Law of Jurisdiction

One major preoccupation with the approach suggested in this paper might be the threat to undermine the unity of the law. This was listed by Brownlie as one of the main risks of an excess of specialisation in international legal theory.[284] Yet, this is quite inevitable given the many changes which the international community has undergone in the past decades. After all, the aim of the law is not the static preservation of the legal order but its progressive development in accordance with the changing demands of the system. In this context, it should be acknowledged that the law of jurisdiction is closely intertwined with the concept of domestic jurisdiction. Undeniably, the latter has dramatically changed recently. Matters which not long ago were of exclusive domestic concern are now regarded as amenable to international regulation and scrutiny and some of the once indisputable sovereign prerogatives of the territorial state have been subjected to a steady process of erosion. Hence, one may legitimately wonder why the cognate question of jurisdictional competence should not change accordingly.

After all, the unity of the law of jurisdiction is already fictitious. *Ad hoc* regimes exist in the law of the sea and in other areas such as outer space and Antarctica.[285] Special jurisdictional rules also govern air law, diplomatic and consular relations and crimes under international law. To hold that all these different regimes can be amenable to a unitary law of jurisdiction is neither tenable nor expedient. In fact, the dynamics of international law making have caused specific jurisdictional rules to emerge and develop over time adjusting to the peculiar needs of the matters to which they are to apply.

International economic law can be no exception to the above trend towards specialisation. The complexity of cases is such that general rules are not particularly well suited to meet the needs of the system, unless they are given a specific content. The inherently general nature of customary jurisdictional rules cannot *per se* guarantee a satisfactory level of predictability and expediency in the solution of complicated factual matrices.

The apparent contradiction between the unity and the fragmentation of the law of jurisdiction might be ultimately solved by focusing on a general customary principle whose specific content has to be determined in the light of the substantive standards which have emerged in the various areas of international practice. At the same time the demands of the international community are met

---

[284] I. Brownlie, 'Problems Concerning the Unity of International Law', in: *International Law at the Time of its Codification. Studies in Honour of Roberto Ago* 153–162 (Milan, 1987, Vol. I).
[285] The existence of special regimes of jurisdiction in contemporary international law is acknowledged by I. Brownlie, *Principles of Public International Law*, note 194 above, at 310–311. The author states that such specific regimes derogate from the customary law and general principles of jurisdiction.

by broadening the jurisdictional powers of states with regard to the enforcement of interests that the same states have indicated as primary values for the international community as a whole.

These are the issues which, I believe, one has to ponder over before proceeding to any attempt at systematisation. If I have taken the liberty of suggesting one possible approach, this was by no means intended to abuse my function as a discussant. On the contrary, it was simply meant to stimulate discussion or, as one might say, to throw a clay pigeon for you to shoot at. Thank you very much for your attention.

Sir Ian Sinclair:

Thank you very much. I think you have given us all a great deal of food for thought. You have not in any sense abused your role as a discussant, rather the contrary. You have given us a great deal of interesting things to discuss. I was personally interested in what you were saying about the relevance of other international law topics. You certainly do have to take into account the total context in which a claim to exercise jurisdiction extraterritorially is being advanced. It is a striking feature of international life that where there has been an assertion of jurisdiction which many countries would regard as being an extraterritorial assertion of jurisdiction, it has been open to objection on that ground alone. But where it has been done in the context of a situation in which, for example, the US has been the victim of an international wrong such as the taking of hostages in Tehran then the reaction to what other countries might otherwise regard as being an excessive use of extraterritorial jurisdiction has been muted, to say the least, if not actually non-existent. That, I think, is a fact we ought to bear in mind. But I want to open the discussion up.

Aurelio Pappalardo:

May I ask for a clarification of Professor Maier's statement? When he presented the territorial principle, he indicated that the objective theory is also called the effects doctrine. Now, at least in the field of antitrust, this identification would raise serious difficulties, since it is generally accepted that objective territoriality goes beyond the doctrine of effects, in that it requires that an essential constituent element of the event take place in the territory.

Karl M. Meessen:

One of the problems, in my opinion, is to distinguish internationally binding rules of jurisdiction from national rules of jurisdiction. The latter are susceptible to change as it may please the law-making agencies of the respective state. Harold Maier covered this point very elegantly by pointing out that the Restatement, if I remember it correctly, 'combines international law and comity' whereas Andrea Bianchi's focus was on international law only. Your suggestion, Andrea, to distinguish between a continental European approach to jurisdiction and an

American approach is illuminating. However, I wonder to what extent the two approaches are mutually exclusive. I would prefer to consider them as supplementary.

Gary Born:

My own sense is that there continue to be substantial differences in opinion internationally about the appropriate jurisdictional principles for legislative jurisdiction. To be sure, I think that the US has in general moderated some of the worst excesses of extraterritorial jurisdiction, at the same time that European and other states have embraced non-territorial jurisdictional concepts not too different from the US.[286]

Nevertheless, it is my sense that the process of convergence still has a considerable way to go. In particular, I believe that the US penchant for a broad effects doctrine, and for liberal definitions of nationality, is not yet accepted in many other countries. Moreover, the Restatement's 'rule of reason' and similar interest analyses in the choice of law context probably submerge jurisdictional differences until specific disputes, involving particular sets of interests, arise. With the general quiet in US regulatory circles over the past decade or so, such disputes have not often arisen. But that does not mean that there is in fact underlying unanimity about the appropriate scope of national regulatory jurisdiction of international business activities.

---

[286] See Born, 'A Reappraisal of the Extraterritorial Reach of US Law', 24 *Law & Policy in Intl Bus.* 1 (1992).

Chapter V

Extraterritorial Application of Criminal Law: Jurisdiction to Prosecute Drug Traffic Conducted by Aliens Abroad

Adelheid Puttler

In the area of criminal law, problems of jurisdiction have been discussed at great length for many decades. However, there remain some open questions. One of them is whether a state has jurisdiction to prosecute foreign drug dealers that operate in regions close to its borders thereby frustrating its drug prevention policy.

1. The Netherlands and Germany: A Clash of Policies

Illicit drug use can create problems for the health of individuals. The supply of such drugs may impair the social or public health of societies. Opinions on how to deal with the drug problem, however, differ. Particularly at issue is what role criminal law should play in carrying out a successful anti-drug policy. Major disagreements seem to exist as to whether it is useful or even necessary to employ criminal law measures where 'soft' drugs are concerned such as cannabis and cannabis derivatives.

When neighbouring countries like the Netherlands and Germany pursue differing drug prevention policies, problems of extraterritorial jurisdiction can emerge. Over the past two decades in several cases before German courts, the question has arisen as to whether a state has jurisdiction to prosecute a foreign national trading in cannabis products abroad. In these cases, usually the cannabis dealer has been a Dutch national and has carried out his activities in the

Netherlands in a region near the German border. Among his customers have been not only local hashish smokers but also 'drug tourists' from other countries, especially German nationals attracted by the more permissive rules for soft drugs in the Netherlands. With the advancement of European integration and the gradual disappearance of border controls in the European Union, daytrips to the Netherlands to buy hashish have become increasingly easy for German tourists.[287]

Although both Dutch law and German law prohibit the sale or distribution of cannabis products without an appropriate licence and qualify such conduct as a criminal offence, there are differences regarding the prosecution of such offences. While in the Netherlands prosecution is discretionary,[288] German prosecutors are under an obligation to prosecute according to the so-called principle of legality.[289] Important elements of the Dutch anti-drug policy include an active campaign against hard drugs but a more lenient approach to the sale and consumption of hashish and marijuana. Under certain conditions, Dutch police and public prosecutors, therefore, tolerate drug dealers who trade only in these substances.[290] It is understandable, therefore, that German authorities pursuing a different drug policy are concerned about Germans travelling to neighbouring Dutch provinces to buy hashish. Sometimes German customers consume the hashish they purchased while still within Dutch territory. In other cases, cannabis products bought in the Netherlands are transported to Germany and either consumed there by their original buyers or resold to others.[291]

2.   Legal Grounds to Prosecute under German Municipal Law

When German police have gathered sufficient information on a hashish dealer in the Dutch border region, the public prosecutor usually applies to a German court for a warrant of arrest and has the person placed on lists for internationally

---

[287] Cf. 'Maastricht 2: A Hot Corner of Drugs and Tolerance', in *Intl Herald Tribune*, 21 Apr. 1994, at 1.

[288] C.F. Rüter, 'Die strafrechtliche Drogenbekämpfung in den Niederlanden – Ein Königreich als Aussteiger?', 100 *Zeitschrift für die gesamte Strafrechtswissenschaft* 385, 388 (1988); K.H. Reuband, *Drogenkonsum und Drogenpolitik – Deutschland und die Niederlande im Vergleich* 15 (1992).

[289] Strafprozeßordnung (StPO) s. 152(2). German law provides the possibility of refraining from prosecution, e.g. in minor cases (StPO ss. 153, 153b), in cases concerning offences committed abroad (StPO s. 153c) or in minor drug cases, where the offence is committed in the interest of personal consumption only (Betäubungsmittelgesetz s. 31a). Of these provisions, however, only StPO s. 153c would be applicable to a foreign cannabis dealer abroad selling regularly to a larger number of customers.

[290] C.F. Rüter, 'Die strafrechtliche Drogenbekämpfung in den Niederlanden – Ein Königreich als Aussteiger?' 100 *Zeitschrift für die gesamte Strafrechtswissenschaft* 385, 397 *passim* (1988).

[291] Cf. 27 Entscheidungen des Bundesgerichtshofs in Strafsachen (BGHSt) 30 = *Universal Jurisdiction over Drug Offences* case, 74 ILR 166, 168 (1987).

wanted persons. Sometimes the police manage to arrest the offender when he either enters German territory[292] or is extradited by a third country.[293]

The German Strafgesetzbuch (Penal Code)[294] s. 3 provides: 'German criminal law applies to offences committed within the domestic territory'. There are, however, several provisions in the German Strafgesetzbuch (StGB), which establish jurisdiction for German criminal courts to try foreigners for drug offences committed abroad. StGB s. 6 states:

> Irrespective of the law of the place where the offence was committed, German criminal law is applicable to the following offences committed abroad:
> 1. ...
> ...
> ...
> ...
> 5. illicit traffic in narcotic drugs ...

Another provision that would permit a drug dealer of foreign nationality to be brought before a German court because of his activities abroad can be found in StGB s. 7(2):

> German criminal law applies to ... offences committed abroad if the act is qualified as a punishable offence at the place where the act was committed ... and if
>
> 1. ...
> 2. ... at the time of commission the offender was a foreign national, the offender was found within domestic territory, and the offender is not extradited, although the Auslieferungsgesetz (German Extradition Law) would permit extradition according to the nature of the offence, because no application for extradition has been made or extradition is not feasible.

3. Jurisdictional Bases to Prosecute under International Law

By applying these provisions of German domestic law, Germany asserts its jurisdiction over drug-related cases involving the conduct of foreign nationals abroad. Public international law, however, determines whether Germany has jurisdiction at all to bring such cases before its courts. It is still a controversial question, whether a state has jurisdiction only when a recognised basis for it can be found in international law or whether it may exercise jurisdiction merely in the absence of any prohibition. This mainly concerns the question of where the

---

[292] There have been cases where German police or their agents lured the suspect across the border by questionable means which led to diplomatic friction between the Netherlands and Germany; see C.F. Rüter, 'Die strafrechtliche Drogenbekämpfung in den Niederlanden – Ein Königreich als Aussteiger?', 100 *Zeitschrift für die gesamte Strafrechtswissenschaft*, 385 (1988).

[293] As in the case of 34 BGHSt 334.

[294] Strafgesetzbuch (StGB) as revised on 10 Mar. 1987, I Bundesgesetzblatt (BGBl) 945 (1987), I BGBl 1160 (1987), as amended most recently by the Law of 2 Aug. 1993, I BGBl 1407 (1993).

burden of proof for jurisdiction lies, either with the state claiming jurisdiction or with the state disputing the right of the other state to claim jurisdiction.[295] In state practice and legal literature there seems to be general agreement now that the right to exercise jurisdiction depends on whether it is possible to identify a sufficiently close connection between the subject matter and the state.[296] In criminal law, several bases of jurisdiction have been discussed which might provide a sufficient nexus between the prosecuting state and the conduct abroad.

For the cannabis cases under discussion here, jurisdiction to prosecute might be based on one or several of the following connecting factors: territoriality, effects, protection of state functions, universality, and representative administration of criminal justice.

A.   Jurisdiction Based on Territoriality

In general, a state has jurisdiction over all persons and things within its territory, territoriality being the closest connection.[297] A state may prosecute a crime on grounds of territoriality only if at least part of the crime was committed in the prosecuting state's territory. This means that a constituent element of the crime must have taken place in its territory.[298] In the Dutch cannabis cases, whether this requirement has been met would depend on the exact facts of the individual case. If the Dutch dealer merely sells hashish to his German clients without knowing or caring where they will consume it or what they will do with the drugs afterwards, a sufficiently close link to German territory can hardly be established. The situation would be different, however, if the Dutch dealer intended to bring cannabis into Germany by giving it to German nationals who then smuggled it for him. Under such special circumstances it could be said that a constituent element of the crime of importing narcotic drugs, i.e. bringing drugs over the border, took place on German territory. The territorial principle would therefore only be applicable to very particular factual situations.

B.   Jurisdiction Based on Effects

Another connecting factor, on which jurisdiction to prosecute conduct abroad can be based, may be found in the effect of the crime felt in the prosecuting state's territory. Where criminal law is concerned, it is acknowledged that a state

---

[295] M. Akehurst, 'Jurisdiction in International Law', 46 *BYIL* 145, 167 (1972/73).

[296] R. Jennings/A. Watts (eds.), *Oppenheim's International Law* 457–58 (9th edn, 1992); B.H. Oxman, 'Jurisdiction of States', in R. Bernhardt (ed.), *Encyclopedia of Public International Law*, Instalment 10 (1987), at 277, 278.

[297] The American Law Institute, Restatement of the Law Third, The Foreign Relations Law of the United States, s. 402(1)(a) and Comment c (1987); D. Oehler, *Internationales Strafrecht*, 155 *passim* (2nd edn, 1983); B.H. Oxman, 'Jurisdiction of States', in: R. Bernhardt (ed.), *Encyclopedia of Public International Law*, Instalment 10 (1987), at 277, 279; J.L. Brierly, *The Law of Nations* 299 (6th edn, 1978); see also German StGB s. 3.

[298] F.A. Mann, *Studies in International Law* 72–73 (1973).

has the right to try and punish an offender whose behaviour outside its territory has caused injury inside its territory.[299] A frequently cited example for the applicability of this principle is that of the offender in state A who fires a gun thereby shooting over the border into state B and injuring someone there. State B would then have jurisdiction to prosecute the offender based on the effect caused by his conduct in state B. In this example the injurious effect itself is a constituent element of the crime.[300] Being closely linked to the territory of the prosecuting state, this basis of jurisdiction is frequently called the objective territorial principle.[301] There are advocates of a wider effects doctrine who acknowledge jurisdiction based on effects even if the effect is not a constituent element of the crime. However, in their view, not every kind of effect resulting from the conduct abroad is sufficient. A crime may produce distant and indirect effects in many countries. Giving jurisdiction to every country where an effect can be felt, even if it is only remotely concerned, might come close to acknowledging universal jurisdiction. Therefore, according to supporters of the effects doctrine, only a state where the primary, direct and substantial effect of the conduct is felt has jurisdiction to prosecute the offender.[302]

In cases of illicit sale of cannabis products abroad, the question arises as to what kind of injury or effect is caused on German territory and whether or not the effect is sufficiently direct and substantial to allow for prosecution.

Medical experts differ as to the concrete physical and psychical effects caused by occasional or permanent consumption of cannabis derivatives. There seems to be agreement, however, that under the acute influence of cannabis the consumer's concentration and perception are disturbed so that driving a car, for example, might be dangerous. Moreover, medical evidence seems to show that occasional consumption of hashish and marijuana in small amounts does not cause immediate bodily harm or lead to physical addiction. Experts disagree as to the potential for adverse mental effects on certain groups of consumers, especially young, unstable persons consuming cannabis frequently and in high doses.[303] It is highly controversial whether cannabis acts as the gateway to

---

[299] R. Jennings/A. Watts (eds.), *Oppenheim's International Law* 459–60 (9th edn, 1992); B.H. Oxman, 'Jurisdiction of States', in R. Bernhardt (ed.), *Encyclopedia of Public International Law*, Instalment 10 (1987), at 277, 279–80; M. Akehurst, 'Jurisdiction in International Law', 46 *BYIL* 145, 152 *passim* (1972/73).

[300] This was also the case in the *Lotus* decision of the Permanent Court of 7 Sept. 1927, PCIJ, Series A, No. 10 at 4–107 (1927).

[301] R. Jennings/A. Watts (eds.), *Oppenheim's International Law* 460 (9th edn, 1992).

[302] The American Law Institute, Restatement of the Law Third, The Foreign Relations Law of the United States, s. 402(1)(c) and Comment d, s. 403(2)(a), s. 421(2)(j) (1987); M. Akehurst, 'Jurisdiction in International Law', 46 *BYIL* 145, 153 *passim* (1972/73); see also F.A. Mann, *Studies in International Law* 34 (1973); but cf. R. Jennings/A. Watts (eds.), *Oppenheim's International Law* 475 (9th edn, 1992).

[303] According to K. Täschner, *Das Cannabisproblem* 154 *passim* (1986) constant cannabis abuse may influence motivation and lead to changes in the consumer's personality; see also Th. Geschwinde, *Rauschdrogen* 42 *passim* (2nd edn, 1990). This is questioned by S. Quensel in S. Scheerer/I. Vogt, *Drogen und Drogenpolitik* 387 *passim* (1989).

cocaine and heroin, the consumption of soft drugs making users more inclined to try dangerous hard drugs as well.[304] German legislative history concerning the German Narcotics Law (Betäubungsmittelgesetz) shows that German legislators have been of the opinion that cannabis abuse may create dangers for the health of individuals and may induce especially young people to turn to hard drugs.[305]

Two different kinds of possible effects of selling drugs to German consumers in the Dutch border region have to be taken into consideration: on the one hand, direct effects on the cannabis consumers and their physical and mental health, and, on the other hand, the effect on public health and social peace of German society resulting from the potential danger that cannabis consumers might turn to hard drugs as well. As mentioned above, there is no conclusive medical evidence to show that substantial adverse effects on the cannabis consumers' health are certain or even probable. The mental effects described seem to occur only in special consumer groups and then only after prolonged use of higher amounts of the drug. It would require a special fact pattern to consider such effects as the direct result of specific sales by Dutch cannabis dealers.

Jurisdiction might exist, however, if clients of the Dutch cannabis dealer drove their cars on German territory under the immediate influence of the cannabis acquired in the border area thereby endangering themselves and other people on the road. But a state could only base its jurisdiction on these effects if they were substantial ones. Driving under the influence of cannabis would therefore have to occur frequently and the dangers caused would have to be considerable.

The second kind of effects, those to public health and social well-being because of the possible move from the recreational use of cannabis to the abuse of hard drugs, would not provide a sufficiently close connection for jurisdiction to prosecute the foreign cannabis dealer. First, among drug experts the gateway effect is highly controversial. Secondly, even if such effect could be established, it would not result directly from the sale of the soft drugs. Not all hashish smokers become cocaine addicts. The easy availability of soft drugs may be one but not the only step on the way to hard drugs.

C.　*Jurisdiction Based on the Protective Principle*

In one of the Dutch cannabis cases the German Bundesgerichtshof based jurisdiction on the so-called protective principle. The court held that the Dutch dealer had violated German interests by having sold over many years considerable amounts of hashish to German nationals who had then brought the drug to Germany to consume or resell it there.[306] In a case before the US Court of Appeals for the 11th Circuit involving the intent to smuggle marijuana into the

---

[304] See Th. Geschwinde, *Rauschdrogen* 44 *passim* (2nd edn, 1990); S. Quensel in S. Scheerer/I. Vogt, *Drogen und Drogenpolitik* 391 (1989).
[305] Bundesrats-Drucksache 665/70 (neu), at 5 *passim*; Bundestags-Drucksache 8/3551, at 24.
[306] 34 BGHSt 334, 339.

US, the court held that the US had jurisdiction based on the protective principle. A Honduran vessel carrying on board a large amount of marijuana had been intercepted by the US Coast Guard on the high seas 125 miles east of the Florida coast. The crew members were charged with having violated the Marijuana on the High Seas Act. [307]

International law recognises the need for states to protect their governmental functions. It allows a state to prosecute foreigners who have committed acts outside the state's territory that are directed against the sovereignty or security of the state or endanger its functions. The protective principle is applicable to a limited class of offences; examples given are espionage, counterfeiting the seal of the state or its currency, falsification of official documents, attacks on diplomats and treason. [308] A distinction has to be made between the effects doctrine discussed above and the protective principle. While jurisdiction based on the effects doctrine requires that the effect or result of the offence occurs in the territory of the state claiming jurisdiction, the protective principle applies if the conduct abroad threatens the security, integrity or the proper functioning of the prosecuting state's government even if there is no effect in the state's territory. [309] Both bases of jurisdiction may overlap when the conduct abroad causes an adverse effect in the territory of the prosecuting state thereby threatening its security or government functions. [310] In the cases mentioned above, German and US authorities had an interest in prosecuting conduct abroad considered as preparatory to smuggling cannabis derivatives into their countries. Germany and the US regarded these activities abroad as weakening their anti-drug policy. The protective principle, however, may not be used merely to impose a state's policy or ideology on foreigners outside its territory. Its purpose is to safeguard the political independence of the state exercising jurisdiction but not to serve as a means of enforcing the state's policy abroad. [311] Jurisdiction based on the protective principle would only exist if the drug sales in the Dutch border region or the carrying of marijuana on board the Honduran vessel threatened the security of the prosecuting state or its state functions. Neither of the two court decisions discussed this point. As has already been pointed out, the consequences of the consumption of cannabis derivatives are controversial. Even if taking soft drugs had adverse effects on the health of individuals and encouraged a number of hashish smokers and marijuana

---

[307] *US v Gonzalez* 776 F.2d 931 (11th Cir., 1985).

[308] M. Akehurst, 'Jurisdiction in International Law', 46 *BYIL* 145, 157 *passim* (1972/73); C. Blakesley, 'Extraterritorial Jurisdiction', in M.C. Bassiouni (ed.), *International Criminal Law*, Vol. 2 Procedure 3, 19 *passim* (1986); The American Law Institute, Restatement of the Law Third, the Foreign Relations Law of the United States, s. 402(3) and Comment f (1987).

[309] See *US v Pizzarusso* 388 F.2d 8, 10–11 (2d Cir. 1968).

[310] C. Blakesley, 'Extraterritorial Jurisdiction', in M.C. Bassiouni (ed.), *International Criminal Law*, Vol. 2 Procedure 3, at 19 (1986).

[311] M. Akehurst, 'Jurisdiction in International Law', 46 *BYIL* 145, 159 (1972/73); F.A. Mann, *Studies in International Law* 80 (1973); see also R. Jennings/A. Watts (eds.), *Oppenheim's International Law* 471 (9th edn 1992).

consumers to turn to hard drugs later on, jurisdiction based on the protective principle could hardly be asserted. While such an argument might possibly be made if imports of large amounts of *hard* drugs into a country were at issue which threatened to cause drug abuse and the addiction of a considerable part of that state's population thereby corrupting the government or destabilising social order, there is no evidence to show that the activities of the Dutch cannabis dealer or the conduct of the Honduran crew members threatened to impair the proper functioning of government authorities or endangered state security.[312]

D.   Universal Jurisdiction

According to the Bundesgerichtshof (German Federal Supreme Court), StGB s. 6 No. 5 bases jurisdiction for prosecution of illicit traffic in all kinds of controlled drugs on the principle of universality.[313] In public international law, however, it is far from settled that the universal principle may be applied to illicit traffic in cannabis products.

Jurisdiction based on the universal principle means that in cases of acts internationally defined as crimes, the state of capture may prosecute the alien offender irrespective of the law of the state where the offence has been committed and irrespective of the possibility of extradition. The applicability of the universal principle to certain crimes can be determined by public international law or can be stipulated for in international agreements. It is a controversial issue whether such a basis of jurisdiction exists in customary international law at all.[314] For its supporters it derives its justification from the character of certain offences which are a danger to the international order and in the repression of which all states have an interest.[315] When applicable, it allows a state to extend its jurisdiction to offences where neither the act nor the offender nor the victim has any relation to its territory. Consequently, the exercise of such jurisdiction often entails the danger of thereby infringing upon the sovereign rights of another state. Therefore, the principle is limited to crimes which the nations of the world have qualified as attacks upon the international order and have mutually agreed to suppress, e.g. piracy on the high seas. Moreover, there are international conventions which provide for the suppression of certain activities. To establish

---

[312] But see C. Blakesley, 'Extraterritorial Jurisdiction', in M.C. Bassiouni (ed.), *International Criminal Law*, Vol. 2 Procedure 3, at 42 and note 180 (1986). The author discusses whether in the special case of the crime of conspiracy to smuggle drugs, as it is known in US law, this offence could present a potential threat to a government function because it violates customs regulations.

[313] 27 BGHSt 30, 32 = *Universal Jurisdiction over Drug Offences* case, 74 ILR 166, 168 (1987); 34 BGHSt 1, 2; 34 BGHSt 334, 336.

[314] See M. Akehurst, 'Jurisdiction in International Law', 46 *BYIL* 145, 163 *passim* (1972/73).

[315] E.g. The American Law Institute, Restatement of the Law Third, Foreign Relations Law of the United States, ss. 404, 423 (1987); F.A. Mann, *Studies in International Law* 81 (1973); D. Oehler, *Internationales Strafrecht* 532 *passim* (2nd edn, 1983); R. Jennings/A. Watts (eds.), *Oppenheim's International Law* 469 (9th edn, 1992).

universal jurisdiction by such a convention, it is not sufficient, however, that the treaty in question qualifies a specific conduct as a crime. In addition, the treaty needs to contain an agreement of the parties as to the applicability of universal jurisdiction to this offence.[316]

Although it has been suggested that trade in narcotic drugs belongs to that limited number of international crimes that may justify recourse to the universal principle,[317] the existence of such state practice has not been established,[318] most particularly with regard to 'soft' drugs like hashish and marijuana.

Jurisdiction based on universality could, however, have been agreed upon by way of treaty. The international community considers international drug control to be a significant issue. The Single Convention on Narcotic Drugs of 1961,[319] replacing all prior international drug treaties, creates a system of international drug control which has subsequently been amended and further enhanced by the Convention on Psychotropic Substances of 1971 and the Convention against Illicit Traffic in Narcotic Drugs and Psychotropic Substances of 1988.[320] International conventions distinguish between two major groups of controlled drugs, narcotic drugs and psychotropic substances. Cannabis and its derivatives are listed among the narcotic drugs to which all control measures are applicable.[321]

Parties to the Single Convention on Narcotic Drugs of 1961 are required to limit to medical and scientific purposes the production, manufacture, export, import, distribution of, trade in, use and possession of drugs. According to art. 4 of the 1961 Convention each party is required to take 'such legislative and administrative measures as may be necessary' to achieve the goals of the convention. Under certain conditions the 1961 Convention and the 1988 Convention also require parties to establish as punishable offences a wide range of activities relating to controlled drugs, among them the sale, distribution, delivery, export and import of such substances.[322] The 1961 Convention and the

---

[316] D. Oehler, *Internationales Strafrecht* 533 *passim* (2nd edn, 1983); M. Akehurst, 'Jurisdiction in International Law', 46 *BYIL* 145, 160–61 (1972/73).

[317] F.A. Mann, *Studies in International Law* 81 (1973); D. Oehler, 'Criminal Law, International', in R. Bernhardt (ed.), *Encyclopedia of Public International Law*, Installment 9 (1986), 52, 53; A. Verdross/B. Simma, *Universelles Völkerrecht* 779 (3rd edn, 1984).

[318] See Ph. Kunig, 'Die Bedeutung des Nichteinmischungsprinzips für das Internationale Strafrecht der Bundesrepublik Deutschland', *Juristische Schulung* 594, 596 (1978).

[319] UN Treaty Series, Vol. 520, No. 7515, as amended by Protocol of 25 Mar. 1972, UN Treaty Series, Vol. 976, No. 14152.

[320] Convention on Psychotropic Substances of 21 Feb. 1971, UN Treaty Series, Vol. 1019, No. 14956; UN Convention against Illicit Traffic in Narcotic Drugs and Psychotropic Substances of 20 Dec. 1988, E/CONF. 82/15 and Corr. 2. The 1988 Convention entered into force for Germany in July 1993 and for the Netherlands in Dec. 1993.

[321] Single Convention on Narcotic Drugs of 1961, note 319 above, art. 2(1) and Schedule I; UN Convention against Illicit Traffic in Narcotic Drugs and Psychotropic Substances of 1988, note 320 above, art. 1(n).

[322] Single Convention on Narcotic Drugs of 1961, note 319 above, art. 36(1); UN Convention against Illicit Traffic in Narcotic Drugs and Psychotropic Substances of 1988, note 320 above, art. 3(1)(a)(i).

1988 Convention both contain provisions on 'jurisdiction'. Article 36(2)(a)(iv) of the Single Convention on Narcotic Drugs of 1961 stipulates that:

> ... offences ... committed either by nationals or by foreigners shall be prosecuted by the Party in whose territory the offence was committed, or by the Party in whose territory the offender is found if extradition is not acceptable in conformity with the law of the Party to which application is made, and if such offender has not already been prosecuted and judgement given.

On the other hand art. 36(3) reads:

> The provisions of this article shall be subject to the provisions of the criminal law of the Party concerned on questions of jurisdiction.

It is therefore doubtful whether the parties to the 1961 Convention intended to regulate questions of international jurisdiction at all. The heading of art. 4 of the 1988 Convention is 'Jurisdiction' and art. 4(2)(b) states that each party:

> May also take such measures as may be necessary to establish its jurisdiction ... when the offender is present in its territory and it does not extradite him to another Party.

But art. 4(3) states that:

> This Convention does not exclude the exercise of any criminal jurisdiction established by a Party in accordance with its domestic law.

The wording of these articles suggests that the 1961 Convention and the 1988 Convention set up minimum standards for provisions of jurisdiction to be included in the internal law of the parties rather than regulate the question of international jurisdiction in general. Moreover, art. 36(2)(a)(iv) of the 1961 Convention and art. 4(2)(b) of the 1988 Convention make the exercise of jurisdiction subject to not having extradited the offender. Universal jurisdiction, however, would entitle a state to prosecute irrespective of an application to extradite or the possibility of extradition. Therefore the provisions in the 1961 and 1988 Conventions do not express an agreement of the parties as to the applicability of the public international principle of universality to drug-related offences.

E.   *Jurisdiction Based on the Principle of Representative Administration of Criminal Justice*

According to German StGB s. 7(2), Germany asserts its jurisdiction to prosecute conduct abroad if, under the law of the state where the offence took place, the conduct would be a punishable offence and the offender is not extradited to this state although under German law extradition would have been permitted. Dutch authorities in general do not prosecute drug dealers trading in cannabis derivatives only. In accordance with its international obligations,[323] however, the Netherlands has qualified dealing in cannabis products as a criminal offence by law.[324] Under StGB s. 7(2), Germany could claim jurisdiction even if the Netherlands had not applied for extradition of the Dutch cannabis dealer because it had not been interested in prosecution.[325] Moreover, trading in cannabis products belongs to those kinds of crimes for which German law would allow extradition.[326]

StGB s. 7(2) derives jurisdiction from the so-called principle of representative administration of criminal justice. This principle is said to be based on an abstract notion of solidarity among states to prosecute offenders.[327] It means that the state where the offender is found has jurisdiction to prosecute if he or she is not extradited to the state where the crime was committed. While in their criminal law a number of states, especially in Europe, claim jurisdiction derived from this principle, it is not universally accepted and its limitations are controversial.[328] It is doubtful, therefore, whether under customary international law Germany could claim jurisdiction under this principle.

However, jurisdiction based on the principle of representative administration of criminal justice can be stipulated for in international agreements. In several treaties the contracting parties have agreed on such a basis of jurisdiction.[329]

The UN Conventions of 1961 and 1988[330] also contain special provisions in this respect. According to art. 36(2)(a)(iv) of the Single Convention on Narcotic Drugs of 1961 the state in whose territory the offender is found has jurisdiction 'if extradition is not acceptable in conformity with the law of the Party to which application is made, and if such offender has not already been prosecuted and judgement given'. The wording of this provision does not make it clear whether art. 36 would permit jurisdiction only in cases where an application for

---

[323] Single Convention on Narcotic Drugs of 1961, note 319 above, art. 36(1); UN Convention against Illicit Traffic in Narcotic Drugs and Psychotropic Substances of 1988, note 320 above, art. 3(1)(a)(i).

[324] K.H. Reuband, *Drogenkonsum und Drogenpolitik – Deutschland und die Niederlande im Vergleich* 15–16 (1992).

[325] E. Dreher/H. Tröndle, *Strafgesetzbuch*, s. 7 para. 11 (annotated part) (46th edn, 1993); A. Schönke/H. Schröder, *Strafgesetzbuch – Kommentar*, s. 7 para. 25 (annotated part) 24th edn, 1991).

[326] i.e. the offence does not fall under the Gesetz über die internationale Rechtshilfe in Strafsachen (German Law on International Assistance in Criminal Matters) of 23 Dec. 1982, I Bundesgesetzblatt 2071 (1982) s. 3 and ss. 6–8, according to which extradition is not permitted, when petty offences and military or political crimes are concerned; for an English translation see S. Uhlig/W. Schomburg/O. Lagodny, *Gesetz über die internationale Rechtshilfe in Strafsachen (IRG)* 390 *passim* (2nd edn, 1992).

[327] D. Oehler, *Internationales Strafrecht* 506 (2nd edn, 1983).

[328] D. Oehler, *Internationales Strafrecht* 144 *passim*, 498 *passim* (2nd edn, 1983).

[329] European Convention on the Suppression of Terrorism of 27 Jan. 1977, art. 6(1), European Treaties Series No. 90, II Bundesgesetzblatt (BGBl) 321 (1978); International Convention against the Taking of Hostages of 18 Dec. 1979, art. 8(1), II BGBl 1361 (1980) = 18 *Intl Leg. Mat.* 1456 *passim* (1979).

[330] Notes 319 and 320 above.

extradition was made by the state where the crime had taken place but was refused by the state where the offender had been found. Moreover, the state claiming jurisdiction would have to ascertain whether the offender had already been brought before a court in another state. The wording of art. 4(2)(b) of the Convention against Illicit Traffic in Narcotic Drugs and Psychotropic Substances of 1988, on the other hand, is simpler and shorter. A state may claim jurisdiction over a foreign offender present in its territory when 'it does not extradite him to another Party'.

In the preamble of the 1988 Convention, the contracting parties have stressed that it has been the objective of this convention to deal especially with the problem of illicit traffic of drugs and to cover aspects not envisaged in the previous treaties thereby reinforcing and supplementing the provisions of the 1961 Convention. Therefore, it can be assumed that the provisions of the 1988 Convention concerning jurisdiction replace those of the 1961 Convention insofar as prosecution of offenders, especially drug dealers, is made easier.

There remains the question, however, whether the state exercising jurisdiction is free to prosecute and punish the offender under its own laws or whether the German court would have to take into consideration a previous trial in the Netherlands or – if no such trial had taken place – the maximum sentence that could be awarded under Dutch law. Contrary to art. 36(2)(a)(iv) of the 1961 Convention, art. 4(2)(b) of the 1988 Convention no longer specifies that the jurisdiction of the state where the offender is found depends on the offender not having been to trial in another state before. Besides, even customary public international law would not prohibit international double jeopardy (*ne bis in idem*).[331]

Moreover, art. 4(2)(b) of the 1988 Convention does not stipulate that the state claiming jurisdiction would have to apply or take into consideration any other law than its own. It has been suggested that when basing jurisdiction on the principle of representative administration of criminal justice the state should not inflict a punishment exceeding that which would be imposed by the state where the offence was committed.[332] This is because first, at the time when the crime was committed the offender did not know the criminal law which is now being applied to its conduct and, secondly, although applying its own laws the state claiming jurisdiction merely represents the state where the offence was committed. The 1961 Convention and the 1988 Convention are silent as to whether the state claiming jurisdiction is limited in its choice of punishment. The Conventions' objective is to fight especially against illicit drug traffic. To make prosecution more effective, the 1988 Convention introduced art. 4(2)(b) which enables a state to claim jurisdiction under the sole condition that the offender

---

[331] D. Oehler, *Internationales Strafrecht* 585 (2nd edn, 1983).
[332] J. Meyer 'The Vicarious Administration of Justice: An Overlooked Basis of Jurisdiction', 31 *Harvard Intl L. J.* 108, 116 (1990); D. Oehler, *Internationales Strafrecht* 146 (2nd edn, 1983).

found in that state is not extradited. It can be argued that the contracting parties did not intend to limit the jurisdiction under art. 4(2)(b) in any other way. Therefore, the prosecuting state would not have to take into consideration the maximum penalty provided for the offence in the law of the state where the crime was committed.

4.   Conclusion

Under customary public international law a state's jurisdiction to prosecute foreign nationals distributing and selling cannabis derivatives in the territory of a neighbouring state is very limited. Only in special circumstances may the principle of territoriality and the effects doctrine provide sufficient connecting factors establishing jurisdiction. The state claiming jurisdiction, on the other hand, cannot rely on the protective principle. This basis of jurisdiction does not enable a state to enforce its policy in foreign countries but merely allows a state to prosecute crimes abroad that are directed against its political independence or security or endanger its government functions. Universal jurisdiction to prosecute offences concerning 'soft' drugs does not exist in customary international law. The fact that in the UN Conventions of 1961 and 1988 a large number of states have agreed on qualifying illicit traffic in cannabis products as a criminal offence does not automatically entail universal jurisdiction. In order to establish universal jurisdiction the contracting parties would have had to stipulate for the applicability of the principle of universality in addition to regarding such offences as crimes.

Jurisdiction to prosecute can be based, however, on the principle of representative administration of criminal justice. Although controversial in customary international law, this basis of jurisdiction has been agreed upon in several treaties. With respect to illicit traffic in drugs the UN Conventions of 1961 and 1988 likewise recognise the principle of representative administration of criminal justice. While the 1961 Convention sets up certain limitations for its applicability, art. 4(2)(b) of the 1988 Convention, replacing the provision of the 1961 Convention in this respect, gives a contracting party the possibility to prosecute a foreign offender present in its territory when it does not extradite him to another state party to the Convention.

Andreas F. Lowenfeld:

Did the Netherlands come to the aid of their national or did they leave him twisting in the wind?

Adelheid Puttler:

No, in general they did not come to the aid of their national. In one of the cases though, there was a problem of evidence. The German police had obtained some evidence from their Dutch colleagues but the Dutch police officers were not authorised to give this evidence to the German police. The Netherlands therefore protested against the use of this evidence and the German court then excluded the evidence. Therefore, the Dutch cannabis dealer was only found guilty of having sold two kilograms instead of the formally charged amount of some 100 kilograms. It is interesting to note that the Netherlands have never asked for extradition in this case. The Netherlands only said that if Germany let the Dutch national go, the Netherlands would consider the question of whether to prosecute him.

Paul Peters:

Was there any evidence of sales having been made to German nationals or residents? As the dealers' activities only took place in the Netherlands, I presume that all or most of the sales were made to nationals or residents of the Netherlands.

Andreas F. Lowenfeld:

That's a German market!

Adelheid Puttler:

Not necessarily. The places where the Dutch cannabis dealers conducted their business in those cases are right across the border and the border is open, so everybody can go there. From the facts of the cases it is not always clear whether the cannabis dealers sold most of the hashish to Dutch nationals or to German nationals. It seems that the consumers come from several different countries.

Paul Peters:

In Holland the retail trade in hashish, i.e. the sale in small quantities, has not been prosecuted during the last 15 years or so.

Andreas F Lowenfeld:

One more evidence of the single market.

Gary Born:

I take it that the nationality of the consumer, the customer, was not an element of the crime. Was there any evidence of the nationality of the consumers?

Adelheid Puttler:

According to the facts of the cases some of the consumers were German and some were Dutch. The German authorities did not exclusively prosecute those offences where the consumers were clearly identified as German nationals.

Harold G. Maier:

But there was specific evidence that there were German consumers, not simply location. Is that right?

Adelheid Puttler:

Yes.

Gary Born:

So people in Washington DC can rest easy.

Adelheid Puttler:

Of course, that was the underlying reason why the German police were interested in the activities of the Dutch cannabis dealers. If there were no German customers concerned, then there would be no interest of the German police to prosecute. German courts, however, base jurisdiction mainly on the universality principle. Already the existence of the universality principle in customary international law is controversial.

Sir Ian Sinclair:

I think, that is a bit controversial itself. The universality principle is accepted basically as being a possible basis for jurisdiction in international law. It is the limits which are controversial. It certainly applies to slavery, torture, crimes of war.

Adelheid Puttler:

Yes, but it is not clear whether it is applicable to offences regarding soft drugs. Neither the Netherlands nor any other state considers the sale of a large amount of heroin as a petty crime. It seems that everybody agrees that selling heroin is an international crime. Moreover everybody seems to agree that every state that gets hold of such an offender has jurisdiction to prosecute. But, in our cases we have only rather small quantities of hashish. It is not clear whether such sales would be considered as international crimes.

Andreas F. Lowenfeld:

But I have one other question, sort of a technical question. I wonder at what level do you ask about jurisdiction. If he is indicted, charged with 200 kilograms, he then says no jurisdiction, the court says, 'yes, there is jurisdiction'. Then the probative evidence that is admitted, because of the objection you pointed out, only shows two kilograms, do you then go back and ask for jurisdiction over again? You keep emphasising the two kilograms. I am not sure that is right if the first charge was not completely fraudulent. That goes to the sentence.

Pieter J. Kuijper:

In the Netherlands where the offences territorially took place, *de facto* they would not have been prosecuted there. What is the position of the Netherlands *de jure*? Is it a breach of the Dutch criminal law to sell cannabis in the Netherlands?

Paul Peters:

As far as the Netherlands are concerned, where the alleged offences took place, *de facto* they would not have been prosecuted there; but the position *de jure* still is that selling cannabis or hashish is a breach of the criminal law. Under the principle of discretionary powers (the principle of opportunism), the public prosecutor has discretion whether or not to prosecute any offence and the authorities concerned decided a long time ago at the national level that small scale sales of soft drugs would not normally be prosecuted in the Netherlands.

Andreas F. Lowenfeld:

Take another example. Suppose instead of selling hashish, he runs a prostitution ring. Suppose he runs a ring of prostitutes just across the border and the poor German youth run over there for their pleasures. You might have a similar case.

Francesco Francioni:

The point I would like to make is that we have cases like the Mexican extradition case (*Alvarez* case), where the Supreme Court of the US missed a great opportunity to decide whether there was US jurisdiction at all. Unfortunately, this was not considered. The point I am coming to is this: When you are considering grounds for challenging the German courts' assertion of jurisdiction, what kind of interests are you referring to? Does the extradited dealer have a personal interest to object to the excessive jurisdiction on grounds of human fundamental rights? And, therefore, I think that maybe an effort could have been made to challenge that in the light of an unrelated treaty concerning civil jurisdiction; i.e. the Brussels Convention, but that clearly states examples of excessive jurisdiction which might be transposed with some imagination to the field of criminal law. You know, we have countries in Europe where jurisdiction can be based on the location of property, but on this point the Brussels Convention is inconsistent. So I do not know what the result would be in that circumstance. But another argument that can be raised relates to the treatment of aliens.

Sir Ian Sinclair:

But as far as the individual is concerned, the person prosecuted: was any consideration given on his behalf to taking proceedings before the European

Commission on Human Rights in Strasbourg on the ground that he had been brought into German jurisdiction essentially, conceivably unlawfully?

Adelheid Puttler:

No, not as far as I know.

Karl M. Meessen:

Andy Lowenfeld last night urged us to spot the conflict. I think in the cases presented by Adelheid somehow the Dutch authorities have not taken a strong interest. But let us just assume that cases of that kind were made a specific policy of the German government. There are thousands of similar cases where some link exists between this policy of leniency and the different policy in Germany. If they tried to lure in the dealers, it could in the long run result in frustrating the Dutch policy and we would thus be confronted, under the dignified heading of the principle of universality, with two different types of enforcement.

Yoshio Ohara:

I have four questions to Pieter Kuijper. The first question regards the application of the nationality principle to technology. The US Export Administration Act of 1979 adopted a phrase 'technology subject to the jurisdiction of the United States' ss. 5 and 6(1)(a). Is that not a violation of art. 4 of the Paris Convention for the Protection of International Property providing for the territoriality of patent? In the case of *Siberian Pipeline*, the French patent was different from the US patent of the gyroscope invented by General Electric Co. In my understanding, the US government is not entitled to expand its jurisdiction to the French patent in order to prohibit the export of goods made on the basis of French patent to Russia. My second question concerns the protest that the EC Commission made to the US government against systematic encouragement in law and in fact to include submission clauses in private contracts as circumvention of limits on national jurisdiction imposed by international law (see the EC Commission's comments on the US regulations trade with the USSR, 21 ILM 891 (1982)). Is it not permissible to encourage in fact the inclusion of such submission clauses, not in a systematic way? My third question relates to the jurisdictional basis for additional sanctions imposed by the US against the export of non-US machinery in violation of the CoCom regulation. (See Protest by the EC Commission and government of Germany to the US government against additional sanction to future violators of CoCom regulations on 15 January 1988.) Although the Japanese Ministry of International Trade and Industry (MITI) prohibited the export of Toshiba Machinery Co's machinery to communist bloc countries for one year and the Tokyo District Court also imposed fines and servitude upon violators of CoCom regulation, the US Omnibus Trade and Competitiveness Act 1988 additionally prohibited that company's export to the US and procurement with the US government for three years and furthermore prohibited its parent company's, Toshiba Co's procurement with the US government for three years. In case of exports made by US technology, expanded application of the nationality principle to corporations might be allowed despite the territoriality of patent. On the other hand, in case of exports made by non-US technology, only the protective principle for the security of not only the US but also Western nations as a whole might be allowed in the period of the Cold War. However, after the end of the Cold War, will the invocation of the protective principle still be justified? My final question concerns the US's opportunistic use of standards for corporate nationality. On one hand, the US has often applied the application of nationality principle to corporations. On the other hand, in *Sumitomo Shoji America Inc v Avigliano* (457 US 176 (1982)), the US Supreme Court adopted the law of the country where corporation is established as a standard of corporate nationality on the basis of the Commerce Treaty between the US and Japan. What is your opinion and that of the EC Commission to such opportunistic use of standards for corporate nationality?

Sir Ian Sinclair:

Pieter, would you care to respond to that?

Pieter J. Kuijper:

Well, I'll do my best. I think that the ideas of Professor Ohara on the Paris Convention are very interesting but I am not a very good patent lawyer. I'm not a patent lawyer at all. And I must admit I do not know the provisions of the Paris Convention very well but I could imagine that indeed that is an area, where the counsel that Andrea Bianchi has been giving us, namely that we should draw on other principles of international law in order to look at some of the problems that we are confronted with, might be of great value and, therefore, I really would like to know, if perhaps Professor Ohara has another occasion to explain his view of it, to what extent territoriality of patents has an influence on our problems.

As far as the diplomatic demarche in the *Pipeline* case is concerned, I must say that personally I have come around to a somewhat milder view of these assurances after it became clear to me through research how many countries were actually using that kind of assurance in their export licensing systems. But there is still probably a grain of truth in the protest from the Community at that time. As I recall the American regulations really enjoined American companies to use this kind of assurance everywhere not just on an *ad hoc* basis, or it was not just in granting an individual export licence that the export control division of the Department of Commerce said, 'Well, we believe that herein assurances indicated given the circumstances of the case but it was a consistent, legal requirement, which was used there'. The question, then, is whether you are not confronted with a kind of abusive right there. I think that it was probably somewhat intended that way in the original remark. That is another additional rule of international law if it exists. I mean the abuse of rights under international law is pretty controversial but might be of some further help to us.

In the additional sanctions contained in the Trade Act of 1988, yes. I have looked at it from the perspective of public infringement of the national security provision of the Procurement Code. But it is quite possible to ask the question that Professor Ohara asked: What is really the jurisdictional basis for prescribing such a sanction at all. If any legal principle is applicable, it must probably be the protective principle. You then get into a policy argument as to whether, in a certain situation, the invocation of such a protective principle is acceptable or not. I would tend to think that even in the present circumstances, there might be situations, not necessarily cold war situations but other very important problems concerning the export of strategic material, which would still justify the protective principle and that was the reason why I was looking more for the infringement of other international norms. As far as the nationality of companies, *Sumitomo*, is concerned, I wholly agree with you.

Sir Ian Sinclair:

Thank you very much, Pieter. But I think at this point we might break for coffee.

Chapter VI

Extraterritorial Application of Environmental Law

Francesco Francioni

1. The Emerging Issue of Extraterritorial Environmental Regulation

Despite the great abundance of scholarly contributions to the general topic of environmental protection, the issue of extraterritorial jurisdiction in the field of environmental law remains relatively unexplored. [333] Yet since the late 1980s a number of developments have added new dimensions to this issue.

First, environmental regulation has become a serious source of barriers to the free movement of goods and technologies across national boundaries. Secondly, the increasing stringency of environmental regulation in advanced industrial countries has stimulated the extraterritorial relocation of polluting industries. This phenomenon, which has been called 'pollution tourism', necessarily involves jurisdictional consequences. Thirdly, the increasing concern for the protection of the domestic environment has stimulated states to adopt legislation restricting the import of environmentally noxious substances. When such legislation extends to production processes and technologies abroad, an issue of extraterritorial jurisdiction arises.

Naturally, the best way to address these issues is with the development of common environmental standards at a global level or at a regional level. The

---

[333] See, for instance, C. Kiss, *Droit international de l'environnement* (1989); P. Birnie and A. Boyle *International Law and the Environment* (1993). For a specific treatment of the issue of extraterritorial environmental regulation, see 'Developments in the Law – International Environmental Law', 104 *Harvard L. Rev.* 1487, 1609 (1991).

latter approach has been followed in Europe with the adoption of the Single European Act, [334] and, to a lesser extent, in North America with the recently enacted NAFTA. [335]

Short of such international common standards, present experience shows that the extraterritorial application of national environmental law remains an attractive option. There are several legal justifications for supporting it. The most obvious one is the nationality link between the regulating state and the entity operating abroad. Another justification is the existence of a significant connection between the extraterritorial activity and the legal system of the regulating state. Such connection may be the implementation in, or the effect on, the national market of the relevant activity. Further, the extraterritorial application of environmental law can be justified on the basis of the policy argument that national regulation must also protect the elements of the global environment, such as the ozone layer and the climate, or contribute to the conservation of common resources, such as those of the high seas, of outer space, and of Antarctica, and to the preservation of biodiversity. [336]

Today there are many examples of extraterritorial jurisdiction based upon the above legal and policy considerations. We can mention the procedural safeguards, such as environmental impact assessment, and the substantive norms on waste disposal, marine pollution, and the protection of flora and fauna, which are normally applicable to national activities that are to be carried out or have effect in areas beyond national jurisdiction such as Antarctica. Granted, this issue is different from the one of extraterritoriality involving the sphere of sovereignty of another state. Nonetheless, it is indicative of the need to extend environmental safeguards beyond the limits of national territory. Moreover, it may generate the same type of jurisdictional conflicts that traditionally have accompanied extraterritorial claims between sovereign states. The recent dispute between the US and Mexico regarding the application of the US Marine Mammals Protection Act 1972 to areas of the sea beyond national jurisdiction amply demonstrates this. [337]

A different, but related problem is that of the transfer abroad of extraordinary environmental risks such as those arising from the use of nuclear plants or management of insidious experimental processes, such as genetic engineering and other ultra-hazardous technologies. In these cases what is in question is not only the *legitimacy* of the extraterritorial regulation by the exporting state, but also that state's *duty* to extend its regulatory reach to those states of import

---

[334] See Arts. 100a and 130r *et seq.* of the Single European Act, OJ, 1987. L169/1.
[335] The North American Free Trade Agreement of 1992, 32 *ILM* 289 (1993), was followed by the North American Agreement on Environmental Cooperation of 1993, 32 *ILM* 1480 (1993) to take into account environmental concerns linked to the increased freedom of trade especially between the US and Mexico.
[336] B. Doos, 'Environmental Issues Requiring International Action', in Lang, Neuhold and Zemanek (eds.) *Environmental Protection and International Law* 1 *et seq.* (1991).
[337] See below, s. XIII.

where the complexity and the high level of the risk involved is not matched by the preparedness and expertise needed to avert or effectively respond to accidents and emergencies.[338]

2.   The Limits of Extraterritorial Environmental Regulation

Faced with these increasing needs for extraterritorial regulation, neither public nor private international law seems to offer any *ad hoc* rule specifically applicable to the field of environmental law. The question thus arises as to what general principles and doctrines may help us to determine the admissibility and scope of extraterritorial environmental jurisdiction. To clarify this, it will be useful to briefly outline some theoretical premises on which the analysis which follows will be based.

The first premise concerns the present writer's belief that a solution to the problem of extraterritorial jurisdiction cannot be based on the assumed existence of a body of customary international rules whose object and function is to validate specific jurisdictional titles for every state's regulatory and adjudicatory functions.[339] Much criticism has been directed to the holding of the Permanent Court of Justice in the *Lotus* case[340] and to the continuing viability of the principle of states' jurisdictional freedom asserted therein.[341] However, despite the assumed obsolescence of this judgment due to its old age as well as to the circumstance that the Permanent Court was notoriously split on the issue, hardly any convincing element may be found in subsequent practice to prove the existence of general norms governing jurisdiction *per se*.

The second premise concerns the unsuitability of an unitary approach to the manifold problems of extraterritorial jurisdiction. If one rejects the theory of the existence of general international law norms validating jurisdictional criteria, then different solutions to different problems of extraterritoriality, antitrust, export controls, environmental regulation, etc., need to be found.

Thirdly, if the above approach is correct, the theory of the balancing of interests in the private international law variant of US jurisprudence,[342] or in the public law notion of a last-resort device inspired by a 'rule of reason' or comity,[343] loses much of its rational foundation. Rather than an all-embracing balancing scheme good for all seasons, resolution of jurisdictional conflicts

---

[338] The paradigmatic case in this subject remains *Bhopal*. On this case see T. McGarity, 'Bhopal and the Export of Hazardous Technologies', 20 *Texas Intl L. J.* 333 (1985) and other contributions in the same issue of this journal.

[339] For literature on this subject, we refer to the contributions by Maier and Bianchi in this volume.

[340] *Lotus* case. PCIJ, 1927, Ser. A., No. 10.

[341] *Ibid.*, at 19.

[342] Restatement (Third) of the Foreign Relations Law of the United States 1987 ss. 402–433.

[343] K. Meessen 'Conflicts of Jurisdiction under the New Restatement', 50 *Law and Contemporary Problems* 47 *et seq.* (1987).

requires the identification of the specific state interests affected by the extraterritorial claim and of the substantive norms of international law by which such interests are protected. Thereupon, one may judge whether or not the assertion of extraterritoriality in a particular form and in a specific sector of the social and economic life of the foreign state constitutes an internationally wrongful act.

In this perspective, it is not difficult to imagine that the most likely candidates to perform such limiting function are the norms governing the condition of aliens and of their economic interests, to the extent that the exercise of extraterritorial jurisdiction may constitute a breach of the minimum standard of justice in their treatment. Such would be the case if a state imposed harsh sanctions or liability on a branch of a foreign company which was unwilling or unable to abide with an extraterritorial order addressed by the sanctioning state to the parent company or other unit of the group operating abroad. Also norms on human rights may acquire a certain relevance in this area. For example, the assertion of extraterritorial adjudicatory jurisdiction over subjects who have no significant relation to the forum except transitory presence there, or an indirect effect on it owing to the activities performed in foreign territory, may well constitute a breach of an international 'due process' standard.[344] Also such principles as freedom of trade and non-intervention in the domestic affairs of a foreign country may provide a parameter for determining the illegality of an extraterritorial claim.

The same considerations apply to norms of international environmental law that concern the present paper more directly. The influence of environmental norms, however, rather than being 'negative', in the sense of restricting the permissible scope of extraterritorial jurisdiction, as a rule is 'positive'. They tend, in fact, to support or enhance the legitimacy of extraterritorial regulation and are consistent with the idea that unilateral state action may help to prevent international environmental harm and to further international policies intended to advance environmental quality. Norms adopted in the past two decades with a view to protecting components of the global environment invariably legitimise extraterritorial effects. This is the case, as we shall see in the following section, with the international regime for the protection of the ozone layer, as well as with the 1973 Washington Convention for the Protection of Endangered Species. The same can be said of the 1991 Madrid Protocol concerning the Protection of the Antarctic Environment. It requires that the contracting parties give effect within their own legal systems to rules and procedures: on environmental impact assessment, on waste disposal, on conservation and management of wildlife and of protected areas which, of necessity require their

---

[344] For a discussion of this specific issue, P. Schlosser, 'Jurisdiction in International Litigation – The Issue of Human Rights in Relation to National Law and to the Brussels Convention', 74 *Rivista diritto internazionale* 5 *et seq.* (1991).

ultraterritorial application to activities (scientific, logistic, recreational) that are to be carried out in Antarctica.

In a different context, the extraterritorial application of environmental law may be the result of a choice of forum or choice of law made by plaintiffs or courts in view of obtaining a more effective remedy or a higher level of reparation with respect to a given harm. The much discussed *Alfaro* case[345] concerning a suit in Texas for serious environmental and personal injury resulting from the use of pesticides in Costa Rica illustrates this paradigm. The Supreme Court of Texas accepted jurisdiction on the expressed theory that opening American courts to claims of extraterritorial application of American standards of liability would induce American companies exporting dangerous substances and technologies to adopt a higher level of precaution for the common good. This approach is commendable in principle. However, it may cause undesirable problems of forum shopping and, thus, as a reaction, a broad resort to the doctrine of *forum non conveniens*. As is known, this doctrine was successfully raised before the US courts in the *Bhopal* litigation, ultimately ended by a settlement between Union Carbide and India.[346]

3. The Legitimacy of Extraterritorial Environmental Regulation: The US–Mexico Tuna Dispute

The two above precedents have not given rise to inter-state conflicts, primarily because of the convergence of the plaintiff's private interests and his home country's public interest in obtaining a higher level of judicial protection (*Alfaro*); or because of the acquiescence (*Bhopal*) of the affected state with a certain measure of extraterritorial jurisdiction. In other cases, instead, assertion of extraterritorial environmental jurisdiction may give rise to sharp conflicts. To the extent that such conflicts are of a legal nature, they must be resolved by legal criteria. The GATT dispute between the US and Mexico over the incidental killing of dolphins in the harvesting of tuna provides a useful case study for discussing a general framework of criteria that may be applicable in resolving this type of conflict.

The facts of the dispute can be summarised, very briefly, as follows. Mexican fleets engaged in commercial harvesting of tuna in the Eastern Tropical Pacific, employ a catching method called 'purse-seine net' fishing. This method involves the use of purse nets which are unfolded by fast auxiliary boats around a bank of fish and then secured at their extremities onto the fishing vessel. All the fish so encircled are then harvested.

This method is efficient, but problematic: it means that since in the Eastern

---

[345] *Dow Chemical Co v Alfaro* 768 S.W. 2D 674, Texas 1990. See, particularly, the concurring opinion by Dogget J. at 689.
[346] 634 F. Supp. 842 (SDNY, 1986).

Tropical Pacific tuna and dolphins live together, the catching of the former entails the killing or maiming of the latter.

Aware of this problem, the US authorities had enacted specific legislation in the early 1970s to protect dolphins from this type of incidental killing. The Marine Mammals Protection Act (MMPA) 1972, amended in 1988 and 1990, established an authorisation regime for tuna fishing in areas where such fishing entails a risk for the life of dolphins. Section 101(a) of the MMPA provides that the Secretary of the Treasury 'shall ban' the import into the US of fish (and fish products) caught with methods that entail killing of dolphins beyond certain tolerable limits as set by the US (in excess of US standards). These provisions apply to the territorial waters and exclusive economic zone of the US as well as to the high seas. A further provision of the MMPA prohibits imports into the US of yellowfin tuna caught by purse-seine nets in the Eastern Tropical Pacific, unless the country of origin proves that it is maintaining a conservation programme for marine mammals which:

(1) is equivalent to the one of the US; and
(2) which in effect permits a rate of incidental damage to dolphins not significantly greater than that of the US.

Between the end of 1990 and the beginning of 1991, the US started suspending the import of tuna from a number of countries including Mexico. It is interesting to note that such measures were not adopted by the federal government *proprio motu* but subsequent to a judicial injunction obtained by a group of concerned environmentalists pursuant to the MMPA.

The tuna embargo had the effect of opening a commercial dispute between Mexico and the US. Faced with the inability to settle it through direct negotiations, Mexico requested and obtained the constitution of a GATT panel under art. XXIII of the General Agreement. The Panel rendered a report in favour of Mexico on 16 August 1991. [347]

The Panel found that the US measures restricting import of tuna were inconsistent with obligations undertaken under GATT and, particularly, under arts. XI and XIII concerning the prohibition of discriminatory requirements in relation to specific geographical areas. No justification for such measures was found in art. III, which permits restrictions in the form of internal regulations governing the sale, purchase or use of products, since, in the view of the Panel, the import restrictions did not apply to an imported product as such (tuna), but to a separate species (dolphins) not subject to commercialisation in the US.

Aside from the great interest that the above GATT provisions present, from the point of view of the reconciliation of free trade and protection of environmental quality, the aspect of the Panel's ruling that is most relevant to our discussion concerns the application of GATT art. XX.

---

[347] *ILM* 1594 *et seq.* (1991).

As is known, this article contains an exception to the general principle of free trade and permits, *inter alia*, the adoption or enforcement of measures

... b) necessary to protect human, animal or plant life or health

... g) relating to the conservation of exhaustible natural resources if such measures are made effective in conjunction with restrictions on domestic production or consumption...

The US argued that the MMPA, insofar as it aimed at the protection of animal life and at the conservation of living resources had to be covered by the art. XX exception. Mexico, on the other hand, contended that art. XX was to be interpreted in the sense of referring only to the conservation of animal or resources located *within the territory of the importing state*, while the US measures had an extraterritorial application to living resources located beyond the limits of national jurisdiction.

The Panel upheld Mexico's position essentially on the basis of two arguments. The first was inferred from GATT legislative history. The Panel found that in the first draft of the Havana Charter, the precursor of GATT which instituted the stillborn International Trade Organisation, the provision corresponding to the present art. XX contained a qualifying clause restricting the exception to human, animal or living resources located 'in the territory of the importing country'. They then concluded that this was sufficient indication of a concern to avoid abuses and thus had to be taken as conclusive evidence of the strictly territorial scope of art. XX.

The second argument used by the Panel rested on policy considerations. These essentially concerned the perceived risk that the ability of a state to unilaterally impose environmental standards on other states would result in the breaking down of the unity of GATT and its transformation into a multiplicity of special regimes applicable among parties with similar environmental or sanitary legislation.

4.   Critique of the Panel's Ruling

Although the reasoning of the GATT Panel is limited to the GATT system, and in no way does it prejudge the way in which the question of extraterritorial application of environmental law should be resolved at the level of customary international law, I believe that the above arguments are not immune from criticism.

With regard to the first one, it appears hardly logical and even bizarre to base a restrictive interpretation of art. XX on the evidence cited by the Panel. Under ordinary rules of interpretation, if GATT negotiations show that an attempt had been made to introduce a restrictive territorial clause in the text of what is today art. XX; if the same negotiations reveal that such attempt was motivated by the concern of some states to limit the discretion of national authorities in the adoption and implementation of measures intended to protect human, animal or plant life; if, this notwithstanding, the restrictive territorial clause did not find its way into the final drafting of art. XX, the only logical conclusion appears to be that the contracting parties chose to leave open the question of the territorial scope of art. XX.

In any event, it seems necessary to conclude that the failure to adopt the restricting clause bears witness to the lack of consensus over the necessity or advisability of confining art. XX exceptions to the territory of the importing state. Further, the strict territorial construction adopted by the Panel does not conform to the practice followed by the states in the period subsequent to the adoption of GATT.

In this period, conservation of living resources and protection of environmental quality have become the object of international concern and have led to the adoption of several important multilateral instruments that entail substantial limitations on freedom of trade. In 1973 the Convention on the International Trade in Endangered Species (CITES) was adopted in Washington.[348] Its art. X permits import bans which concern the protection of species found primarily or exclusively within the territory of the state from which the import is banned. Article XX did not expressly permit this restriction; but all GATT parties which are also parties to CITES have accepted it. In 1987, the Protocol on Substances that Deplete the Ozone Layer was adopted in Montreal.[349] Most of its contracting parties are also parties to GATT. Article 4 of the Protocol requires that '. . . each Party shall ban the import of controlled substances from any State not Party to this Protocol'. It is clear that this provision postulates the lawfulness of import restrictions with respect to products causing hazard primarily in and from the territory of a state other than the importing one.

The rationale for this ultra-territorial effect of the Protocol rests in the belief that ozone depletion constitutes a hazard to human, animal and plant life and health the world over. Similarly, art. 4 of the 1989 Basle Convention on Transboundary Movement of Hazardous Waste proscribes export of noxious waste to states which are not parties.[350] Also in this case, the international scheme takes it for granted that under GATT art. XX trade restrictions are permissible to safeguard the health and the environment of other states which are not parties to the Basle Convention but, possibly, to GATT.

This treaty practice is essential for a correct contextual interpretation of art. XX. Its scope has to be defined in light of the emerging need to integrate the GATT system with environmental quality considerations which, perhaps, were not so compelling in 1947 as they are today. The urgency of infusing environmental standards into the international trade system is proven by the

---

[348] Ruester and Simma (eds.), *The International Protection of the Environment*, Vol. V, 2228, *et seq.* (1976).
[349] 26 *ILM* 1542 *et seq.* (1987).
[350] 28 *ILM* 657 *et seq.* (1989).

decision to convene a specific conference on the matter in the spring of 1994 after the successful completion of the Uruguay Round.

It is unfortunate that no trace of such considerations can be found in the Panel's report. As regards the policy considerations stressed by the Panel with respect to the risk of jeopardising the unity of GATT by allowing extraterritorial application of environmental standards, doubtless they must be given proper weight. In an epoch such as the present one, which is characterised by lingering economic recession and fierce international competition, the erection of trade barriers under the seductive garb of environmental protection may be politically appealing. This risk, however, rather than by attaching unwarranted qualifications to art. XX, could be averted by following its language faithfully. In essence, this language prescribes three requirements for a state to lawfully resort to trade bans:

(1)   The purpose of the ban must not be protectionist but must genuinely be one of those listed in art. XX. The author's opinion is that the object and purpose of the MMPA, the circumstance that the US authorities adopted the ban in compliance with an impartial court's order sought by concerned environmentalist groups, should be taken as *prima facie* evidence that the primary purpose of the ban was the conservation of dolphins rather than commercial protectionism.

(2)   The second requirement is that the measure must be necessary for attaining one of the goals listed in art. XX. It is debatable whether alternative means, with lower impact on trade, were available to the US. What is certain is that denial of access to national markets of foreign products has already been considered a necessary means for inducing compliance with environmental standards in the already mentioned treaty practice on endangered species and on substances harmful to the ozone layer.

(3)   The third requirement is that exclusionary measures should not be discriminatory. At first sight, the singling out of the Eastern Tropical Pacific as a target area in the MMPA could appear as discriminatory against Mexico. However, the reason for the singling out of this zone appears to be the circumstance that, in the opinion of experts, it is unique in the sense of offering a habitat where tuna and dolphins are systematically found together. This, apparently, does not occur in other marine areas of the world.

Looking beyond the specificity of the present case, we find it important to note, from a general point of view, that a proper application of the above three requirements can be a sufficient tool to control abuses and distortions of art. XX, without resorting to an *a priori* preclusion of the extraterritorial application of environmental standards. Such a preclusion would be inconsistent with the notion that states have obligations *erga omnes* in matters such as the protection of the global environment as well as the protection of human rights and international peace. Naturally, one could object that the protection of dolphins is not yet the object of a general obligation, not even of a multilateral treaty similar to CITES or the Montreal Protocol. Besides, dolphins are not (yet) an endangered species. However, several provisions of the Law of the Sea Convention, particularly arts. 65 and 120, show that at least a basis for protection already exists and that a certain *communis opinio* as to the desirability of furthering the protection of marine mammals has been expressed in an authoritative forum. In the last analysis, what one must take into account in addressing the issue of the legitimacy of extraterritorial environmental regulation is that national legislation has always played an important role as a catalyst for the progressive development of international law. This is all the more so in the law of the sea and of marine resources, where the assertion of regulatory claims beyond national jurisdiction has been the decisive force behind the shaping of new norms such as those on the EEZ and on the 100 mile anti-pollution zone in ice-covered areas.[351] With regard to the specific issue of protecting marine mammals against the risk of indiscriminate methods of fishing, not only has national legislation in concerned countries begun to emerge – in the US with the MMPA, in New Zealand with the 1991 law prohibiting pelagic driftnets,[352] and, again in the US with the International Dolphin Conservation Act of 26 October 1992.[353] But an international practice is also beginning to take shape. One needs only to recall the Wellington Convention of 24 November 1989 on the prohibition of pelagic driftnets, the Noumea Protocol of 20 October 1990,[354] and the series of General Assembly resolutions of 1989, 1990 and 1991[355] which reiterate the need to proscribe indiscriminate and irresponsible methods of fishing.

These instruments may not be conclusive to the finding of a generalised *opinio juris* and, thus, of a binding customary norm. They are enough, however, in our view, to support the opinion that extraterritorial application of national environmental standards pursuant to such instruments is legitimate and consistent with a modern interpretation of GATT art. XX.

5. Is there a Duty to Apply Environmental Law Extraterritorially?

In light of the above conclusion, the last question that needs to be addressed is whether, in the field of environmental law, circumstances exist where extraterritorial application of national safety standards should be considered the object of a duty.

---

[351] See Canada's Arctic Waters Pollution Act 1970 and art. 234 of the UN Convention on the Law of the Sea.
[352] 31 *ILM* 214 *et seq.* (1992).
[353] 32 *ILM* 540 *et seq.* (1993).
[354] 29 *ILM* 1449 *et seq.* (1990).
[355] *Id.*, at 1555 and 31 *ILM* 241 *et seq.* (1992).
[355a] *bis* in a subsequent dispute settlement procedure requested by the EEC with respect to the same issue, the panel has essentially accepted this conclusion. See the report published in 33 *ILM* 839 (1994) paras. 5.32 and 5.33.

In a world of sovereign states where each claims exclusive control over its own territory, it is natural that even positing this question may appear inconsistent with sovereign equality and the principle of non-intervention. For however relevant these facts may be, it is our view that in the specific area of environmental protection they should not be deemed capable of outweighing the need to ensure a minimum level of co-operation between states. Extraterritorial application of environmental law may be an element in such co-operation.

First of all, one must note that much of the doctrinal and political controversy over the issue of extraterritorial jurisdiction stems from, or is exacerbated by, the recurrent 'double standard' practised by states which, while they are keen on exporting their economic, social or political values by an assertion of extraterritoriality, at the same time they do not hesitate to resist reciprocal intrusions by foreign claims of extraterritorial jurisdiction within their sphere of sovereignty. A similar double standard also characterises the attitude of a state which, while asserting the right to apply its environmental law extraterritorially in a situation in which extraterritoriality results in protection for domestic industry (as in the case of the US with the MMPA) at the same time denies its responsibility for exercising similar extraterritorial control when this would entail a cost in terms of reduced exports or competition in foreign markets.

A coherent doctrine of extraterritoriality requires the abandonment of such double standards and the linking of the right to assert extraterritoriality with the responsibility to exercise extraterritorial jurisdiction whenever it is appropriate in order to avoid serious environmental harm or the exposure of the public to an uncontrolled hazard in foreign territory.

This responsibility, obviously, is not an unqualified one. The complexities of the contemporary world and the great disparities in economic and technological development may require that less affluent and less developed states accept lower environmental standards as compared to those of advanced industrialised countries from which they import technologies and products liable to harm the environment.

However, certain highly hazardous industries, such as production of nuclear energy, experimental genetic engineering and certain chemical industries, should not become grounds for the competitive devaluation of national safety standards in order to conquer foreign markets or to relocate multinational enterprises looking for a better bargain in production processes. If international standards are absent, the best way to prevent dangerous competition toward the lowest level of environmental standards – which would involve the exporting of the most polluting industries or allowing the export of sub-standard technologies and plants – is to uphold a principle of responsible co-operation between exporting and importing countries under which a certain measure of extraterritorial application of environmental standards is required. This means, first of all, that all the appropriate procedural safeguards concerning information and transparency about the risk involved in exported products and technologies be applied also with respect to the importing country in view of facilitating its informed consent and the development of appropriate preparedness and response action in the event of accidents or emergencies. It means also that substantive safety standards should be responsibly applied extraterritorially by the exporting country when the nature and the scale of the risk is such as to expose foreign communities and their environment to extremely serious injury. In the case of toxic wastes, nuclear plants, biotechnologies and ultra-hazardous chemical industries – to give only some examples – the argument for refusing export to a country with a weak safety regime, which is based on an extraterritorial application of a strong national regime, ultimately rests on the duty of every state to ensure that 'activities within their jurisdiction or control do not cause damage to the environment of other States'. This duty is affirmed in Principle 21 of the Stockholm Declaration and is restated in Principle 2 of the 1992 Rio Declaration.

In a world where the protection of environmental quality is increasingly intertwined with fundamental human rights, one should conclude that, ultimately, conscious discrimination based on the location or nationality of the people exposed to serious risks is not consistent with the fundamental right of individuals and peoples to live in a safe environment.

Sir Ian Sinclair:

Thank you very much indeed: I think I will call straight away on our discussant Ernesto Hizon.

Ernesto M. Hizon:

The interests of trade and the environment have always been portrayed as being at odds with each other. Environmentalists blame the existing GATT framework for its inflexibility in adapting itself to justified environmental concerns through its tendency to adhere to narrow, legalistic definitions. In contrast, the GATT zealously guards the liberal trading system it spawned, fending off any attack – notwithstanding its possible merits – that may undermine the basic principle of non-discrimination.

This suggested 'innate conflict' between seemingly diametrically opposed philosophies is more illusory than real. Since the fallout from the controversial 'Tuna Fish' GATT Panel Report resulting from the complaint filed by Mexico against the US, the battle between environment and trade has assumed mythical proportions, and one is usually compelled to take sides in the never-ending dispute.

What is often conveniently overlooked in this passionate debate is that those who argue in favour of the extraterritorial application of environmental norms proceed from the premise that the country with the apparently more stringent environmental standards is tacitly empowered to impose the same on another sovereign state simply because its heightened level of environmental conscious-ness cloaks it with the authority to be a spokesman for the good of the environment. Unfortunately, an enhanced degree of environmentalism does not mean that the ordained environmental standards are universal, nor do they automatically blossom into accepted customary international law. It is likewise a gross oversimplification to argue that when another state disagrees or does not conform to the purported elevated environmental norm, such state betrays itself to be an opponent of the pro-environment movement.

This thumbnail sketch of what we believe are reasonable requirements for acceptable environmental measures, and the brief discussion of the 'Tuna' dispute and its repercussions in sum, advance the following arguments:

(1) internationally accepted environmental standards and requirements do not clash with the principles of free trade but on the contrary, complement them;

(2) the issue of extraterritorial jurisdiction becomes relevant only when there is a multilateral consensus on what constitutes a legitimate environmental standard;

(3) a country cannot and must not unilaterally impose its own environmental standards on another sovereign state when it concerns conduct which occurs outside its territorial jurisdiction.

Before proceeding to the specifics of the 'Tuna Fish' ruling, and to the question of extraterritorial jurisdiction, it is important to establish a consensus on what would be reasonable prerequisites for 'justifiable' environmental protection measures. We propose the following:

(1) the environmental threat is global;

(2) a multilateral consensus exists;

(3) the primary aim of the measures is environmental protection;

(4) the measures are proportional to the danger;

(5) corrective intervention should be 'optimal', i.e. should occur as close as possible to the source of the market distortion.

The potential abuse inherent in the imposition of extraterritorial environmental measures is as grave a peril to the world's economic system as is the risk of neglecting the environment to the detriment of the world's ecological system. If one state clothes itself with the power to force its environmental norms on another state, not only is the essential international law principle of sovereignty violated, but the practice also transforms the rule-oriented framework of our international trading system, or international legal system for that matter, into one that is purely based on the relative economic and political might of the parties involved. In this world of *realpolitik*, it would be too idealistic, if not naive, to presume that the behaviour of a state proceeds primarily from altruistic motives. As the tuna fish dispute indicates, narrower trade or economic interests often lurk behind environmental measures. Developing countries always find themselves at a great disadvantage because they are powerless economically and politically to resist such pressures. Moreover, we must consider that the economic conditions of less affluent countries may not permit them to survive the imposition of stricter conditions on their traded goods. If this were the case, the cost for arbitrarily determined environmental standards, even if they were valid, would be too high. A 'big brother' mentality in the adoption of environmental rules possesses the potential for chaos, anarchy and emnity in the world trading system.

It is thus fundamental that environmental standards be instituted from a broad consensus on a multilateral basis and further, be formalised in a document to be recognised as part of international law. In other words, the environmental threat must be global, i.e. one which affects the world as a whole, and not limited to the interests or the geographical area of a particular state. While forging agreement on a wide variety of environmental issues between nations with varying degrees of economic development and environmental consciousness may be difficult, only a multilateral approach can guarantee some form of order and fairness in the implementation of such standards. It is essential that this prudent path towards environmental regulation recognises the equality of all nations and balances their shifting interests in economic development and the environment.

Equally important as this requisite broad multilateral agreement on environmental norms, is the condition that the primary aim of the measure is environmental protection. The effect of the environmental standard on trade should be merely incidental or peripheral and not the underlying purpose of the measure. Its likely consequences on the welfare of affected domestic producers should not be the real reason for its implementation. Since an environmental measure has the potential to interfere with the free flow of trade, a distortion of trade should be confined to those cases where genuine environmental interests are at stake. If the disguised objective of an environmental standard is the protection of certain domestic producers, then the use of trade policy instruments is the more appropriate form of response or retaliation. Linkage between environmental policy and trade – a fashionable practice of late – merely muddles the issue and lends itself to abuse. But, as is often the case, smaller countries are the targets of these environmental restrictions on trade as they are not in a strong position to counteract the notion that the environmental laws passed by the more developed economies are indeed the accepted international norm.

The fourth proposed requirement for justifiable environmental protection complements the aforesaid element of intention: the measures should be proportional to the environmental threat. The protective measures imposed should be limited to those necessary to accomplish the environmental objective.

Finally, the corrective government intervention should occur as closely as possible to the market distortion in the country of origin. Under this theory of 'optimal intervention', environmental damage is prevented through the control of production processes, that is to say, at the precise point of environmental injury. Since damage is checked within the confines of the producing country (and prejudices only the producing country), intervention does not occur at the trade level and the issue of sovereignty, or the extraterritorial reach of environmental laws, does not even enter into the picture.[356]

This proposed checklist of preconditions for justifiable environmental protection measures dovetails with the most recent provisions of customary international law on the environment as exemplified by the Rio Declaration on Environment and Development (UNCED) of June 1992.[357] The Rio Declaration attempts to codify certain recognised environmental standards in international law and practice which in effect constitute the body of customary international law on the environment. Notably, the Declaration in forthright language:

(1) respects the fundamental principle of national sovereignty in the issue of jurisdiction;

(2) confirms the right of each state to institute environmental measures pursuant to its own policies and in the context of its socio-economic situation; and

(3) harmonises the thrust of the environmental agenda with existing international trade law.

In fact, there is a constant effort on the part of this Declaration to reject any notion of an intrinsic conflict between environment and trade.

Principle 2 of the Declaration, an echo of Principle 21 of the Stockholm Declaration on the Human Environment of 1972, reiterates the basic principle of a state's territorial jurisdiction over its natural resources and its prerogative to protect the environment within and without its jurisdiction pursuant to its environmental policies. This Principle intimates that the extraterritorial reach of environmental law, if it exists, or is granted, should be restrictive in its application, and should be clearly in pursuit of legitimate environmental objectives for the benefit of all affected states. Principle 2 speaks clearly when it provides:

> States have, in accordance with the Charter of the United Nations and the principles of international law, the sovereign right to exploit their own resources pursuant to their own environmental and developmental policies, and the responsibility to ensure that activities within their jurisdiction or control do not cause damage to the environment of other States or of areas beyond the limits of national jurisdiction.

Principle 11 of the same 1992 Rio Declaration not only provides that a state maintains the right to establish its own environmental norms, it can also set its

---

[356] The basic theory of 'optimal intervention' in the light of environmental policy is found in P.J. Lloyd, 'The Problem of Optimal Environmental Choice', in K. Anderson and R. Blackhurst (eds.), *The Greening of World Trade Issues* 49, (London: Harvester Wheatsheaf, 1992). See also E.U. Petersmann, 'Trade Policy, Environmental Policy and the GATT', in *Außenwirtschaft* 197 *et seq.* (1991) and E.U. Petersmann, 'International Trade Law and International Environmental Law', in 27 *Journal of World Trade* 1, at 43 *et seq.* (1993).

[357] Reproduced in 31 *ILM* 818 (1992).

environmental objectives in conjunction with its environmental objectives in conjunction with its development policies. It reads:

> States shall enact effective environmental legislation. Environmental standards, management objectives and priorities should reflect the environmental context to which they apply. Standards applied by some countries may be inappropriate and of unwarranted economic and social cost to other countries, in particular, developing countries.

Principle 12 of the Rio Declaration underscores that environmental concerns need not collide with the prevailing liberal trading system and further adds the proviso that trade policy measures aimed at the protection of the environment should not be disguised restrictions of trade. Principle 12 is a crucial provision to the environment–trade debate because it responds to the criticism of the school of environmentalists who claim that the trading system inherently prejudices the attainment of environmental goals. The Principle properly acknowledges that liberal trade goes hand in hand with a protected environment. What is noteworthy is that the Rio Declaration does not shy away from the controversial issue of the potential extrajurisdictional effects of environmental laws. The intent of the Principle in this respect, is clearly stated, to wit:

> States should co-operate to promote a supportive and open international economic system that would lead to economic growth and sustainable development in all countries, to better address the problems of environmental degradation. Trade policy measures for environmental purposes should not constitute a means of arbitrary or unjustifiable discrimination or a disguised restriction on international trade. Unilateral actions to deal with environmental challenges outside the jurisdiction of the importing country should be avoided. Environmental measures addressing transboundary or global environmental problems should, as far as possible, be based on an international consensus.

What the above Principle declares is that unilateral measures aimed at protecting the global environment, notwithstanding their possible merits, are not looked upon with favour, unless such are based on a multilateral consensus. In this respect, the Declaration's emphasis on the multilateral characteristics of viable environmental standards parallels the GATT's inherent bias in furnishing multilaterally agreed regulations and remedies.

'Agenda 21', also adopted by the UNCED along with the Rio Declaration, spells out this sensible policy in greater detail. Chapter 2.11 among others, provides, in part:

> 2.11 Governments should encourage GATT, UNCTAD and other relevant international and regional economic institutions to examine, in accordance with their respective mandates and competence, the following propositions and principles:
>
> (g) ensure that special factors affecting environment and trade policies in the developing countries are borne in mind in the application of environmental standards, as well as in the use of any trade measures. It is worth noting that standards that are

valid in the most advanced countries may be inappropriate and of unwarranted social cost for the developing countries.

(i) avoid unilateral actions to deal with environmental challenge outside the jurisdiction of the importing country. Environmental measures addressing transborder or global environmental problems should, as far as possible, be based on an international consensus. Domestic measures targeted to achieve certain environmental objectives may need trade measures to render them effective. Should trade policy measures be found necessary for the enforcement of environmental policies, certain principles and rules should apply. These could include, *inter alia*, the principle of non-discrimination; the principle that the trade measure chosen should be the least trade-restrictive necessary to achieve the objectives; an obligation to ensure transparency in the use of trade measures related to the environment and to provide adequate notification of national regulation; and the need to give consideration to the special conditions and developmental requirements of developing countries as they move towards internationally agreed environmental objectives.

In the preceding sections, extreme caution is advised in allowing environmental rules with extraterritorial effect due to the anticipated socio-economic burdens which may befall developing countries. It is of course logical that developed countries would have higher standards on the environment; less developed countries would be preoccupied with their economic development. There is also no disputing the contention that developed economies are much more capable in implementing more ambitious environmental protection measures than the poorer nations. This state of affairs, however, does not give those in a position of advantage in the maintenance of higher environmental standards the licence to force them upon those who are not equipped to do so. In many instances, the developing countries 'guilty' of employing environmentally damaging technologies have merely inherited them from developed country firms. These industries may have either disposed of their less environment-friendly industrial techniques to technology-hungry states, or the latter may have just settled for the polluting technologies they could barely afford. The case of the CFC air-conditioners, refrigerators and aerosol spray cans is one of many that comes to mind.

Admittedly, the Rio Declaration and the UNCED 'Agenda 21' are still 'soft law' rules that may be disregarded, especially by the powerful nations who will continue to insist on their respective environmental and trade policies. But the orientation towards multilateralism and trade liberalism, as well as the conservative stance in the extrajurisdictional dimension are all too evident. If subsequent international conventions perpetuate this trend, the interests of the environment and that of trade would gradually converge.

If we proceed from the conclusions drawn from the foregoing discussion, it would be safe to say that the much ballyhooed controversy in the 'Tuna Fish' GATT Panel Report is actually overblown and neither represents an irreconcilable conflict between environmental law and trade law, nor does it embody any critical precedent on the issue of extraterritorial jurisdiction.

In a 1991 complaint by Mexico against the US, it was claimed that the American prohibition of imports of yellowfin tuna and tuna products caught by

Mexican vessels in the Eastern Tropical Pacific Area (ETPA) in the Pacific Ocean with the purse-seine net fishing method resulting in the incidental killing of dolphins, over and above the US standards was inconsistent with arts. XI and XIII of GATT and, moreover, did not fall under the environmental exceptions specified in GATT art. XX. Under the disputed US Marine Mammal Protection Act (MMPA) and s. 8 of the Fisherman's Protective Act (the Pelly Amendment), imports of tuna which caused a dolphin-kill rate more than 1.25 times the US fishermen's taking rate recorded for the same period fell under the prohibition. The US embargo was also extended to similar imports from 'intermediary nations' who re-exported the banned tuna products to the US.[358]

Since the Panel Report was submitted in September 1991, the Report has not been adopted by the parties to the dispute. Despite the ruling in its favour, Mexico did not seek its adoption due to its possible repercussions to the NAFTA agreement negotiations pending at that time. However, because the MMPA effected a parallel embargo on countries that refused to prohibit the import of tuna from countries under the first embargo from the US, opposition to the MMPA grew. In mid-1992, even the European Community filed a new complaint against the MMPA with GATT.[359]

The other issues raised in the Report on national treatment on quantitative restrictions are not relevant here. The environmental and extrajurisdictional controversy arises from the US's assertion that the import prohibition on tuna is justified under the art. XX(b) exception in GATT which permits trade distorting measures 'necessary to protect human, animal or plant life or health'. Article XX(g) also provides the additional exception for measures 'relating to the conservation of exhaustible natural resources if such measures are made effective in conjunction with restrictions on domestic production or consumption'. The US argued that it had to rely on the embargo measures because there was no other measure that was reasonably available to it to protect the dolphin population in the ETPA.

The Panel Report reasoned that the US should have tried to exhaust GATT-consistent approaches before it resorted to the import prohibition. The Panel proposed that 'international co-operative arrangements' on dolphin protection should have been secured before imposing the embargo.[360] Pivotal was the Panel's assertion that even assuming that the embargo was the single resort reasonably available to the US, the measure could not be deemed 'necessary' in the context of art. XX(b) because:

> ... The United States linked the maximum incidental dolphin-taking rate which Mexico had to meet during a particular period in order to be able to export tuna to

---

[358] US Restrictions on Imports of Tuna, GATT Doc. DS21/R, reprinted in 30 *ILM* 1594 (1991).

[359] For a discussion on US legislation subsequent to the *Tuna Fish* ruling, see Steve Charnovitz, 'Environmentalism Confronts GATT Rules: Recent Developments and New Opportunities', in 27 *Journal of World Trade* 2, at 37 *et seq.* (1993).

[360] Panel Report, note 358 above, at 5.28.

the United States to the taking rate actually recorded for US fishermen during the same period. Consequently, the Mexican authorities could not know whether, at a given point of time, their policies conformed to US dolphin protection standards. The panel considered that a limitation on trade based on such unpredictable conditions could not be regarded as necessary to protect the health or life of dolphins.[361]

The Panel interpreted the art. XX(b) exception as one which allows each GATT contracting party to determine its own human, animal, plant life and health standards:

> ...if the broad interpretation of Article XX(b) suggested by the United States were accepted, each contracting party could unilaterally determine the life or health protection policies from which other contracting parties could not deviate without jeopardizing their rights under the General Agreement. The General Agreement would then no longer constitute a multilateral framework for trade among all contracting parties but would provide legal security only in respect of trade between a limited number of contracting parties with identical internal regulations.[362]

On the question of art. XX(g) of GATT regarding the conservation of exhaustible natural resources, the Panel Report explained that for considerations similar to those in support of the ruling that there was no extrajurisdictional application of art. XX(b), the argument in favour of the extraterritorial scope of art. XX(g) should be rejected. Referring to a previous Panel decision,[363] the Report stated that the conservation measures taken 'in conjunction with restrictions on domestic production or consumption' should be 'primarily aimed at rendering effective these restrictions'.[364] Since a country can effectively control its production and consumption of an exhaustible natural resource only when they occur within its jurisdiction, the Report concluded that the art. XX(g) exception permits contracting parties to use such trade measures limiting production and consumption *within* their jurisdiction.[365]

The GATT ruling predictably leans heavily on upholding the GATT's basic tenets and favours a restrictive interpretation of the environmental exceptions of art. XX. It may also be said that its approach is either too legalistic or too diplomatic, depending on which side one is on. Conclusions drawn from the historical circumstances giving birth to the provisions can vary according to the methodologies used and sources selected. But this is all understandable, considering that the GATT Panel was reviewing the dispute in the light of GATT provisions,[366] and did not wish to make any value judgments on the environmental policies of the countries involved.[367]

---

[361] *Ibid.*, at 5.33.
[362] Panel Report, note 358 above, at 5.27.
[363] Canada Measures Affecting Exports of Unprocessed Herring and Salmon, GATT, 22, BISD 35th Supp., 98 (1988).
[364] *Ibid.*, at 114.
[365] Panel Report, note 358 above, at 5.31.
[366] Panel Report, note 358 above, at 6.1.
[367] Panel Report, note 358 above, at 5.44.

A recurring parallel to GATT law which is evident in the treatment of the environmental issue in the case is the recognition of the need for an established multilaterally agreed consensus on standards that would apply with more or less equal favour and prejudice to all contracting parties. This is the prevailing philosophy in the Report which both the environmentalists and GATT proponents cannot ignore.

Realities are such that neither Mexico, the US, nor the third countries affected by the second embargo, advance into the legal arena with purely judicial interests in mind. The 'Tuna Fish' issue has elicited tremendous interest because a powerful nation is involved and environmentalists have transformed the enforcement of the MMPA into a battleground for environmental interests. While a country may indeed legislate statutes aimed at environmental protection, their effects on other countries may be extremely prejudicial, so as to negate any advantages to the environment.

For example, a European Community Council Regulation prohibits the introduction into the Community of pelts and manufactured goods of certain wild animal species originating in countries which catch them by means of leghold traps or trapping methods which do not meet international humane trapping standards.[368] Before even considering the legal issues on the required 'humane trapping methods', in the Regulation, it should be noted that the trade of pelts from wild animal species exists because there is a market for the product in the developed countries. The widespread use of pelts for fashionable clothing and for manufactured goods can only occur where the consuming public possesses a considerable amount of purchasing power for these goods. In other words, without the market for these wild animal furs, the number of wild animals killed for this purpose would be considerably less. *Ergo*, the number of animals caught by 'inhumane' methods would also diminish.

Taking a step further, if a small village or group of hunters in some impoverished country were solely dependent for a living on catching wild animals for their skin using the traditional method, then a regulation such as that mentioned above would, in one sweep, remove their single means of livelihood. This is not to say that the objective of the regulation is wrong; but it is the extraterritorial scope of the prohibition and the linkage between the non-trade related condition and trade which breed problems beyond the legal issues.

In the 'Tuna Fish' issue, there was clearly a lack of any established environmental standard that would have merited the invocation of the art. XX(b) and (g) exceptions. The fatal flaw in the US's case is its reliance on the comparative dolphin mortality rates under the MMPA. As stated above, the tuna embargo operates in cases where the dolphin-kill rate is in excess of 1.25 times the recorded US rate for a specific period. This trigger mechanism indicates that the so-called basis for the environmental standard is not a recognised

---

[368] EEC Council Regulation No. 3254/91, 4 Nov. 1991, O.J. (1991) L308/1.

international rule, but the variable, unpredictable incidental kill rate arising from US fishermen's tuna fishing. Although dolphin mortality is a legitimate concern for all nations, the killing of dolphins becomes objectionable only when it exceeds a certain percentage of the number of dolphins killed by US fishing practices. Thus, if US fishermen kill a relatively large number of dolphins for a particular year, due to a higher tuna fish catch, then other countries would be absolved of any violation, so long as it does not top the US level by more than 25 per cent. There is actually *no* environmental norm sought to be followed here. Dolphin mortality shifts in importance according to the tuna yields of US fishermen (since higher harvests mean more incidental killing of dolphins). The conflict in the 'Tuna Fish' dispute, therefore, does not go beyond the level of a trade issue; with no fixed, accepted environmental threshold, the environmental exceptions in art. XX cannot be invoked. And if such is the case, the question of the extraterritorial jurisdiction of environmental legislation does not enter at all into the picture. It is a pity that because of this fundamental defect in the MMPA provision, and the misguided approach of the US in the dispute, the development of a valid standard for the prohibition of the incidental killing of dolphins was sidetracked.

The 'Tuna Fish' Panel report remains, at best, a shaky jump-off point for a discussion of extraterritorial jurisdiction. Neither does the controversy feature a genuine conflict between trade and the environment. In many ways, environmental and trade policies do complement, and should be mutually supportive of, each other. The multilateral approach that permeated the development of international trade law should also serve the peculiar needs of environmental law. Restrictions on trade in the guise of environmental protection measures diminish the intrinsic value of the latter. The urgency of drafting internationally accepted environmental rules should not neglect the balance of interests between states with varying levels of economic development and environmental consciousness. The general effects of such measures are as important as the protection they offer to the environment. Environmental law demands a consensus for it to be effective on an international level; consistency with the existing trading system guarantees its ultimate success.

Sir Ian Sinclair:

Thank you very much. If I were to open discussion on this, I think that we would certainly continue until well after one o'clock. One thing I think I will say, however, and that is that the two contributions that we have had this morning on the application of principles of extraterritoriality in the area of environmental law demonstrate, at least to me, that this raises a whole variety of issues that are not the same issues we have traditionally encountered in the context of jurisdiction. In that sense, I agree entirely to what Francesco was saying at the beginning, that one almost has to, in a sense, divorce this from the traditional discussion we have had about extraterritoriality in other areas of activity. And I think what has just been said also by our colleague, Mr Hizon, in the context of the effect upon third world countries, of environmental measures taken by developed countries which are applied extraterritorially, certainly deserves to be called strongly in mind. However, I think, perhaps, we ought to reflect on this and come back to it tomorrow in the context of our general discussion on drafting rules on extraterritorial jurisdiction.

I am very grateful to our two contributors this morning who have opened our minds to all kinds of new possibilities and developments. One thing I would simply say, I guess purely personally, in relation to what Francesco was saying, I wonder if Antarctica is not almost a kind of what you might call a special case. I know that you know Antarctica, certainly it is an area beyond the limits of national jurisdiction, but the kind of problems that you are going to find with relation to the application of environmental standards in Antarctica are typically, for the treaty part, for those who are involved in giving effect to environmental measures. I don't think they raise the same kind of problems of conflict with other jurisdictions. So, again, they are not a classic extraterritorial problem. With those few points right off the top of my head, I think that we ought to perhaps adjourn.

Francesco Francioni:

As I will be leaving, I just want to make a brief comment. I don't think we disagree with what Ernesto said. I think there is a very large area of agreement. But one point that I would like to make is this: whether the intent of the restrictive measures is protection in disguise or not. I am focusing on what he said regarding the protective motivation of the US's application of the Marine Mammals Protection Act because in this case it was not an initiative of the US government. It was an environmental group that obtained an injunction in California and the Secretary of the Treasury had to do it. So, I do not know why you are really so sure about the protectionist motivation. Of course, if we look at the history you are right and I agree entirely with you. The US has sold a portion of the fleet to Mexican interests and the Mexicans were about to lose their market. So there was a genuine concern on the part of the American population and they even went into court and obtained an injunction.

And the second point I would like to make, I will not dispute your interpretation of art. 3 of GATT and so on, my critique really goes to your interpretation of art. 20 which in light of the context today I believe is a little bit narrow. I would finally make the point that you are right that we should look at the point of view of less developed countries. You may add to the references that you found in the Rio Declaration the very telling expression of 'common but differentiated responsibilities' in which is a whole programme. It is an interesting problem. It may be applicable here, too. And it is a part of the soft law Rio Declaration in which I will be very much interested in developing further studies. But nevertheless, we must realise that in the field of marine resources, in the field of regimes of areas which used to be beyond national jurisdiction, the unilateral action of individual states in building international regimes has been the rule of the past 30 years. Why should we discount, after the continental shelf, after the exclusivity of the economic zone, even the unilateral action of more enlightened states no matter whether they are third world countries or industrial countries. We really have a genuine interest in prohibiting devastating techniques for fishing or incredibly cruel methods of harvesting or catching animals. Should we wait for an international standard? That is my argument. I think that the Marine Mammals Protection Act can achieve what unilateral legislation had achieved in the field of the exclusive economic zone, i.e. certain international standards proscribing drift net fishing or purse-seine net fishing whether it is done in the Pacific or anywhere else.

Cynthia C. Lichtenstein:

That was the point that I wish to mention. I would just like to ask, Francesco a question. You began your talk by saying that there is an international prohibition on certain damaging methods of fishing. What is the source of that international prohibition which you are stating?

Francesco Francioni:

What I said, that there is today's international law trend that is evidenced by resolutions of the General Assembly. The Convention on Drift Net Fishing is at a formative stage which may serve as the nucleus of customary public international law in the field of drift net fishing.

Pieter J. Kuijper:

Would you mind, if I may just briefly react to this, having been the person who argued the tuna/dolphin case to the European Community? I agree to a certain extent with Francesco's critique of the interpretative methods used in GATT. I think that GATT has functioned too long outside the normal disciplines of the system of international law. Panels have usually gone to immediately historic sources. That is not always bad in a certain sense because the historic sources include the Havana Charter which arguably is a much more complete and coherent instrument than GATT itself, so sometimes that historic interpretation has been to the good and has helped the system. But I believe that GATT panels cannot go on like this. They must pay some attention to art. 31. And it is interesting to see that the US was enormously relying on art. 31 in the argument before the GATT panel and we will see what happens. On that interpretation, I wonder, nevertheless, to what extent the treaties that you have mentioned are in any way an indication of how art. 20 should be interpreted when it concerns unilateral measures. Because those are admittedly treaties that exist and that either have ignored the existence of GATT or have just assumed that they could create certain restrictions without hindering the GATT. If you look, for instance at CITES, the Washington Convention on Endangered Species, trade in some of the dolphin species is indeed prohibited. That has never brought any difficulty between the European Community and the US because they both regard that kind of restriction as a kind of later treaty which regulated that specific matter so it was either on the basis of later in time treaty or on the basis of specificity. But that kind of thing was applied without a problem. I admit that in the context of the Basle Convention that might be a bit more complicated. But I hesitate to say, quite apart from our position before the Panel, that this is really decisive or unilateral actions have been undertaken.

Andreas F. Lowenfeld:

You know, I incurred the permanent wrath of the government of the US by being one of the authors of an opinion of the European Community on precisely the question of art. 20. That is in the famous *337* case in which the Americans said let us first look and see if it is necessary and the Panel, following the European submission, said 'no' let us first see what is the violation and then see if there is any other way before they will solve your problem.

Pieter J. Kuijper:

But the environmental problem.

Andreas F. Lowenfeld:

Is that different?

Pieter J. Kuijper:

It's the same because again here in this case the US wanted to go directly to art. 20 and not argue the violations at all so the position is exactly the same. But, for the future, there is another test case before GATT which is going to be extremely interesting which is going to bring forth the wrath from environmental groups and that is various car taxes which exist in the US which also have, or originally had, an environmental goal, such as the gas guzzler tax and other taxes which are structured in such a way that American producers largely escape them and the European Community producers pay them. The same is true for the luxury tax on cars which has a cut-off point of $30,000, which is not indexed, so that American cars largely escape that tax while the higher rate BMWs, Mercedes and, needless to say Rolls Royce come fully under it. These are going to be very interesting test cases also because they are going to develop the requirement of substantive discrimination under art. 3 of GATT, but anyway that has nothing to do with extraterritoriality. Sorry about that.

Ernesto M. Hizon:

I would like to say a final word here. GATT has really become the whipping boy of everybody because it really depends on which side you are on. In another case, which is very well know, the case involving importing cigarettes, the *Thailand* case, Thailand imposed a special tax on imported cigarettes primarily coming from the US on the basis of the art. 20 exception for public health. Now the US was on the other side. It was saying no, that was wrong.

Pieter J. Kuijper:

Well Mr Hizon you can be certain that that was something fully exploited by the person pleading for the European Community.

Sir Ian Sinclair:

The only thing that I would add by way of personal comment on this is that during the entire period of 34 years in which I worked as a legal adviser in the Foreign Office in London I was not permitted to offer any legal advice concerning GATT or any development or question relating to it.

Philip Bovey:

That is still so!

Chapter VII

The UK Government's Experience in Accommodating the Extraterritorial Application of Foreign Laws

*Philip Bovey**

Sir Ian Sinclair:

We are happy to have with us today, Philip Bovey, who is with our Department of Trade and Industry in London who has had and continues to have a degree of experience in this area.

Philip Bovey:

This presentation was not intended for publication and is cast in an appropriate mode. I am sorry that Campbell McLachlan is not here or else I would have invited people to interrupt, thus saving me from getting to the end. But I shall do so, nonetheless, because it is a flexible talk. This itself may provoke an interruption and I may not have to talk at all. There have already been in the course of the conference three substantial swipes at her Britannic Majesty's stance on extraterritoriality: one from Professor Lowenfeld who was supposed to be on our side, to the effect that our *amicus curiae* briefs in the US courts were simply cranked out of the word processor; the second from Professor Lichtenstein, who suggested that there was some inconsistency between our line on the *California and Hartford* case, which was, as Professor Lowenfeld

---

* Mr Bovey would like to point out that what follows is a verbatim record of largely off the cuff remarks made in the course of private discussion. The views expressed are his own and not necessarily those of HMG and the factual statements were included purely to illustrate the point. Some of the accounts of past events may be incomplete or apocryphal.

© Kluwer Law International 1996

just explained, our membership in the Community given the existing territorial ambit of art. 85. The third swipe from the other British delegate here, Campbell McLachlan, was the reference to the degree of schadenfreude which a number of commentators had shown in relation to the fact that we have now got extraterritorial injunctions. In the face of this sustained attack, mostly from people who, with the honourable exception of Professor Lichtenstein, happen not to be present at this particular moment to defend themselves.

Let me begin by explaining what my credentials are. The bit of the UK government which deals with extraterritoriality is in the Department of Trade and Industry which, if I slip into acronym, I will call the DTI. I don't know how many other governments do actually have a special unit with a specific responsibility for extraterritoriality, but we do and my colleague on my right, Michael Johnson, is the head of the unit with responsibility for the subject. He was also, I might say, jointly responsible for the UK Protection of Trading Interest Act which was the high point of UK resistance. He worked on it, I think, with Sir Ian and with another colleague who is not here.

I have only started doing this stuff recently. For ten years I was on the other side of the fence. I was responsible for the law on securities, insurance, corporations, insolvency and we were a regular thorn, if I might change the metaphor, in the side of Michael's branch. In my time, I have done things which they regarded as absolutely outrageous and made them squirm. For example, I was responsible for a UK statute which makes it a criminal offence to manipulate the UK securities market from anywhere in the world wherever the manipulator is. Similarly, I was responsible for a statute which makes it a criminal offence, and indeed void, for one foreign company, to take over another foreign company neither of them having a place of business in the UK or any connection with the UK other than owning 15 per cent of an insurance company – the insurance company not necessarily being a UK based insurance company.

Now I have crossed the fence and I am responsible for the legal aspects of extraterritoriality. In the UK civil service, it is standard form that they ship you across to something which you know nothing about, usually at very short notice. But I am not, in fact, in the slightest bit ashamed of my background in the unit of the UK government that was least comfortable about our stance on extraterritoriality.

Of the provisions I have just mentioned, the one about market manipulation simply codified the common law which had been the common law for a hundred years. The one about insurance had been there long before the Trading Interest Act, and we were merely repeating it. The only provision on which I do feel a bit close to the line was that we provided that it was not an excuse not to provide information about insider dealing, even for an intermediary, for this involves not the alleged perpetrator himself at all, but one who acts for a bank or somebody. We said that it was not an excuse not to provide information about insider dealing merely because your law prevented it. So I do think that that was marginally close to the line, but in my defence we were asked to invent it on a Tuesday to be put down as a Parliamentary Amendment on a Wednesday. But the fact is, and these illustrations show it, that the acceptable limit of extraterritoriality is a very difficult line to draw. The UK has traditionally been the country that has taken the strongest line on it, but we ourselves entirely recognise that line has to be drawn at particular places balancing a number of considerations. There is no simple answer as to what is unacceptably extraterritorial. Many of the papers that we have heard already have demonstrated that that is amply so. But that does not in any way, it seems to us, detract from the importance of the matter nor the need for government as well as the courts and practitioners to consider constantly where we stand and how to react to questions as they arise. That is why conferences such as this one are so valuable. And I am very grateful to Sir Ian and Professor Meessen for inviting me.

What we have to do, what is essential, is to identify and analyse what is and is not acceptable as ET, and that has to be done not just as a matter of theoretical principle. It is essential if business and individuals are to be able to conduct themselves with any degree of confidence. It is also essential if governments are going to legislate extraterritorially because one of the consequences of an unacceptable claim to extraterritoriality is that your legislation is simply ignored. I have little or no doubt that in a number of your countries there are insurance companies that have merged in a way that is void under UK law and you did not take any notice and you were right. There is nothing more important to the maintenance of a stable society, in which business can thrive, than the rule of law and getting this issue right is essential to the preservation of a rule of law in an international context. So against that background what I would like to do is to describe some of the things we as government do.

Government has been very little mentioned apart from the swipes at us and I would like to show you the kind of things which we feel it is our job to do. Now we have got two fundamental rules. The first is that we should try and be consistent. That is, and we are not always successful in this, we try not to object to something that we do ourselves. Do as you would be done by is a rule that has already been mentioned. I am reminded of a story. Every so often, every five or ten years, somebody decides that they are going to sort out extraterritoriality and there is a great conference fixed with the Americans, and at one of these bilateral or trilateral, sometimes the Canadians take part, in one of these conferences the UK delegation presented a list of principles (perhaps the sort we are going to draw up tomorrow) to the Americans and invited them to accept them and the Americans looked down at the list and they ruled out the first nine without question, I mean those were simply not on. They agreed to consider overnight the tenth one, and when they came back in the morning they said well they were terribly sorry but they didn't think they could accept that either. And that principle (I was not there at the conference but my predecessor was) I am reliably informed was 'the rules should be the same for both sides'.

The second fundamental principle that we adopt is that we should act on principle, in principle. I cannot claim that we have always been beyond reproach. It is, after all, our job to protect UK interests but we try very hard not to intervene in a bad case. Michael was talking just before we started about a case in the last couple of weeks where considerable UK interests were involved and we have after a lot of thought decided not to intervene. So it may be true that we crank out the *amicus* brief but we put the most enormous thought and trouble into deciding whether to do so or not. We do try and claim, put forward our line on extraterritoriality only where we would be prepared to defend it as a matter of principle. Apart from anything else we believe that this is in our own self-interest because we do believe that our interventions are taken seriously. The actual words may not be read – they may just note that the UK government has put in a brief – but we do believe that they are taken seriously and we do believe that it is important to maintain our line that we do not intervene merely because a British interest is at stake.

So how do we do it on the ground? The first point that I would make, and I was fascinated how very much a theme this has been of the conference so far, is that we approach the matter from bottom up. If I have learned anything about this area it is that there is no single, simple framework in which you can fit grand principles of extraterritoriality. Andrea Bianchi made very much the same point in his speech. You have to get down into the nitty gritty. You have got to understand the detail of the individual areas of the law and they will not necessarily be the same in each case. I was fascinated by the discussion on this. Within government we are primarily concerned with four areas:

(1) antitrust;
(2) financial services in which I include securities, banking and insurance;
(3) export control; and
(4) fraud.

Maybe we ought to be more interested in the environment or tax but nobody comes to us with these things and there is a limit to the amount we can go out and find. Interestingly, my own division, as well as dealing with questions of extraterritoriality and various purely domestic things, deals with two of these areas. I am also responsible for antitrust and for export control, in both of which we are pushing up against the border in one or two respects.

By far the largest area of our actual activity, in purely numerical terms, is responding to requests for assistance from other governments. There has been a revolution in this respect in the last ten years. Ten years ago we had not acceded to the Council of Europe Convention on Mutual Assistance, declaring it to be fundamentally contrary to the common law. We now have a number of statutory provisions which enable us to exercise compulsory powers to collect information and evidence for other enforcement authorities. We also claim, although again not always successfully, that foreign investigators should not come into the UK even by telephone without our agreement. They do it, but at least if we find out we make a fuss. So we have quite a little industry going of people who look at these requests for assistance and consider whether they are territorially acceptable. In each of the statutory provisions is a requirement that the claim by the foreign state must be territorially acceptable.

Andreas F. Lowenfeld:

These are foreign government requests? We are not talking about civil discovery?

Philip Bovey:

No. These are foreign government requests. That actually takes up most of the time that the people who are doing it on the ground, spend on it. They emphasise very strongly, that which confirms all we have been saying about bottom up and nitty gritty, that it is only possible to do it if they know the facts. There is no general proposition by which you can say, we do not help in this area or we don't help that area. It depends whether it is a US company or a UK company. It depends on where people were. It depends on what market was being operated on. So the second thing that we do and . . .

Sir Ian Sinclair:

I am sorry, Philip, but are all these things being done pursuant to a Council of Europe Convention?

Philip Bovey:

There was a Council of Europe Convention which we did not sign for a long time.

Sir Ian Sinclair:

Yes, I knew that.

Philip Bovey:

We have now signed it and whether by accident or whether the two were linked, we have taken part in a number of respects, the one with the most immediate concern to us in the DTI is the Companies Act 1989. We have taken power to assist regulators worldwide.

Sir Ian Sinclair:

So, it could cover a question from the US.

Philip Bovey:

Oh it does. The US is our main customer.

Andreas F. Lowenfeld:

There is a memorandum of understanding.

Philip Bovey:

There is a memorandum of understanding (MOU). And why I say that the two may not have been closely connected is because the memorandum of understanding on securities matters with the US significantly preceded the accession to the Council of Europe Convention, and again, was done by the thorns in the side, if you like, against the wishes, perhaps, of other parts of government. But it has proved to work. It has proved to draw the fire of the many difficulties that arose. Because what it has done among the elements has been to identify the particular facts that we need in order to judge by doing it.

You turn down requests, but comparatively rarely, but there is a middle category where we help but not enthusiastically and we would normally indicate that we were doing that so that they know where they stand. And by this I think we have developed a much closer understanding with particular bits of the US government at any rate on where the borderlines fall, whose job it is to chase after things. I think that the negotiation of that original MOU, which has been followed up by a number of others, and now by a mutual assistance treaty with the US, which I think has not quite been signed but is very close to being signed, all of that has considerably assisted in developing our respective common understanding.

The third thing that we have spent a lot of time on, I have already mentioned, are *amicus* briefs. I have already said that we spend a lot of time trying to work out what to do. What I think we will have to do, in the light of *California and Hartford*, is to reconsider what we say in purely civil litigation, and although for these purposes *California and Hartford* were not purely civil litigation, the attorneys in the US were acting as *parens patriae* not as enforcers, it was a case that was much closer to civil litigation than to Department of Justice or other enforcement cases. The difficulty is, as a number of people have pointed out, that in an enforcement case you can ultimately appeal to the balancing of the interests of governments. But you cannot do that where two private parties are involved because the one that is deprived of his remedy does not feel that his interest should be subordinated to those of the state and we will certainly have to look again carefully at the form of our briefs and what we are going to say in light of *California and Hartford*. I do not think it will in any respect cause us not to intervene but it has made us think again.

One point that I could perhaps mention on *amicus* briefs in passing is that we do not observe the do-as-you-would-be-done-by rule on them. There is provision for them in our law but we are not welcoming *amicus* briefs from other countries. We have not been very welcoming to the Commission proposal that they should come and intervene in our domestic cases on the antitrust side. We have ourselves intervened, and if this is anything that demonstrates our openhandedness, the other side of the coin of *California and Hartford* is that we have a domestic policyholders' protection scheme and that policyholders' protection scheme is exposed to just this long-tail business that Professor Lowenfeld was talking about on our first evening. We have actually intervened in a case – it is a statutory scheme – against the statutory body which was trying to say that the scheme did not cover US policyholders and we intervened to say that it did, which has cost the UK insurance industry quite a substantial amount.

Andreas F. Lowenfeld:

But it sounds good in the New York cases and in the Chicago cases, because it says to them: don't worry, they have a real remedy in England. That's the consideration.

Philip Bovey:

I think that there is a case for wider use of *amicus* briefs in the UK. I was recently subjected to rather close questioning by Lord Slynn who used to be our UK judge on the European Court of Justice but is now back in the House of Lords; and he conducted a public inquiry in which he invited the Department to answer why they should not be more widely used and I did not find it an easy question to respond to.

Andreas F. Lowenfeld:

Is that published? It is very interesting.

Philip Bovey:

It is about to be published. For the record, Lord Slynn is the Chairman for the European Committee for the House of Lords and the European Committee has just done a study into the Commission's handling of art. 85 and it arose out of that. Judging from the questions he asked us, it is going to be an extremely interesting report.

Finally, we spent quite a lot of time trying to get the law right in the first place. Again, if extraterritoriality is not something that you add on at the end, you have to identify the territorial nexus of your law in the formative state. The conflicts that arise and the cases that one comes across that we have so far talked about in this conference have not arisen as often because the legislature has failed to make its position clear. If the legislature decided and went out and consulted other governments, which we spend some of our time doing, then there would be a good deal less angst and unpleasantness when it finally came to court. So, we do try, this is why, when I was on the other side of the fence, why Michael's branch came and looked at us and said well justify yourself, why are you doing this and why are you doing that? And had we not been actually doing something defensible they would have in the end stopped us. They did not like what we were doing very much but they did not stop us. We have that function within the UK government and we have the function of seeking to respond to other governments although obviously on the subject matter stuff, it's normally those with the particular expertise in the subject matter.

I may say just as one final thought, because most domestic legislation is now made in Brussels and not in London, that we have the greatest possible difficulty in persuading the Commission in their preparation of legislation to take this issue seriously. They keep on trying to confuse it with private international law and sorting out choice of law questions. It is not that. It is about the territorial nexus of mandatory provisions of law.

If I can just, to conclude, give you two examples, one external from the Community and one internal. The external example was on a directive called the Major Shareholdings Directive which is about declaration of direct or indirect interest in shares. We have a rule of law that says that even an indirect interest has to be disclosed provided it is in a UK company. We have a strong defence, we say that a UK company is UK property and therefore we have a sufficient connection. The Community followed our law in the Major Shareholdings Directive but provided that indirect interests, and we are talking about tiny interests here, nothing like control, an indirect interest even in a non-Community company was disclosable even if held by somebody outside the Community if the company was listed. There are possible arguments, you can put forward an argument as to why that is justifiable but what we found most difficult was that the issue did not seem to be one that the Community legislator, in the bits that we deal with, found [...] he was ready to consider and to concern himself with.

Andreas F. Lowenfeld:

What do you mean by this? That it was traded on the market?

Philip Bovey:

Yes. In the Community there is now a whole block of stock exchange and listing directives. The other example is almost to try and end on a light-hearted note, and it is a purely internal one within the Community but we still have substantial concerns within the Community about who regulates things and legislates things. With directives they have to be transposed into national law and the national legislator has to know what the scope of his legislation is and a broad proposition which just declares that motherhood and apple pie is good does not say anything about whose motherhood and whose apple pie it is.

The example, I want to end on, is a directive called the Package Travel Directive, which regulates package travel companies, and it is all about cross-border trade, the whole preamble is all about how this directive is going to enable cross-border trade and it says that package travel companies have got to protect their consumers. In the case of a cross-border sale where a French company is selling to an English consumer, whose law is to apply? Who is actually to make the regulations about the planned accounts and the insurance schemes and all the rest of it?

Andreas F. Lowenfeld:

Brussels.

Philip Bovey:

No! Because these are directives. The result is that we have taken one view. We have taken the view that the *situs* is where the consumer is. I give this purely as an example, but I believe that the French have taken the *situs* as being where the package travel company is. The result is that UK consumers are protected by two laws and French consumers of UK holidays are not protected by any laws. Now we have pressed the Commission very hard as to what they meant because the thing is simply incapable of interpretation. I think that their best answer is, well I wish you had asked us that question at the time, but surely this is their job. If there is any fundamental job of the executive, it is that in preparing legislation they should think about this at the beginning as part of the structure of it and not as an add-on at the end.

Sir Ian Sinclair:

Thank you very much, Philip. As I said before, in this area I am practically in a time warp in the sense that my major involvement in this area of extraterritoriality was some ten years ago or even earlier. And I simply would like to say that I was somewhat encouraged by what you said about certain developments which quite frankly I was not fully aware of. I think that that is certainly a healthy step forward. Maybe this is being overly optimistic, but perhaps no longer is it a dialogue of the deaf which it certainly was ten years ago. But now I will call upon Paul Peters, who is going to comment on this presentation.

Paul Peters:

Thank you. I will talk from a somewhat different point of view. I worked for 30 years in a large international group of companies and was at the bottom of all this activity with the governments. Philip said just now, that the British government when dealing with these kinds of problems looks at it from the bottom up. Well, we were at the bottom.

Andreas F. Lowenfeld:

Ah, we'll pass the hat around.

Paul Peters:

Philip Bovey looked at the problems of extraterritorial jurisdiction from the point of view of the government of a big country. My perspective is that of the business community in a small country. Directors of a company confronted by legislation of a foreign country claiming extraterritorial application, or by orders of a foreign court to disclose documents, are in a predicament; compliance with such legislation or orders will often be contrary to their corporate interests and duties; and sometimes it is in conflict with their own national law. The problems they face have legal, economic and political aspects. Politically and economically, extraterritorial jurisdiction is often perceived as a big stick wielded by the high and mighty ('might is right') or as economic imperialism. The legal position under the domestic law of the company is not always clear, nor is it easy to judge the legality of the application (in particular because some US extraterritorial measures of recent years are contrary to the rules of US law on the subject as set out in the latest Restatement); and from the point of view of international law the position is controversial.

During the 30 years that I worked for Shell companies in several countries, I came across all sorts of problems that arose from the extraterritorial exercise of jurisdiction: discovery orders, antitrust actions, expropriation of assets situated outside the expropriating country, unitary taxation, export controls and security trading regulations; the one thing that I did not experience is the extraterritorial application of penal law on drugs offences, which we discussed earlier today.

My understanding of the rule of international law is close to that expressed in the 1986 Restatement, ss. 401 *et seq.*, although I have strong reservations on some issues, such as the right, however limited, claimed for the US to regulate activities of foreign subsidiaries of American companies (s. 414.2) and those on disclosure (s. 442).

In some cases extraterritorial legislative and judicial jurisdiction (but not enforcement jurisdiction) may be unavoidable and acceptable, but in many cases it is impossible or difficult to justify, even with concepts such as comity. Nevertheless, even when acceptable, such extraterritorial jurisdiction will cause problems. These problems are twofold:

(1) usurpation of jurisdiction by a foreign authority which, under the law of the 'victim' and its home government, has no right to do so (i.e. an infringement of the sovereignty of the home state); and

(2) the creation of legal confusion (and costs) resulting from the fact that there are now two concurrent jurisdictions with which the 'victim' may be confronted: that of the foreign state in competition with that of the home state.

There are of course other cases where concurrent jurisdiction exists and which we have learned to live with, such as the concurrent jurisdiction of the flag state of a ship and the coastal or port state where the ship has infringed the law, but there are strong practical reasons for avoiding concurrence of jurisdiction whenever possible.

The problem of extraterritorial jurisdiction is particularly obnoxious when it hurts not merely the pride of states but when a company gets caught between the jaws of one country's government and the laws of another country where it does its business (to paraphrase the judgment in the *Incandescent Lamp* case).[369] This is the problem of 'conflicting requirements'.

---

[369] *US v General Electric Co*, 115 F. Supp. 835 (D.N.J. 1953), quoted in Restatement 5441, Reporters' Notes No. 1, at 344.

In the last 40 years, states have reacted in different ways to extraterritorial jurisdiction:

(1) Confrontation, by the adoption of blocking statutes. There are now blocking statutes in 20 countries, all established to counter US extraterritorial legislation or court orders. The Dutch statute, which is art. 39 of the 1956 Act on economic competition, forbids compliance with certain foreign measures except with the permission of the Dutch government. This blocking statute has not had to be used in recent years: no requests for dispensation have been received since 1988. A similar series of statutes exists in response to the Arab boycott of Israel. Blocking statutes tend to be unduly confrontational and, in my view, there are better solutions (see below). I don't think that any new blocking statutes have been enacted in recent years, nor do I think that the 20 statutes on record are being used very often. The institution of blocking statutes seems to have gone out of fashion.

(2) Multilateral conciliation, e.g. by creating a consultation procedure in the OECD.

(3) Bilateral procedures and consultations (or merely unilateral diplomatic representations).

(4) In many cases the reaction of the aggrieved state amounts to resignation and compliance, either because it sympathises with the object of the extraterritorial jurisdiction (but why doesn't it legislate itself?) or because the interests at stake are not sufficiently important to the government (though they may be important to the companies affected) or because it is subject to political pressure.

It is widely recognised that, when in a particular case extraterritorial jurisdiction is legitimate, i.e. its exercise is not ruled out by international law, any conflicts arising from it should be resolved by weighing the interests involved (thus Restatement s. 403.3). In my view the national courts of the state exercising the extraterritorial jurisdiction are not the best organs for the balancing act. The weighing should be done by an independent court or arbitrator or, failing that, in an international context. For this and other reasons[370] the OECD Decision of 1976 on Intergovernmental Consultation Procedures on the guidelines for Multinational Enterprises has created an appropriate forum for resolving conflicts

---

[370] There are several other reasons. The problem is not only legal, but requires a multidisciplinary approach, taking economic and political aspects as well as legal considerations into account. In the OECD context there may be a possibility of trade-offs which would not be available in a bilateral context. A problem, even though it is raised as a problem between two states, usually concerns all member states and any settlement reached will work as a precedent; as in GATT dispute settlement procedures, it would be helpful if within the CIME procedures a body of experience and *stare decisis* is built up over the years which will clarify the position with regard to extraterritorial jurisdiction within the OECD membership.

arising from extraterritorial jurisdiction. This Decision, as amended and reconfirmed in 1991, provides for consultations to be held in the Committee on International Investment and Multinational Enterprises (CIME) on any problem arising from the fact that MNEs are made subject to conflicting requirements. The Decision provides that 'governments concerned will co-operate in good faith with a view to resolving such problems, either within the Committee [CIME] or through other mutually acceptable arrangements'. While the guidelines to which the Decision relates constitute 'soft law', and consist of recommendations without binding legal force, the Decision itself, and the obligations it contains, do have binding force.

In 1986 CIME issued a report entitled 'Minimising Conflicting Require-ments, Approaches of Moderation and Restraint', in which the views of a number of member states on extraterritorial jurisdiction are set out and commented upon.

Not all problems relating to accommodating extraterritorial jurisdiction of foreign law give rise to conflicting requirements upon MNEs and are covered by the OECD instrument, but in practice this instrument could probably be applied to the great majority of such problems; and the case law – albeit soft law – so created would help to resolve the rest.

In practice it appears that the CIME consultative procedure has not often been used effectively. One reason may well be the reluctance of states to wash their dirty linen in public, or in a committee, rather than trying to resolve such matters by quiet diplomacy. The available machinery appears to be under-used, as is also the case with the dispute settlement machinery available under the so-called Invisible Codes (the codes of conduct on capital movements and invisible transactions of the OECD).

The EC Convention on the law applicable to contractual obligations, concluded in 1980 in Rome, gives wide discretion to the courts with regard to the extraterritorial application of mandatory rules of foreign law. Article 3.3 provides that, even if the parties to a contract have chosen a foreign law, this does not prejudice the application of mandatory rules of law of another country if all the other relevant elements are connected with that country only. Under art. 7.1 a court, when applying the law of country A, *may* nevertheless (but need not) give effect to mandatory rules of the law of country B with which the situation has a close connection. In some situations these rules may frustrate the extraterritorial reach of the law the parties had chosen. For example, if two Dutch companies have a contract subject to US law, for manufacturing equipment ultimately destined for Cuba, and the contract is subject to US sanctions, a court in the EC may hold that Dutch mandatory law must prevail and that the US sanctions do not apply. In other situations they may facilitate the application of the extraterritorial application of a foreign law. For example, assume that two Americans enter into a contract in Holland, subject to Dutch law, further assume that the performance of the contract has effects in the US and that the contract is illegal, null and void under US law, a court in the EC may give effect to the US law.

Sir Ian Sinclair:

Thank you very much indeed, Paul. Now would anyone like to make a comment?

Yoshio Ohara:

I have two questions. My first question concerns the difference between the British government or expert opinion about extraterritorial application of the EEC competition law before and after the UK's accession to the EC. In the *Dyestuffs* case, Professor Robert Y. Jennings stated an expert opinion, which was quite negative to extraterritoriality, for ICI before the EC Court. On the contrary, in the *Woodpulp* case, Professor Rosalyn Higgins, who wrote the submissions of the UK government as *amicus curiae*, admitted attributive theory on the basis of common law doctrine of agency. Does such difference reflect compromise between the UK's consistent opposition to effect theory and her necessity to observe the EEC competition law as one member state of the EC?

Philip Bovey:

You are absolutely right that the *ICI* decision was there before we joined the Community. We joined the Community with the knowledge of it and of a number of other things that we didn't like in the Community. There are still a number of things that we would rather were otherwise. We went in on *Woodpulp* arguing strongly for something other than straight effects and on our own interpretation, which I know not everybody else shares, but we have at least achieved something because there is a requirement in the judgments that the agreements should have been implemented in the Community, although exactly what that means is not clear. Well, we invented the effects doctrine long before the Americans did. We called it result crimes. I cannot really give you an answer except to say that it was not really the accession to the Community itself that led to a change. What we are doing now is we have published a white paper, a formal government proposal for legislation on antitrust in 1989 and if you look at paragraph 2.11 of that you will find us musing as to what jurisdictional reach to give to our new legislation which will be modelled on art. 85 and that musing has not yet stopped so I cannot give you a clear answer.

Yoshio Ohara:

My second question related to whether the UK plans to conclude an antitrust co-operation agreement with the US in the future like Australia and Canada which have both blocking statutes and antitrust co-operation agreements.

Philip Bovey:

We have no current proposals. We have not ruled it out but our current line is that it is too difficult. That the issues are insufficiently resolved but that is not to rule it out as a matter of principle in any way.

Andreas F. Lowenfeld:

In securities they have a co-operative agreement.

Cynthia C. Lichtenstein:

If you know, why is it that when the UK went to implement the Package Travel Directive it decided to do it from the point of view of the consumer, since these are really rules of conduct for a service provider?

Philip Bovey:

Two reasons. One because we actually thought it was the better interpretation of the law. The directive says that this shall apply to packages sold within the Community so the best guess we had was that the consumer was the recipient. Secondly, was that legally . . .

Andreas F. Lowenfeld:

So, it applied to an American package company too?

Philip Bovey:

Exactly. And that is the other reason that the same rule had to be adopted or otherwise everyone would just go to the Isle of Man or some other place so that they would not be subject to the law. But it is deeply unsatisfactory because it means that the company within the Community may be subject to 12 different sets of requirements about bonding which is just ludicrous.

Michael D.C. Johnson:

I might add a word from the point of view of an administrator to what Philip said about the legal background to the handling by the UK of these cases. First of all, he said we must try to be consistent, which we do and secondly, we must be principled and act on the basis of legal principle which indeed we also do. This does not mean, of course, that every approach that we might have, say from the government of the US for instance, would in itself be objectionable. Certainly not. Or that even if in principle it might look objectionable, it would if carried out necessarily be damaging. It depends on the facts in each case. That is the principle underlying the whole of our so-called blocking legislation (actually not a term that I care for very much, but let us use it for shorthand), essentially a balancing action to judge what is or is not in the circumstances damaging to the trading interests of the UK.

Andreas F. Lowenfeld:

It has never been used.

Michael D.C. Johnson:

Oh yes it has. I was actually going on to give the precise example of the Cuban Democracy Act because in the 13 years that the Protection of Trading Interests Act has been on the statute book, the so-called blocking powers under it have been used in four instances to make statutory instruments, the basic action under the Act to specify a particular area of foreign action as objectionable. Directions have been given on 15 separate occasions to individuals or companies in the UK not to comply with foreign requirements. Now these are 15 different instances, they are not 15 different cases. Four of the 15, for example, were on the *Soviet Pipeline* case and most recently another two were on the Cuban assets control regulations. So I suppose that perhaps half a dozen cases exist. It actually has been effective. Mr Peters said that he regarded blocking statutes as out of fashion. I think that that was the phrase he used. I wish that were so. But the whole point of this Act was essentially as a persuasive devise, to try and persuade our partners in other countries to find a better way of working these things out.

The final point that I would like to make is indeed to echo Philip that we do not have any formal agreement on the handling of antitrust cases with the US. However, we do have a limited agreement on an informal and personal basis between the head of my department, the Department of Trade and Industry, and the Antitrust Department of the Department of Justice, for prior warning of cases where the Antitrust Division is looking into cases with a UK nexus and where it may seek information from persons in the UK. That agreement works well. I personally see perhaps two or three letters a week which come from the American Embassy in London saying that the Antitrust Division is looking into this or that merger or this or that allegation of restrictive business practices and wants to interview the following persons in the following companies in the UK about the following matters. We take these cases very seriously. We do not just rubber stamp them. We actually contact the people concerned. We satisfy ourselves as to the facts of the case and we always reply to the US authorities and in almost every case the interviews go ahead on a voluntary basis.

Andreas F. Lowenfeld:

Do you sit in on them?

Michael D.C. Johnson:

We reserve the right to sit in on them and that has been done. It is not always done. In fact, I do have in my branch two people who are employed virtually full time processing these cases. So it is actually taken very seriously. But the arrangement for consultation works by and large. I think, in recent years there has been little cause for complaint about the way it works.

Sir Ian Sinclair:

Michael, I was going to ask one particular question. In your experience, as a result of the development of this system, which certainly did not exist in my time, I wonder whether you can say whether it has resulted in a greater understanding and a greater degree of co-operation?

Michael D.C. Johnson:

Well, I too have only been back on this work for a few months. But I inherited a very experienced staff as a going concern when I took it over again. My answer would be yes to both questions. Essentially, this is a prior warning procedure which avoids the sort of nasty surprise or the sort of semi-considered action on the part of enforcement authorities overseas which in the past did give rise to jurisdictional disputes. We now try to catch them before they happen.

Andreas F. Lowenfeld:

But you do not get private prior cases which are often the most contentious?

Michael D.C. Johnson:

No.

Andreas F. Lowenfeld:

Did you have one on the *Insurance Antitrust*? Do you know, which is semi-private?

Michael D.C. Johnson:

I cannot answer that question without the colleagues I mentioned. They could probably answer that off the cuff. I cannot because I was not there at the time. I'm afraid I can't remember.

Philip Bovey:

I do not believe we did.

Andreas F. Lowenfeld:

Probably not. Although the US government knew about it and was asked to join and said 'no' but they did not pass the warning on because it is not within the scope.

Philip Bovey:

Just one point on what Mr Peters said on the Cuban Democracy Act, where we did use our blocking statute. I think the difficulty was that every time a moderately relevant bill came before Parliament Senator Mack added his amendment to it.

Andreas F. Lowenfeld:

Bill Clinton said he was for it when campaigning.

Philip Bovey:

I think that the trouble was that Mack finally succeeded because he did veto two at least, and I think that Mack finally succeeded in getting on something that was so hard fought and very much in the government's interest and the balance of political interest just went too far. There are probably lots of people here who know far more about it than I do.

Karl M. Meessen:

I would like to inquire into this concept of private interest on the one hand and governmental interest on the other. At one point you listed several areas in which you did intervene and then you mentioned that in the environmental and tax areas you never did intervene since you were not urged to do so. There was no private interest in soliciting this. And regarding the *amicus* briefs, in purely private litigation? I wonder what is purely private litigation. Is the *Hartford Insurance* case a purely private litigation case involving government when it promotes a certain location as a centre of the insurance industry? Judging from the reaction of the government in Germany, every single private matter can be perceived as a public governmental interest as well in view of financial setbacks for a company that could translate into job losses in Germany and therefore I just wondered how you view this and where you would draw the line? At what point would the UK government get involved?

Philip Bovey:

I think Mr Peters put his finger very much on it with his reference to the Rome Convention and the mandatory rules because I think that the most difficult problems are arising from the increasing tendency of governments, and indeed courts, to use civil sanctions to enforce public policy ideas. Antitrust is the classic example of this but it is in no means the only one. The case that Campbell McLachlan yesterday mentioned, *SIB v Pantell*, was another one where there is a statutory provision applying to a purely domestic contract. It is those cases where the plaintiff, in effect, is being given a bounty or reward almost for enforcing public policy. I am not talking about treble damages here. What I am saying is that it is the cases where the government has decided that the mandatory rule of public principle can be enforced privately – that is a technique that we have freely used and continue to use – rather than direct government to subject regulation. It is those cases that give rise to most difficulty. The pure exchange subject to Dutch law with no relevant American law declaring it to be void would not be of interest to us even if the result would be that jobs would be lost in the UK. It is the ones where there is some kind of legislative requirement at the heart of the private action.

Cynthia C. Lichtenstein:

How do you sort out the difference when a private plaintiff can be viewed as a private attorney general and when, as I would suggest, in *Goldfields* it was simply a private party trying to delay the tender offer and taking advantage of our securities law that does allow private causes of action?

Philip Bovey:

With great difficulty. I did spend a lot of time on that case.

Cynthia C. Lichtenstein:

You do try to decide, it is a factor in which cases you will intervene and the ones in which you will not?

Philip Bovey:

Yes, it is a factor.

Michael D.C. Johnson:

It is one of the ironies underlying our Protection of Trading Interests Act that although it is obviously aimed mainly against government acts, in fact one of the principal stimuli for the discovery provisions in that Act was actually the excessive discovery efforts of the American courts in a civil case. That of course was the *Westinghouse* case in the late 1970s, and it had very wide-ranging discovery demands which led the British government, just at the time when I began to be concerned with these issues, to think that we had to update the much more limited Act that we had on the statute book at the time.

Andreas F. Lowenfeld:

Well that was not Britain's finest hour let us face it. There was a cartel, knowledge of which Britain, France, South Africa, Canada and Australia tried to suppress. It's not my view. Lord Denning thought it all should be discovery rules and you had an excuse because somehow, stupidly, the US Attorney General agreed. That was his fault. And we tried it again in *Laker* and the House of Lords said stay out of this, we can handle it, and really in some sense rebuked the invocation of British Airways.

Philip Bovey:

With the discovery cases now, and they continue, one of our great difficulties is precisely if we suspect that there may be some underlying dirt there. It is very much easier if there is not. It is actually an embarrassment to us, too. We make people sign things saying that they have disclosed all the dirt to us before we will go in and support them. I do not claim, of course, we are not lily white but actually we do not set off to cover up dirt. We generally believe that US discovery goes too wide.

Sir Ian Sinclair:

That has been a view held by British lawyers, public and private, who operate in this field for years and years about US discovery orders. No question about it. But at this point perhaps we should adjourn.

Chapter VIII

New US Policy on the Extraterritorial Application of Antitrust Law and Foreign Responses

Yoshio Ohara

On 3 April 1992, the US Department of Justice announced that it will challenge foreign restraints on US exports under antitrust laws through deleting footnote 159 in its 1988 Antitrust Enforcement Guidelines for International Operations that had been interpreted as prohibiting challenges to anticompetitive conduct in foreign markets unless there was direct harm to US consumers. As the new US policy on extraterritorial application of antitrust laws must cause much more serious impact on importing countries, governments of several countries including Japan and Canada made protests against the US government. Thus, let us try to seek a method to solve such conflict of jurisdiction.

1. The Impact of the New US Policy on the Extraterritorial Application of Antitrust Laws on Importing Countries

The US Department of Justice's Antitrust Guide for International Operations (1 March 1977), which was supervised by Donald I. Baker, Assistant Attorney General under the Carter Administration, stated:

> Antitrust enforcement by the United States Government has two major purposes with respect to international commerce. The first is to protect the American consuming public by assuring it the benefit of competitive products and ideas produced by foreign competitors as well as domestic competitors .... An agreement or set of private agreements designed to raise the price of imports ... raises most

serious antitrust concerns. The second is to protect American *export* and investment opportunities against privately imposed restrictions. The concern is that each US-based firm engaged in the export of goods, services, or capital should be allowed to compete on the merits and not be shut out by some restriction.[371]

However, the 1988 Antitrust Enforcement Guidelines, which was supervised by Charles F. Rule, Assistant Attorney General under the Reagan Administration, showed self-restraint by putting footnote 159 as follows:

> Although the FTAIA [Foreign Trade Antitrust Improvements Act] extends jurisdiction under the Sherman Act to conduct that has a direct, substantial, and reasonably foreseeable effect on the export trade or export commerce of a person engaged in such commerce in the United States, the Department is concerned only with adverse effects on competition that would harm US *consumers* by reducing output or raising prices.[372]

On the contrary, on 3 April 1992, James F. Rill, Assistant Attorney General in charge of the Antitrust Division under the Bush Administration said:

> Applying the antitrust laws to anticompetitive conduct that harms US exports is consistent with the enforcement policy the Department had followed for many years prior to 1988. [The Department review of antitrust enforcement policy on export restraints] confirms that Congress did not intend the antitrust laws to be limited to cases based on direct harm to consumers. Today, when both imports and exports are of importance to [US] economy, we would not limit our concern to competition in only half of our trade.[373]

Attorney General William P. Barr also stated that the new policy is consistent with the text of the Sherman Act, which prohibits restraints of trade or commerce with foreign nations, because 'foreign commerce' includes exports as well as imports.[374] Certainly, it is true from the viewpoint of a literal interpretation of the Sherman Act, but the new policy must have a much more serious impact on importing countries than the old one. The US Department of Justice mentioned the *Canadian Patent Pool* case as one of the judicial precedents supporting the new policy.[375] However, this case is really a typical example of conflict between the industrial policy of the importing country and the competition policy of the exporting country. The members of the Canadian Patent Pool conspired, on the basis of Canadian industrial policy, to give licences only to firms manufacturing in Canada, and to refuse licences which the Zenith Radio Corporation needed to export US-made radios and televisions to Canada. The US Department of Justice brought an antitrust civil suit on the ground that such refusal of licence conspired by Canadian subsidiaries of US manufacturers such as the General Electric Company and the Westinghouse Corporation

---

[371] US Department of Justice, 'Antitrust Guide for International Operations' 4–5 (1977).
[372] *Id.*, 'Antitrust Enforcement Guidelines for International Operations' 30 n. 159 (1988).
[373] *Id.*, Press Release of 3 April 1992, at 2.
[374] John McLaughlin's 'One on One' with US Attorney General William P. Barr, taped on 21 Feb. 1992 for broadcast on 23 Feb. 1992, 2.
[375] US Department of Justice, 'Antitrust Enforcement Policy Regarding Anticompetitive Conduct that Restricts US Exports', Background, 2 (3 April 1992).

violated ss. 1 and 2 of the Sherman Act.[376] Accordingly, the government of Canada made a diplomatic protest to the US government that such civil suit infringed the Canadian sovereignty to formulate its own industrial policy. In order to solve such conflict of jurisdiction, in 1959 the Justice Departments of both the US and Canada concluded the Fulton-Rogers Arrangement on Antitrust Notification and Consultation Procedure,[377] which is a forerunner of the multilateral arrangement made through the OECD Council of 1967. On the other hand, when Hazeltine Research, Inc brought a patent infringement suit against Zenith, the latter counterclaimed that the former violated s. 1 of the Sherman Act.[378] Although the US Supreme Court admitted this counterclaim,[379] due to the nature of a private suit, the Court failed to balance the Canadian interest to establish its own manufacturing industry against the US interest to promote her exports.[380] This failure to adopt the interest-balancing approach later led to a request to the US government to participate in a private suit as *amicus curiae* by art. 6 of the US/Australian Antitrust Co-operation Agreement (1982)[381] and also s. 11 of the US/Canadian Antitrust Co-operation Understanding (1984).[382]

As shown by the *Canadian Patent Pool* case, the US extraterritorial jurisdiction on export restraints before the new policy raised serious problems.

2.   Foreign Responses to the New US Antitrust Enforcement Policy

The governments of several countries made diplomatic protests against the new US policy of extraterritorial application of antitrust laws. Among them,[383] the

---

[376] *US v General Electric Co, Westinghouse Corp, et al* [1962] Trade Cas. (CCH), paras. 70, 342; 70, 420. Mr James M. Spears, General Counsel of the FTC criticised at his address before the International Law Section of the Canadian Bar Association held in Toronto on 15 Sept. 1992 that US extraterritorial jurisdiction over Canadian subsidiaries of American corporations in this case was justified by the nationality principle so that this case would not support the new policy, which will be applied over foreign companies without any links with American corporations. However, the US court obtained personal jurisdiction over N.V. Philips through service of process on its service agent in New York in this case. Thus, Spears' criticism is not persuasive.

[377] As to the Basford-Mitchel Arrangement replacing the Fulton-Rogers Arrangement, Canada-US: 'Joint Statement concerning Cooperation in Antitrust Matters', 8 *ILM* 305 (1969).

[378] *Hazeltine Research, Inc v Zenith Radio Corp* 239 F. Supp. 51 (ND Ill 1965); 288 F.2d 25 (7th Cir. 1967).

[379] *Zenith Radio Corp v Hazeltine Research, Inc* 395 US 100 (1969).

[380] Douglas E. Rosenthal & William M. Knighton, *National Law and International Commerce: The Problem of Extraterritoriality* 30–31 (1982); Alan D. Neal & Melville Stephens, *International Business and National Jurisdiction* 64–65 (1988).

[381] Agreement between the Government of the United States of America and the Government of Australia relating to Cooperation on Antitrust Matter, 29 June 1982, 21 *ILM* 275 (1984).

[382] Memorandum of Understanding between the Government of the United States of America and the Government of Canada as to Notification, Consultation and Cooperation with respect to the Application of National Antitrust Laws, 9 Mar. 1984, 23 *ILM* 275 (1984).

[383] The content of the protest by the UK government has not yet become public.

contents of such protests by Japan and Canada have become publicly known, so let us examine them.

Assistant Attorney General Rill emphasised that 'the policy change has general application and is not aimed at particular foreign markets'.[384] However, many US Congressmen consider the Japanese 'keiretsu', which means close co-operation between parts suppliers and assembly manufacturers or vertical integration between car manufacturers and dealers, as a vertical restraint of trade so that it must be a target of the new policy. The government of Japan, which was assumed as a potential target of the new policy, made diplomatic protests to the US government immediately after the announcement of the new US policy. Earlier the governments of Canada and the UK and the Japanese Ministry of Foreign Affairs[385] and Ministry of International Trade and Industry (MITI) insisted that:

(1) such application would constitute extraterritorial application of domestic laws which is not permissible under international law, without mentioning, in particular, the effects doctrine;

(2) the US government should notify and consult with a country where illegal conduct was occurring so that the competition authority of such country could regulate the conduct under its own law.

Furthermore, the MITI complained that the new US policy would supplement the reprisal measures against unfair trade under s. 301 of the Omnibus Trade and Competitiveness Act 1988 with the result of transforming antitrust laws into trade law.[386] Japan's Fair Trade Commission (JFTC) also expressed serious concern that such application of the US antitrust laws against anti-competitive conduct overseas would come into fundamental conflict with the position of other countries, including Japan, on the jurisdiction of national competition laws and would raise problems under international law, and also that such application might result in antitrust enforcement for the purpose of protecting US exporters. If the interests of US exporters would be protected by US antitrust laws, the JFTC apprehended that exporters might bring numerous private suits in order to obtain profit.[387] Thus, Chairman Umezawa of the JFTC requested US Assistant Attorney General Rill to withdraw the new US policy, but the latter refused.[388]

The government of Canada, to which the US antitrust laws have often been extraterritorially applied, complained that the application of the effects doctrine to the area of export foreclosure is insufficiently established by state practice to be consistent with international law.[389] Such a view is the same as the British one.

---

[384] See note 373 above, at 3.
[385] 'Statement by the Spokesman of Japan's Ministry of Foreign Affairs', Press Release of 4 April 1992.
[386] MITI (ed.), 'Report on Unfair Trade Policies by Major Trading Partners', 116–17 (1992).
[387] Statement by the JFTC of 9 April 1992.
[388] *Nikkei* Newspaper of 16 April 1992.
[389] Note No. 074 by the Embassy of Canada in Washington D.C. on 5 May 1992.

3.   Possible Solution of Conflict of Jurisdiction

The above-mentioned protests by Japan and Canada against the new US antitrust enforcement policy insisted upon the necessity of both negative and positive comity.

As to negative comity, the US antitrust authorities should accord good faith consideration to the national interests of other countries which may lead to the avoidance or minimisation of a conflict of national interests during consultation. Even if each country asserts that its own national interest is predominant and it is unable to defer to the expressed national interest of the other, it should nonetheless seek to reduce the scope and intensity of the conflict (see s. 7 of the US/Canadian Antitrust Cooperation Understanding). The interest-balancing approach for such purpose has been accepted by US judgments such as *Timberlane*[390] and *Mannington Mills,*[391] Restatement (Third) of the Foreign Relations Law of the United States (1987),[392] the 1988 Antitrust Enforcement Guidelines,[393] and the EC/US Antitrust Cooperation Agreement[394] (art. VI). However, in reality, US courts have been prone to balance favourably US interests so as to exercise US jurisdiction even if the US interest is barely discernible.[395] Therefore, the US should reflect upon the factors that necessitated the interest-balancing approach as a critique to the unilateral exercise of extraterritorial jurisdiction based on the effects doctrine.

With respect to positive comity, not only the two protesting countries but also the US government itself take the same position, namely: 'if the importing country is better situated to remedy the anti-competitive conduct overseas and is ready to act, the US antitrust authorities are prepared to work with them'.[396] Article V(2) of the EC/US Antitrust Cooperation Agreement provides the ability of the antitrust authorities of the exporting country to request enforcement action by the authorities of the importing country, if the former believes that the anti-competitive conduct carried out on the territory of the latter is adversely affecting the important interests of the former. Finally, co-ordination of concurrent antitrust investigations or proceedings in both importing and exporting countries,[397] which are related or affect each other, is

---

[390] *Timberlane Lumber Co v Bank of America* 549 F.2d 597 (9th Cir. 1977).
[391] *Mannington Mills Inc v Congoleum Corp* 595 F.2d. 1287 (3rd Cir. 1979).
[392] Sections 403, 442(1)(c).
[393] See note 372 above, at 32, No. 170 at 32 *et seq.*
[394] Agreement between the Commission of the European Communities and the Government of the United States of America regarding the Application of their Competition Law, 30 *ILM* 1487 (1991).
[395] Eleanor M. Fox, 'Extraterritoriality and Antitrust – Is "Reasonableness" The Answer?', in 1986 Proceedings of Fordham Corporate Law Institute 49, 59.
[396] See note 373 above, at 3.
[397] For the example of such co-ordination of concurrent proceedings between the German Federal Cartel Office and the JFTC without a basis in a bilateral antitrust co-operation agreement in the case on international cartel agreements between Europe and Japan concerning manmade fibres,

found in art. 2(5) of the US/German Antitrust Cooperation Agreement (1976)[398] and also art. IV of the EC/US Antitrust Cooperation Agreement.

Mr James R. Atwood is sceptical as to the effectiveness of positive comity, as follows:

> It is not realistic to expect one government to prosecute its citizens solely for the benefit of another. It is no accident that this has not happened in the past, and it is unlikely to happen in the future. We should not expect the principle of positive comity ... to impact dramatically on the proposition that laws are written and enforced to protect national interests. [399]

However, as US Assistant Attorney General Rill pointed out, '(i)n most cases conduct that harms [US] exporters also harms foreign [e.g. Japanese] consumers, and may be actionable under the other country's antitrust laws'. [400] In fact, in cases regarding the US Naval Base in Yokosuka[401] and the US Air Force Base in Yokota, [402] probably on the basis of notification by the US antitrust authorities, the JFTC ordered Japanese constructors to stop bid-rigging. The US government succeeded in obtaining compensation for damages suffered from such bid-rigging from Japanese constructors who participated in such anti-competitive conduct. [403]

Despite the JFTC's apprehension of the potential increase of private antitrust suits following the new antitrust enforcement policy, no case has been brought. Several learned American lawyers view vertical restraints of trade as having been

---

cont.

    see Yoshio Ohara, 'International Application of the Japanese Antimonopoly Act', *Swiss Rev. of Intl Competition L.* No. 28, 5, 14 *et seq.* (1986).

[398] Agreement between the Government of the United States of America and the Government of the Federal Republic of Germany Relating to Mutual Cooperation Regarding Restrictive Business Practices, 23 June 1976, 15 *ILM* 1282 (1976).

[399] James R. Atwood, 'Positive Comity – Is it a Positive Step?', in Proceedings of Fordham Corp. L. Inst. 79, at 87 (1992).

[400] See note 373 above, at 3. Mr Atwood himself admitted it by stating that 'The Opening of Japanese markets would help American exporters, but it would also help the buyers of goods and services within Japan' (see note 399 above *id.*).

[401] 35 Collection of JFTC's Decisions 57, 8 Dec. 1988. The total sum of administrative fines imposed on 70 companies, which implemented bid-rigging, amounted to ¥ 289m.

[402] 38 Collection of JFTC's Decisions 187, 9 May 1991. The total sum of administrative fines imposed on three companies amounted to ¥ 275m.

[403] US Department of Justice, Press Release of 19, 22 Dec. 1989. The US government was compensated as much as US$33m (approximately ¥ 5bn) from 100 companies which participated in bid-rigging in the *Yokosuka* case. It was also compensated as much as $36.7m (approximately ¥ 5.5bn) from 11 companies in the *Yokota* case. The US government succeeded in obtaining such huge compensation by threatening to bring a suit before the US courts against Japanese constructors, which had established American subsidiaries or branches. However, I doubt the use of American subsidiaries or branches, which had never participated in bid-rigging within the territory of Japan, for the purpose of obtaining personal jurisdiction over its parent company in Japan because it is too much of a mechanical application of the alter ego theory or expanded principle of nationality.

[404] However, the Vertical Restraints Guidelines (1985) were withdrawn by the US Department of Justice on 10 Aug. 1993.

handled on the basis of the 'rule of reason',[404] and not as '*per se* illegal' unlike horizontal agreements on price. Thus, it is not easy to get a court ruling that keiretsu in Japan violates the US antitrust laws.[405]

Let us hope that the conflict of jurisdiction resulting from the expansion of US extraterritorial jurisdiction can be avoided or reduced through intergovernmental notification, consultation and co-operation on the basis of both negative and positive comity.

Aurelio Pappalardo:

I can be very brief, since several of the points I have included in my outlines have already been mentioned, while others have been even if only briefly discussed. The problem of what is called the extraterritorial application of the EC antitrust rules has mainly been seen from a specific angle, i.e. the conflict between the 'doctrine of effects' and the requirement, dictated by the principle of territoriality, that jurisdiction should be based on something more than the effects of foreign behaviour. This is the basic point, which I have briefly mentioned this morning.

Let me summarise the terms of the debate. One starts from the fact that art. 85 of the EC Treaty prohibits agreements between undertakings which:

(1) restrict competition; and
(2) affect trade between member states.

If both conditions are met, the provision applies irrespective of where the actors are located. As the Commission said in its *Dyestuffs* decision (1969) 'there is no reason to consider whether the undertakings which originated these restrictions on competition have their registered office within or without the Community'. Similarly, in its Notice on Japanese Imports (1972), the Commission said that 'the fact that the headquarters of some or all of the firms involved are located outside the Community does not vitiate [art. 85] if the effects of such agreements are felt within the Common Market'. Interestingly enough, however, while the Commission relied both on *Lotus* and *Alcoa*, it apparently tried to qualify its approach, emphasising that only *direct effects* would justify jurisdiction. Such a qualified approach, the Commission believed, would constitute an acceptable compromise between *Alcoa's* 'pure' doctrine of effects and a too rigid interpretation of the 'objective territorial jurisdiction' principle (which requires that an essential constituent element of the event take place in the territory). It remained unclear what 'direct effects' precisely means.

---

[405] Joseph P. Griffin, 'New US Enforcement Policy Is Assessed', *Nat. L. J.* (16 Mar. 1992) 32; Donald I. Baker, 'A Misguided Assault on Keiretsu', New York Times Forum, 22 Mar. 1992; Daniel J. Plaine, *Proposed Changes in International Antitrust Enforcement Policy* (31 Mar. 1992); Robert T. Greig, *Competition Policy, Its Enforcement and Its Impact on Business* (15 Apr. 1992).

Even this qualified approach was rejected by the non-EC defendants (plaintiffs in the *Dyestuffs* cases before the EC Court), in particular ICI (for whom Professor Jennings wrote a long and learned opinion). The principle of objective territorial jurisdiction, they claimed, requires that the (allegedly illegal) behaviour has taken place, at least in part, within the territory. International law does not recognise the 'effects doctrine' as interpreted by the EC Commission (at least not in the field of economic law). Advocate General Mayras further qualified the Commission's view, suggesting that the EC could base its jurisdiction only on direct, immediate, reasonably foreseeable and substantial effects.

The Court however disregarded both the Commission's and the Advocate General's views and founded jurisdiction on a quite different ground, i.e. the economic unity of the group of undertakings. The non-EC defendants controlled several subsidiaries in the EC; it is the activities of the latter that the Court imputed to the parents, which constituted the basis for the conclusion that the parents had infringed art. 85. 'In view of the unity of the group' the Court said 'the actions of the subsidiaries may in certain circumstances be attributed to the parent company. The applicant [i.e. the parent] was able to exercise decisive influence over the policy of the subsidiaries as regards selling prices in the Common Market and in fact used this power'. Jurisdiction was thus found without discussing the 'effects doctrine' at all.

This is where we were until *Woodpulp*, which presented a significant difference in that the allegedly illegal activity, i.e. price fixing, had been entirely organised outside the EC. As in the previous case, agents and subsidiaries operated in the EC, but apparently they did not carry on any activity relevant for the purposes of the case. *Woodpulp* thus presented some features of a pure 'effects' case, and some thought that the Court would now be compelled to face squarely the doctrine of effects. The Commission still heavily relied on the 'effects doctrine', although it endeavoured to further qualify it, in comparison to the *Dyestuffs* decision. First, it justified the application of art. 85 by the fact that the effect of the price collusion was 'not only substantial but intended, and was the primary and direct result of the agreements and practices'. Secondly, in order to establish jurisdiction, it also relied on the implementation test, according to which a restrictive agreement by parties located in third countries can be implemented in the EC 'either by trading directly into the Community or by using agents or sales offices within the Community'. While the latter way to implement goes back to the *Dyestuffs* case, 'trading directly' constituted a novelty.

The point of view of the UK government, which intervened to support the Commission, is also worth mentioning. According to this view, the decisive factor in order to find jurisdiction is whether the foreign firms, parties to restrictive agreements, have implemented such agreements within the EC; since many of those firms had indeed sold their goods in the EC through subsidiaries or agents, the latter activities were essential to justify the applicability of art. 85. The UK government apparently tried to convince the Court to adopt a solution which would be consistent with the *Dyestuffs* ruling.

Andreas F. Lowenfeld:

The State Department in Washington was passing out press releases.

Aurelio Pappalardo:

Surprisingly, the Court decided that the role of agents or subsidiaries is 'immaterial' to the jurisdictional analysis. It said that a restrictive agreement 'consists of conduct made up of two elements, the formation of the agreement and the implementation thereof. The decisive factor is the place where it is implemented'.

Implementation, which the Court does not define, apparently corresponds to 'trading directly' in the EC (i.e. with the third country company concluding a sales agreement with an EC-located buyer). As to the case under discussion, the Court concluded that the producers had 'implemented their pricing agreement within the Common Market. Accordingly, the Community's jurisdiction to apply its competition rules to such conduct is covered by the territorial principle as universally recognized in public international law'.

Let me briefly comment. If one asks whether the Court has endorsed the effects doctrine, the answer depends on what 'implementation' means. Neither the Court, nor the Commission has seriously tried to clarify this point. Implementation appears to be the fact that a foreign company is involved in some commercially and/or legally relevant relationship with a buyer. If we neglect the role of subsidiaries or agents, which in the Court's words is immaterial, what remains is a seller, located in a third country, and a buyer, located in the EC, who pays a price which has been agreed upon by a number of sellers, i.e. a cartel price. This is the implementation. But if this is all, I think we can say that it comes very close to 'effects' in the sense of the 'effects doctrine'. It is indeed not clear where that constituent element of the behaviour which would characterise the territorial principle is to be found.

Sir Ian Sinclair:

Thank you very much indeed. To be quite frank and again if I may make a purely personal comment, the citation that you have given to support your statement, '. . . accordingly Community jurisdiction to apply its competition rules to such conduct, is covered by the territorial principle universally recognized in international law' could hardly be more cryptic.

Andreas F. Lowenfeld:

They did it on purpose. Think how long this case is and how short the opinion of the Court is. They tried to say as little as possible with it all coming out right.

Karl M. Meessen:

I just wondered whether anyone in this room believed that the Court should have denied jurisdiction to those parties.

Sir Ian Sinclair:

I am reserving my position.

Philip Bovey:

The British government has expressed no view.

Karl M. Meessen:

Leaving the technicalities aside, I think it was a poor case to argue the jurisdictional issue. There should have been a more serious occasion to challenge the reach of jurisdiction under Arts. 85 and 86.

Andreas F. Lowenfeld:

It is the perfect example of the trouble of having an anonymous opinion and no dissents and no separate opinions. So they ended up with something that pleases nobody.

Philip Bovey:

It is a fudge.

Sir Ian Sinclair:

I do not object to that description but only because, contrary to what my friend to the right thinks (Professor Lowenfeld), I do not regard the Court's decision in *Woodpulp* as, in fact, endorsing the effects doctrine.

Pieter J. Kuijper:

Could I just say something at least remotely related to the substance of the dispute? I totally agree with Andy Lowenfeld that this is a good example of what you get when you have a court where you have no dissents. There are two elements that ought to be added to what Mr Pappalardo has said, first of all there were a few companies involved there, notably the Canadian companies, who had no agents, or at least we had no evidence that we found in the hands of the agents, so there was only the evidence which came from other sources that they had directly traded between the Community, that they had made offers even without going through agents to certain people. So there you had direct trading into the Community. And you have the problem of KEA the Webb-Pomerene cartel of American and Canadian woodpulp producers and the Commission had separately, as it had done on previous occasions, attacked the organisation of the cartel in addition to the members. We had to fine them separately and the Court could only find a compromise by keeping KEA out of the case and saying that, contrary to what it said on earlier occasions, the organisation of the cartel was not separate from its members and deserved no separate fine. Why did the Court want to rule that out? Because KEA posed the question of the effects doctrine in its starkest fashion. KEA did not do any trading into the Community, did not even have any telephone contacts with anyone in the Community. KEA was organising the cartel in the US. By ruling that one out, the Court gave itself the opportunity to reach this kind of compromise. The problem, of course, is that they have now said that the producers implemented their agreement within the Common Market but they have not said what would happen if the implementation of the agreement consisted of the act of an omission.

Philip Bovey:

Absolutely. If you get a refusal to trade is that still an implementation? The Commission would say, yes. And I think the present position of the Commission is that in that case we would still go for it and there may soon be a case before the Commission which poses that test but that would mean, and I think that is more or less the position of the Commission, that you are, in effect, applying the effects doctrine. Well the Commission would never say so, after this ruling of the Court, they would simply say that this was an implementation through omission.

Just one point for Professor Ohara, also because he asked whether the Community had protested the new American policy announced in 1992 of the American Department of Justice Antitrust Division, and my recollection is that we have not done so but that has to do with the fact that just at that time the Commission concluded a rather, at least as far as competency is concerned, controversial agreement with the US about consultations in antitrust matters like Germany has, etc., and since the new US policy was considered in that forum there has never been an open statement about it. I can tell you that my colleagues in contact expressed their greatest doubts about this policy but they were assured that the US would want to apply the rules of positive comity precisely through this discussion with the Commission whenever there would be a case for it involving conflict with the Community.

Andreas F. Lowenfeld:

I want to comment a little bit on Professor Ohara's paper, I think that is either the new frontier or its end. The analogy to the effects doctrine that we've had over the years is the guy shooting a gun across the border and the river makes the border and you shoot across and that has been almost everywhere accepted. Next, we have pretty much acceptance of, for example, product liability cases, a harmful drug that is exported, but the analogy is always that the bullet goes into the target state. The US proposal in 1988 is, to me, quite a new departure. I don't think the Restatement, for instance, which tries to cover everything, ever mentioned this. It is also quite clear that the reason that the Europeans did not comment is that it was an anti-Japanese move. There is no doubt about that. It was part of the frustration of the American administration with structural impediments and with tariffs which they do not quite understand and with the balance of trade that they cannot get out from under, they lowered the value of the dollar versus the yen and that has had almost no effect. I do not think, I am not certain, but I do not think that the American courts would sustain such an action unless there were really a predatory intent as well. Simply a notion that, let us say, Toyota has its group of suppliers whom it has always dealt with and with whom it is satisfied and some Americans cannot break in. It may be that the president is concerned with that but I do not think that American courts would accept that and certainly I do not think that they would accept it as part of the effects doctrine. Everything is possible, everything has an effect on everything else, but that is very different from the effects doctrine as we have seen it because it goes in the other direction.

Sir Ian Sinclair:

It is a kind of mirror image of it.

Andreas F. Lowenfeld:

It is a mirror image and I just want to tell you that, since I on the whole believe in the effects doctrine, I do not believe in this.

Aurelio Pappalardo:

Let me add a last brief remark on the controversy between the US and the Community, which followed the attempt by the US, in 1982, to use its export control laws to enforce an embargo on sales by foreign subsidiaries of US companies of material for the Trans-Siberian gas pipeline. The diplomatic note of protest sent by the EC Commission to the US government seemed to suggest that international law does not provide a sufficient basis for jurisdiction founded only on effects. The explanation of what might appear as a contradiction with the point of view strongly defended by the Commission in the antitrust field probably resides in the fact that the effects claimed by the US appeared to the Commission to be too attenuated to support jurisdiction.

Pieter J. Kuijper:

I have never understood people who say that that is contradictory with our position on the effects doctrine. It doesn't say so.

Andreas F. Lowenfeld:

I remember that the note cites or the later démarche cites the Restatement which was then in draft form and we were strongly criticised for undercutting US policy to which we said that if US policy obeyed international law we would not have any problem.

Cynthia C. Lichtenstein:

In terms of the analogy that comes from the bullet, the difficulty with the analogy is that when you are in the securities law field, whether it is fraud or, say, market manipulation, in both those cases, the US has insisted that these are effects on the US markets without any conduct, any kind of thing that you can visualise being implemented in the US. That is why I was wondering when in the discussion of *Woodpulp*, I understood you to say that the UK does have a law sanctioning market manipulation as having a direct effect upon the UK market wherever the manipulation takes place.

Philip Bovey:

You are absolutely right that it does raise these kind of difficulties. Our proposition, which is reflected in s. 47(2) of the Financial Services Act 1986, is that it has to be intended to affect the UK market. Obviously, if you trade in a particular way in a foreign market it is going to affect every other world market – that is true of securities and commodities and of a wide range of financial instruments and the proposition, which we derived from the original nineteenth century case law, was that it has to be intended to have that effect.

Andreas F. Lowenfeld:

Will you presume the intent if the effect . . .?

Philip Bovey:

The burden of proof is on the defendant.

Cynthia C. Lichtenstein:

It is a stricter requirement.

Philip Bovey:

Yes.

Harold G. Maier:

It seems to me that this may be the perfect place to apply the Restatement's analysis – that there may be an effect if the effect is not unreasonable. In other words, to use the reasonableness criteria. There is jurisdiction, but when you look at the question, in this kind of a case it would still not be reasonable to apply the local law to this kind of effect. If we develop a jurisprudence in this manner, we avoid the buzz word concept. When someone says, 'the effects doctrine', all of a sudden everybody shakes. Well that is crazy. It does not make any difference what you call it. The question is: Is the effect the kind of effect that ought to permit this local regulator to regulate external acts.

Andreas F. Lowenfeld:

That is why we put effects in s. 402 which is a minimum and then s. 403 makes its application subject to reasonableness.

Sir Ian Sinclair:

If I could just make a personal comment. The kind of visceral reaction that I have to the mention of the effects doctrine is that it is the effects doctrine, as practised by US courts and agencies over many years, which has given rise to many of the problems in this field. I entirely agree with you that when one looks to the substance of a particular case one may find very good reasons why, in particular circumstances, an exercise of jurisdiction may not be objectionable.

Harold G. Maier:

It may be good for us to start thinking about it, not in terms of what the history is but rather to try to explain the parts of the history that make sense. These can be retained; the parts that do not make sense can be rejected.

Sir Ian Sinclair:

I think that all of us who have practised in this field know that we have been guilty of major inconsistencies. I could certainly say *mea culpa* for the next hour.

Andreas F. Lowenfeld:

Can I just make one final point here? The mention of securities is very interesting because, I have said this to the British here and elsewhere, in fact, no country likes securities fraud, no country likes insider trading. The remedies are somewhat different, but even so you do not really get substantive conflicts, the only conflicts you get are quote 'sovereignty conflicts'. Whereas in the competition law field there are underlying differences.

Sir Ian Sinclair:

No country likes the laundering of drug money.

Andreas F. Lowenfeld:

That's correct.

Sir Ian Sinclair:

And that is why we had an agreement with the US government in 1984 which was designed *inter alia* to deal with this problem of banking secrecy laws in the Cayman Islands.

Philip Bovey:

But the area of securities does give rise to very great difficulty because the way in which different securities regulators regulate their market differs in detail. The overall objective is the same, but it differs in detail and things that are permitted in the market, and it gets down to the finest definitions about who is an affiliate of whom and whether they can buy shares during a public offering. All that sort of stuff, and there are substantial differences, much more in the detail, but those details because of the nature of the securities markets are worth billions of pounds to people. So yes it is easier to deal with it because there is a common objective. I mean there is no common identification as to what insider trading actually is and for so much of securities law if you are not breaking the law you are not doing anything wrong.

Andreas Weitbrecht:

Going back to *Woodpulp* for a minute to say a word in defence of jurisdiction and of applying art. 85 in this case, whether you call this effects doctrine or implementation or whatever. If the European chemical producers get together and set prices and allocate market shares between themselves, they are fined by the European Commission, as has happened, hundreds of millions of ECUs. The Community doesn't happen to have producers of woodpulp. So they're all outside the Community and if they get together and decide we will not have subsidiaries within the Community, we will not have agents in the Community, we will, since there are no producers in the Community, sell into the Community only from outside and we will agree to set prices and allocate customers between ourselves, should they not in the same way be subject to art. 85, as are the producers of Polyprophene, PVC and Polyethelene?

Yoshio Ohara:

Although both the Court and the Commission of the EC found that the price recommendation by the KEA was binding to members of the woodpulp trade association so that it was not distinguishable from price fixing of its members, the Court rescinded the Commission's decision which imposed a fine on the KEA. This fact shows the limitation of the implementation theory on which the Court relied because that theory cannot admit extraterritorial application of the EC competition law to the American trade association which provided the opportunity for price fixing with its members but did not itself sell pulp within the territory of the EC. If the Court had adopted the effect theory likewise, the Commission and Advocate General Mr Darmon, the Court might support the Commission's decision. The Court might decide not to adopt the effects theory, to which the UK had consistently objected, by considering that as long as the EC competition law was applied to price fixing of members of the American trade association, the objective of keeping competition within the EC was accomplished without accusing the association.

Pieter J. Kuijper:

The Court could only reach that conclusion by leaving its earlier policy, or acceptance of Commission policy, to impose fines both on the organisation of a cartel and the members of the cartel. And here they said, 'Well, we quashed the fine as far as the organisation of the cartel is concerned because it cannot properly be distinguished from its members'. And that gave them the possibility of keeping only to the implementation theory. If they had not followed the first démarche, they would have had to confront the question that Mr Ohara would pose, namely that the cartel had not implemented anything within the Community. The organisation of the cartel implemented the cartel in the US and therefore that put the question of the effects doctrine squarely before the Court. If the Court hadn't found the technique of excluding KEA from the case altogether by saying that it was not distinguishable from its members and therefore didn't deserve to be fined . . .

Karl M. Meessen:

I think the effects doctrine has reached a new dimension. The point is that effects so far were understood to be domestic effects and now the reverse is also true. Positive comity precisely obliges us to care about foreign effects and the embarrassing point about all this is that it was accepted some 13 years ago by all our governments. In this Restrictive Business Practices Code, the effect on international trade wherever it occurs was supposed to trigger antitrust action and this concept, which has been broadened ever since, is now being used to turn around the effects doctrine to make it more or less a fair trade issue rather than an antitrust issue in an effort on the part of the American government to protect its exporting industry in its not so overwhelmingly successful efforts to enter . . .

Andreas F. Lowenfeld:

Their assault on the Japanese fortress!

Karl M. Meessen:

And this, I think, is the conceptual problem. It's separating effects from the domestic state. It was the domestic state where the effects occurred that took action. In the future, it could be any state in view of effects occurring elsewhere.

Yoshio Ohara:

I personally admit the well defined effects doctrine together with the principle of reasonableness and positive comity.

Ernesto M. Hizon:

I just wanted to ask Professor Ohara about resolving the conflict of jurisdiction, the last point, that he mentioned. Well, I do believe that this measure is really another anti-Japanese measure and you can go on and on talking about anti-dumping but from the other point of view if you say Japan, in the interests of so-called positive comity, is prepared to work with the US or with any country which opens Japan to these attacks on let's say antitrust law. Isn't this always the way Japan tries to run away from the consequences of its so-called ... system – meaning to say, 'okay, let's always cut a deal. Let's make a deal'. This is done in anti-dumping. This is done in antitrust. Isn't this a bit hypocritical on the part of Japan? I mean, sure, we're going to get the best lawyers. We'll talk about how unfair it is and how the effects doctrine shouldn't be applied but the bottom line is when the coast is clear we are going to cut a deal. Isn't that inherently unfair, too, if you come to think of it?

Sir Ian Sinclair:

I don't think I will ask Professor Ohara to respond to that. I suggest you take it up with him in private afterwards. I think this is the point at which we should move on to our next topic for this afternoon. That, of course, is national control of international mergers and acquisitions. Here we are fortunate to have Andreas Weitbrecht intervening.

Chapter IX

National Control over International Mergers and Acquisitions

Andreas Weitbrecht

Thank you, Sir Ian. Mergers and acquisitions are controlled by states for a variety of reasons. They may wish to control foreign investment. They may be concerned about national security, a topic on which I understand Ed Sherman will speak in a minute. They may wish to control the behaviour of players during corporate takeover battles. That is, again, not the subject on which I will talk. States also control mergers and acquisitions in order to preserve the competitive structure of domestic markets. I will devote my introductory statement exclusively to competition and antitrust law aspects within antitrust. I will not talk about the mandatory notification requirements that are part of most of the merger control regimes. They are often quite burdensome on enterprises in an international setting. Two Japanese banks merging have to notify the EC Commission under the EC Merger Regulation from the statutory thresholds that are set. But, however burdensome and expensive this may be, it has in the end raised little controversy between states and I will consequently disregard that. I will draw on the experience from the US, from Germany and from the EC, as the three jurisdictions that have perhaps contributed most to the body of learning that there is in the field of international merger control.

There are basically four different scenarios – disregarding more complicated things like joint ventures. There is the case where you have a domestic acquirer and a foreign target. I will give you an example of a case that has recently been decided by the Federal Cartel Office and we will discuss that at some length. It has also been the situation of the *de Havilland* case decided by the European Commission where Aerospatiale and Alenia, a French and an Italian company, were trying to take over de Havilland, the Canadian producer of regional aircraft.

That merger has been prohibited by the European Commission under the EC Merger Control Regulation. In the reverse, you have a domestic target and a foreign acquirer. You have a third situation where you have a foreign acquirer and a foreign target and both have subsidiaries in the state that is trying to assert jurisdiction. In the 1960s that was, for instance, the situation in the US in the *Ciba/Geigy* case. It has recently been the subject of a District Court decision by Judge Gesell in the D.C. District involving a case between a Finnish manufacturer of mining and underground drilling equipment, the kind of things that are used to build the channel tunnel. They were seeking to acquire the French subsidiary of Baker Hughes making the same kind of equipment. Both had small sales subsidiaries in the US and the US thought that this was so substantial that they had to sue them in the US District Court. There was no mention made of *Timberlane* or any of its progeny. There is one footnote referring to the fact that the Department of State had received a note from the Finnish government, but the Department of State had concluded that US interests of comity were not at stake and that was the end of that discussion. Of course, the case did not reach the real test because Judge Gesell concluded that there was enough competition in the US market even after that merger. But it is, nevertheless, interesting to note that there was no mention made, as one might have expected, of the *Timberlane* case and the cases following that body of law.

Andreas F. Lowenfeld:

That is a good example, if you have a good case on the merits do not spend all your time on jurisdictional issues. The typical lawyers' approach is to cite jurisdiction as far as you can. But that is a very good case for it.

Andreas Weitbrecht:

So this is the third scenario and the fourth scenario is the easiest one for us and we will not deal with it. It is where you have a purely domestic acquirer and a domestic target. The case that I want to discuss here today is the recent decision by the Federal Cartel Office prohibiting the acquisition of the Allison transmission division of GM, which the German company, Zahnradfabrik Friedrichshafen or ZF for short, sought to acquire. So you have, from the German point of view, a domestic acquirer and a foreign target. The case has also been taken up in the US where I understand the decision on whether to bring a case to court is about to be made. Of course, from the US perspective, the case takes on the reverse posture: a foreign buyer and a domestic target, but in the end it does not make a difference in the analysis. At least that is my opinion.

I will give you briefly the facts of this case. The case concerns the market of transmissions for trucks, for buses, and for heavy construction vehicles. These are rather specialised markets and their precise definition need not concern us here. ZF is the leading player in the world in these markets. It has a worldwide market share of about 50 per cent and Allison is the second player with a worldwide market share of about 20 per cent. The Federal Cartel Office concluded that ZF had a dominant position on the German market and all other geographical markets that you might consider and that this dominant position would be strengthened by the acquisition of Allison. Therefore, they prohibited the merger. The case is now being appealed. The turnover that Allison has in Germany is exclusively within the field of transmissions and it is not substantial.

Looking at this case now under international law, I will put aside whether it was properly decided under German domestic law and I will also assume as correct what the Federal Cartel Office concluded, namely that not only would the combined entity have a market share of 70 per cent on the German and European market but basically on the world market and that they would have such a great technological advantage over any competitor that entry by other firms into this market was unlikely. Under international law we start again with the effects doctrine but only because Germany is a country which has the effects doctrine incorporated into its domestic competition law. But I do not think that the effects doctrine is at issue here at all, certainly not the way I would understand the effects doctrine. In my interpretation, you are not looking just for any effects in the domestic territory. You are looking for just the kind of detrimental effects that the statute which you are about to apply seeks to enjoin. So it is the constituent element of the conduct and of the effects on the market which occur on the territory of the state that assumes jurisdiction, and if you prefer to call that objective territoriality, fine. So if the threshold for prohibition under domestic merger control law is met, then I would think there is at least a basis under international law for assuming jurisdiction.

But of course that is just the beginning and not the end. Because it is then that we have to start to look for the proper remedy and it is there that the discussion starts because the remedy must be reasonable and must meet the requirement of proportionality. One solution has been to try and limit the remedy to the domestic territory. So you would leave the foreign parts of the merger transaction intact. Often this can easily be done. For instance, it was the solution in *Ciba/Geigy* where a certain product line, where the competitive problems were greatest, was spun off to someone else. That solution is not available in cases where you have basically one product or products that are very much interrelated, as in this case where you have transmissions for trucks and for buses, and for heavy construction equipment vehicles. It is easy to limit the remedy if you have problems in one product market but if you try and limit your remedy to one geographical market you find great difficulties. In this case, how can you limit the effects of a prohibition order to Germany? There is simply no way because the gravamen of the problem is that one major player on the world market ceases to exist. The remedy must be prohibition, it seems, which has a worldwide effect.

Sir Ian Sinclair:

I am sorry but correct me if I am wrong. I really want to understand this. At the moment I do not actually see any jurisdictional problem at all. The

Bundeskartellamt is considering a possible acquisition by a German firm of an American firm in the US. To the extent that the Bundeskartellamt is going to prohibit the German company from making the acquisition, that prohibition, certainly would apply territorially. It is applied to the German company in Germany. Certainly, it may have a serious effect upon the US company in the US, but the actual order is territorial.

Andreas Weitbrecht:

Assuming that the US decides that this merger is okay.

Andreas F. Lowenfeld:

It will not compel the merger.

Andreas Weitbrecht:

It will not compel it but assuming the US would support this merger because it saves jobs in the US by keeping Allison alive which otherwise could be closed. We would then have to face a conflict. In my mind it cannot be the watershed issue of the US issuing an order addressed to GM prohibiting the sale.

Philip Bovey:

The only logical way to solve that problem is to have a worldwide one stop shop and that is not practical. It always comes up when people say that you should only have one government deciding it but even if you went that way how do you decide which government it is? It's difficult enough in the EC.

Cynthia C. Lichtenstein:

There is no question that Germany does have jurisdiction. Whatever the US reaction may be it will not be on the basis of an assertion that international law forbids Germany to take that decision.

Andreas Weitbrecht:

That is because ZF is a domestic corporation.

Peter von Stoephasius:

I am from the Bundeskartellamt but I do not see any problem with that case. We did have jurisdiction over that case because it certainly is a German company. A company which would have been strengthened by that merger just made, financially, but I think a better case would have been if you had mentioned the *Philip Rothman's* case. That was a merger completely outside Germany except that both countries had subsidiaries in Germany and we have a fiction in our domestic law that this would be enough for jurisdiction over the subject matter.

We interdicted that merger, not the whole merger, but only limited to our territory. The solution was that the merger did not proceed in the territory of Germany.

Andreas Weitbrecht:

The solution in that case, with the foreign companies in a foreign country and two domestic subsidiaries, the solution that was aimed by the Bundeskartellamt was to limit the remedy to Germany. But that is hardly possible in the cigarettes market. What is valuable there is the trademark.

Andreas F. Lowenfeld:

The whole world is Marlboro country.

Andreas Weitbrecht:

Yes, you may take the German Marlboro trademark and give that to a competitor in order to keep the effects of the merger from the German territory. But you cannot easily keep the Marlboro cigarettes manufactured in the UK by the merged enterprise from entering the German market and so you end up with confusion. You have two Marlboro cigarettes on the German market. And that is exactly the point. It is increasingly difficult to limit the remedy in these cases to the domestic territory and I would think that in a case like the *Allison-ZF* case Germany can prohibit such a merger. The reason why it is justified under international law, to me, is not so much a question of: is this a German corporation so Germany can do anything to them? It is more a question of why it is not so shocking that Germany can prohibit this merger with worldwide effects. Rather, it is due to the fact that there is now an emerging consensus that mergers which damage the market structure are a bad thing. One of the reasons why cases such as *Ciba/Geigy* seemed so unusual at the time was that at that time, no one had merger control laws except the US and the reason why the *Dupont/ICI* case was so unusual was that at that time no one had a competition law, an antitrust law, except for the US. Today, certainly between Europe and the US there is a consensus about a certain core of antitrust or competition law. There are differences at the fringes. I submit that the approximation of the laws on the substantive level contributes a great deal to alleviation of the jurisdictional conflicts. Thank you.

Peter von Stoephasius:

May I add just a simple example which can help even if a German company is involved in such a merger? Maybe two subsidiaries of German companies will merge with a small company abroad so no one will see any effects on our territory. So there we would deny jurisdiction in that case. It could have also been that in the *ZF* case, if ZF was the daughter of another parent company abroad and if it was clear that this new merger abroad, would not spend any money in ZF, no effect would have occurred in our country. But in that case it was a principle target to take over that German company.

Andreas F. Lowenfeld:

Suppose it is the other way around. That is, Allison says we are going to buy the technology of ZF and we are going to make the stuff in Detroit. Would you prohibit it?

Peter von Stoephasius:

Well, yes, if it was clear that the process in Germany would be developed also by the parent company, to exploit it and to have it strengthened in our country and that would be the case here.

Karl M. Meessen:

How about a cigarette type reservation in that case? Is a German company serving only the German market viable in this product market? I doubt it and, therefore, you would have to go beyond the line respected in the *Cigarettes* case by making it a worldwide prohibition order and that, in my opinion, would cause serious problems.

Peter von Stoephasius:

Allison is a strong, big company, only maybe DM30bn. Our definition of a very small market which will not be subject to control is DM10m. So beyond that limitation we control everything we want to control.

Gary Born:

The more I think about this case the more intriguing it becomes. It is not a case of territorial jurisdiction. It cannot be, because the conduct that is being prohibited is the acquisition of shares in the US. That purchase of the shares, looking at this from a formalistic traditional perspective, is conducted in the US. So the German regulation is not territorial. Perhaps the basis for the regulation is nationality, except that if you look at it carefully, I bet they buy the shares through a US subsidiary which they set up for that purpose. And indeed when you look at it very carefully what you really care about is the effects on the German market which brings us back to where we started. It is the fact that you are taking the leading German producer, or the entity that has the largest German market share, and putting it together with another entity that has the second largest German market share, it is those effects on the German market which you care about and this leads me to the final question. Suppose that the acquiring company had been French. Would you and could you have done anything?

Peter von Stoephasius:

We would have done it I think, because it is not only to take over the shares but to have the financial sources. It has the same effect on our market.

Sir Ian Sinclair:

We have got a bit diverted from our main theme although it is an interesting discussion. We have to call on Professor Sherman to talk about the presentation made by Mr Weitbrecht and I call upon him now to comment on that presentation.

Edward R. Sherman:

Thank you very much, Chairman. Actually, I am not a Professor but rather a wissenschaftlicher Mitarbeiter at the Lehrstuhl for Professor Meessen. In any event, I wish to talk about another means by which states can regulate inward foreign investment, another technique for restricting foreign control over domestic assets and technology and that is by simply deeming such acts contrary to or an impairment of national security interests. In particular, I want to talk briefly about the provisions which comprise the Exon-Florio Amendment which was first enacted as part of the Omnibus Trade and Competitiveness Act 1988, [406] draw some conclusions and then open the floor up for discussion.

Before I begin to actually touch upon the Amendment's provisions, I would like to give a little historical background to its enactment as I believe, in this case at least, it sheds more light on the Amendment's purpose than does the legislative history. In 1986, Fujitsu Ltd, a Japanese Electronics company, announced plans to acquire the Fairchild Semiconductor Corporation. Fujitsu's announcement came at a time when there were prevailing allegations that Japanese manufacturers were dumping semiconductors on to the US market. [407] Fujitsu's proposal was vehemently opposed by various US government officials, including Caspar Weinberger, at that time Secretary of Defense, and Malcolm Baldridge the then Secretary of Commerce, on the grounds of national security. [408] Opponents to the acquisition used the Committee on Foreign

---

[406] Omnibus Trade and Competitiveness Act of 1988, Pub. L. No. 100–418, s. 5021, 102 Stat. 1107, 1425–26 (1989) (codified as amended at 19 U.S.C. s. 2901 (1988)). The Exon-Florio provisions are found in the Defense Production Act 1950, 50 U.S.C. app. s. 2170 (1988).

[407] Holmer, Bello, Preiss: 'The Final Exon-Florio Regulations on Foreign Direct Investment: The Final Word or Prelude To Tighter Controls?', 23 *Law and Policy in Intl Bus.* No. 3, at 593, 596.

[408] See Brenton R. Schlender, 'Fujitsu Drops Plans to Acquire U.S. Chip Maker', *Wall St. J.* 17 Mar. 1987, at 3.

Investment in the US (hereinafter the Committee)[409] to apply pressure upon Fujitsu despite the fact that at this time the Committee was without authority to block the acquisition. Eventually, Fujitsu succumbed to the pressure placed upon it and withdrew its plans.[410] Nevertheless, in the aftermath of the Fujitsu affair, it became apparent that the President of the US lacked the express statutory authority to block or suspend mergers which may threaten to impair national security.[411] Legislation was thereafter drawn up, sponsored by Senators Exon and Florio, and it came in the form of an amendment to the Omnibus Trade and Competitiveness Act 1988.

Basically you have the relevant provisions before you. They are listed on the outline that has been distributed. Very briefly let me read over them. Simply, the Amendment authorises the President to investigate mergers and acquisitions with foreign persons which could result in foreign control to determine the effects on national security.[412] If the President finds that the foreign interests exercising control might take action which threatens national security and that other provisions do not provide adequate authority to safeguard national security[413] the President is authorised to suspend or prohibit the transaction.[414]

On 21 November 1991, the Committee published its final regulations regarding the Exon-Florio provisions.[415] The relevant regulations are as follows: Concerning filing, the regulatory strategy adopted relies on a 'voluntary' notice by the parties or notice by a government agency to trigger an inquiry by the Committee. The parties must submit detailed information to the Committee with the notice.[416] If voluntary notice is provided and the Committee declines to

---

[409] Regarding the history of the interagency Committee on Foreign Investment in the United States (Committee) and its composition see Holmer Bello, Preis, note 407 above.

> [Committee] which is chaired by the US Trade Representative, was originally created in 1975 by executive order to review, on an interagency basis, foreign acquisitions of U.S. companies. Exec. Order No. 11,858, 40 Fed. Reg. 20,263 (1975), as amended by Exec. Order No. 12,188, 45 Fed. Reg. 989 (1980). An executive order issued in December 1989 named CFIUS [Committee] as the body 'to receive investigations' under Exon-Florio, Exec. Order No. 12,661, 54 Fed. Reg. 779, 780 (1989). In addition to the U.S. Trade Representative, CFIUS is comprised of representatives from the Departments of Defense, Commerce, Justice, State, Treasury, Interior, Agriculture, Labor, Transportation and Energy, the Office of Management and Budget, the Council of Economic Advisors, the National Security Council, and the U.S. International Development Cooperation Agency. Exec. Order No. 11, 858, 40 Fed. Reg. 20,263 (1975), as amended by Exec. Order No. 12,188, 45 Fed. Reg. 989 (1980).

[410] *Id.*

[411] *Id.* (citing 134 Cong. Rec. 8881 (1988) (statement of Sen. Exon)).

[412] 50 U.S.C. app. s. 2170(a) (1988).

[413] *Id.*, s. 2170(d).

[414] *Id.*, s. 2170(c).

[415] Regulations Pertaining to Mergers, Acquisitions, and Takeovers by Foreign Persons, (31 C.F.R. pt. 800).

[416] Confidential business information is protected from disclosure under the Freedom of Information Act. The information which must be furnished includes the following:

1) the transaction at issue;
2) the assets of the US entity being acquired;

conduct a formal investigation, then the matter is concluded. However, if notice of the merger is never given to the Committee, then the President has the power to suspend, block or divest the merger at any future date. The only limitation placed upon the President's power in this respect, is that the President must review the merger under the facts as they existed at the time of the merger.[417]

Regarding the definitions of a US person, foreign person, and control under the provisions, the three most important terms in the regulations: a US person is defined as 'any natural person or entity but, in the case of the latter, only to the extent of its business activities in interstate commerce in the United States, irrespective of the nationality of the natural persons or entities which control it'.[418] In other words, pursuant to this definition, a US-based subsidiary of a foreign corporation, i.e. a corporation organised under the laws of a foreign state and wholly owned and controlled by a foreign national, is a US person. On the other hand, a foreign subsidiary of a US corporation is not a US person, even if it exports goods to its parents and unaffiliated US companies.[419] Here one might want to note the difference with the 1979 Export Administration Act whereby export controls applied to all foreign firms controlled by US firms[420] and which gave rise to quite a bit of international tension.[421]

A 'foreign person' is defined as any foreign national or any entity over which control is exercised or exercisable by a foreign interest.[422] Therefore, a foreign-based subsidiary owned and controlled by a US parent corporation is not a foreign person. However, a US subsidiary, owned and controlled by a foreign parent organised under the laws of a foreign state, is a 'foreign person'.

'Control' is defined broadly and it includes 'the power, direct or indirect, whether or not exercised . . . to determine, direct or decide matters affecting an

---

cont.

    3) the target entity's business activities, product lines, US facilities, identification numbers of government contracts (including those to which the entity was a party within the last five years that involved classified information), products and services supplied to the military services and the Defense Department, and any of its technologies that have military applications;

    4) the line of business of the foreign entity making the acquisition, including any parent and affiliate relationships; and

    5) any plans of the foreign entity regarding the acquired US company's R&D efforts, its corporate structure (e.g. the relocation, shut down, consolidation, or sale of product lines or technology that is defence-related or otherwise bears on national security), changes in its product quality and any modifications or terminations of its contracts.

[417] The regulations state that such future action shall only be for a purpose based on 'facts, conditions or circumstances existing at the time the transaction was concluded . . .'.

[418] Regulations Pertaining to Mergers, Acquisitions, and Takeovers by Foreign Persons, note 415 above, at C.F.R. s. 800.220.

[419] *Id.*

[420] The Export Administration Act of 1979, 50 U.S.C. app. ss. 2401–2420 (Supp. V 1981).

[421] See e.g. *Dresser Industries, Inc v Baldridge* No. 82–2385 (D.D.C. filed 23 Aug. 1982), *dismissed per stipulation,* 23 Dec. 1982.

[422] Regulations Pertaining to Mergers, Acquisitions, and Takeovers by Foreign Persons, note 415 above, at 31 C.F.R. s. 800.21(a)–(b).

entity'.[423] Examples of control listed in the regulations include: business decisions regarding the sale or transfer of the entity's principal assets, the dissolution of the entity, the closing or relocation of the entity's research and development and production facilities, the termination or non-fulfilment of business contracts, or the amendment of the entity's articles of incorporation.[424]

Concerning the action of the President, after the parties submit their information and their notice to the Committee, the Committee must decide within 30 days whether to open a formal investigation[425] and the length of the investigation can not exceed 45 days.[426] Thereafter, the President has 15 days in which to act.[427] It is important to note that the President's findings are not reviewable.[428]

Lastly, essentially almost every type of transaction is covered. Included are tender offers, joint ventures, asset acquisitions, and basically all transactions which could result in foreign control.

The two observations I wish to make and which I hope will spark an interesting discussion are as follows: First, the Amendment does not define 'national security' and the published Committee Regulations do not provide any guidance on how the term is to be interpreted.[429] The Committee was of the opinion that because there was no attempt to define 'national security', or at least none could be found within the legislative history of the Amendment, Congress intended that the President's power be unencumbered. For example, Congress failed to highlight any particular industry or particular products which may implicate national security concerns.[430] However, regardless of Congress' motives, the Amendment's failure to define 'national security' speaks to its elusive nature and it is for this very same reason that the President's findings are not reviewable. Under American jurisprudence, the question of 'national security' is a political one and non-justiciable.

The difficulty in defining 'national security' is compounded by the fact that we are moving away from an era of direct military aggression and toward one of economic statecraft. Thus, national security concerns are becoming increasingly

---

[423] *Id.*, at s. 800.204(a).
[424] *Id.*, at 31 C.F.R. s. 800.204(a).
[425] *Id.*, at 31 C.F.R. s. 800.402(h).
[426] *Id.*, at 31 C.F.R. s. 800.504.
[427] *Id.*, at 31 C.F.R. s. 800.601(a).
[428] *Id.*, at 31 C.F.R. s. 800.601(b)(2).
[429] See Holmer, Bello, Preiss, note 407 above, at 608 (citing one Committee report):

'that came close to offering "some guidance by identifying business sectors, according to Standard Industry Classification (SIC) codes, which could be considered outside the scope of national security". However, the agencies could not reach a consensus as to where the lines should be drawn, so no guidelines were drafted.'

(quoting Joseph F. Dennin & Mark Shonkwiler, 'CFIUS and the Proposed Exon-Florio Regulations, 1 Foreign Investment in the U.S.': *News & Analysis*, (BNA) No. 3, at 4–7 (Aug. 1989)).
[430] *Id.*

predicated upon economic claims and in the context of the Exon-Florio Amendment this is evidenced by proposed legislation seeking to broaden the Exon-Florio inquiry to expressly encompass 'economic security'.[431]

Andreas F. Lowenfeld:

Proposed?

Edward R. Sherman:

Yes, proposed. But what difference does it make whether the supplemental legislation is proposed or not if 'national security' is not defined and the President's findings are not reviewable. In other words, nothing prevents US foreign policy, which is to a large degree shaped by economic considerations, from falling under the general rubric of 'national security' for the purposes of the Exon-Florio Amendment regardless of whether the scope of inquiry is expressly broadened or not.

Sir Ian Sinclair:

Were protests made by foreign governments, not necessarily against the definition or non-definition of national security, but against the actual definition of 'persons'?

Michael D.C. Johnson:

Yes. The Community protested repeatedly against the certainly detailed rules made under the Exon-Florio Amendment because I had the pleasure of presiding during the UK presidency over a number of discussions in the Article 103 Committee when those protests were being agreed on.

Sir Ian Sinclair:

I would have been very surprised if there had not been any!

Edward R. Sherman:

In any event, regarding the lack of a definition for 'national security', if industrial policy and national security become inextricably linked, if delimitation in a meaningful sense is not possible in this age of economic warfare, then compliance with pre-existing trade obligations and the creation of new ones will

---

[431] See Holmer, Bello, Preiss, note 407 above, at 615 (citing H.R. 5225, 101st Cong., 2nd Sess. s. 3 (1990)) (Congressman Doug Walgren introduced a bill that would broaden the scope of the Exon-Florio Amendment to include: 'the control of domestic industries and commercial activities by foreign citizens as it affects the industrial and technological base of the United States').

constitute nothing more than a foreign policy decision.[432] Economic considerations will replace political ones and the principles of MFN and national treatment will be rendered illusory.[433] In this respect, it should be further noted that similar language which permits contracting parties to circumvent their treaty obligations based on national security grounds, exists in GATT. Article XXI states that '[n]othing in this Agreement shall be construed to prevent any contracting party from taking any action which it considers necessary for the protection of its essential security interests'. Moreover, similarly to the Exon-Florio Amendment, it is questionable whether under GATT a claim of national security can ever be examined. Article XXI(a) states that a party may not disclose information which may be contrary to its security interests. Thus, there are two problems: defining 'national security' and reviewing the merits of the claim.

Sir Ian Sinclair:

Well, it is not only those two problems, but it is also another problem and that is the actual reach of the regulation in terms of the persons to whom it may be applied.

Edward R. Sherman:

That is the second point I would like to address. Although it is doubtful that the regulations will produce the problems associated with the *Pipeline* cases, because a foreign subsidiary of a US corporation is not regarded as a US person under the Amendment, unlike in the Export Administration Act 1979, nevertheless there are two concerns. First, where two foreign companies seek a merger and one company has a US subsidiary involved in the national security field their deal may have to be reworked. The assertion has been made that this produces a '*de facto* protectionism' for US firms.[434] Secondly, extraterritorial problems exist if one simply changes the definition of 'territoriality' which perhaps needs to be

---

[432] See e.g. Riddell, 'The foreign takeover exception that "proves the rule"', *World Trade News*, 6 Feb. 1990 p. 7 col. 3. (In defending its decision ordering China National Aero-Technology Import Export Company (CATIC) to dispose within three months of Mamco, an aircraft parts manufacturer in Seattle which it bought two months ago, the Bush Administration insisted that the decision unanimously recommended by the Committee had 'nothing to do with US foreign policy towards China and is strictly based on enforcing the law on national security grounds'.)

[433] It was noted by the corporate secretary for International Investment in response to the Bush Administration's decision in the *CATCO* case that '[w]e hope this will not set a precedent for reviewing foreign investment on political grounds. That would seriously erode the US commitment to the principle of national treatment'. *Id.*

[434] See Dennin & Shonkwiler, note 429 above, at 6 ('De facto protectionism' would occur when 'a French company wishing to acquire a German company that has a U.S. subsidiary potentially involved in the national security field faces the possibility of losing the sub-element of its acquisition or being forced to make certain concessions [and meanwhile] a U.S. company competing for the right to acquire the German company and its U.S. subsidiary faces no such risk and therefore can afford to pay a higher price than that offered by the French firm'.).

done in light of existing treaties such as the GATT and the notion of economic free trade which . . .

Andreas F. Lowenfeld:

But think how it has been used. It was used to cancel an acquisition by a company established by the Peoples Republic of China to make some kind of ball bearings used in some high technology aircraft. It is possible that it is abused. We have not used it for soybean mills or anything like that. Some congressmen claim that far from the regulations being too restrictive they are too lax and that the government, at least the Bush Administration, really did not believe in this.

Philip Bovey:

But how many French firms were dissuaded from buying soybean mills? You have no idea.

Edward R. Sherman:

Exactly. Because 'national security' is not defined, you simply do not know what industries, what deals will be subject to Committee review. Furthermore, although you are right, there has been only one divesture under the Amendment, the *CATCO* case, there have been a number of deals that had to be reworked for fear that otherwise they would be viewed as an impairment to 'national security' and subject to the strictures under the Amendment. For instance, in 1989, ASEA Brown Boveri Ltd (ABB), a Swiss-Swedish engineering company, proposed the creation of a joint venture with Westinghouse. After the Committee undertook an investigation, apparently members were concerned that the joint venture would have adverse consequences for the US electrical equipment market, ABB announced that it would maintain production and R&D facilities in the US.[435] Does this constitute a trade-related investment measure in violation of future GATT provisions . . .

Andreas F. Lowenfeld:

Strict security control and to make sure the technology does not get transferred, those were Japanese companies and the Japanese are somehow not as great a threat as the Chinese in Washington's view. In other words, this is one more game.

---

[435] Holmer, Bello, Preiss, note 407 above, at 611 (citing 'Bush Won't Block Swiss Electrical Deal After CFIUS Exon-Florio Investigation', 6 *Intl Trade Rep.* (BNA) No. 26, at 664 (24 May 1989)).

Michael D.C. Johnson:

Can I comment, Chairman? Perhaps a slightly broader point concerns the national security let-out under the GATT, because Mr Sherman referred to it. Article XXI is perhaps the least defined and in some ways the most abused article of GATT because the definition, as was rightly said, is a self-definition. It is up to countries to decide what their own national security interests are and the US certainly has invoked art. XXI in a number of trade cases. I think one of the most recent ones concerns fuel tanks for aircraft containing a certain type of synthetic fabric (I forget the details) as inimical to US interests and therefore the materials are kept out or restricted. There is at least implied or potential invocation of art. XXI of GATT as the excuse. In fact, there is no jurisprudence on that article. There was a panel case in GATT some years ago under which Nicaragua brought a case against the US on the trade embargo of Nicaragua. The Panel found that indeed Nicaragua had been severely damaged economically by the embargo but it then also cut away any basis for its own argumentation for the report by saying that its terms of reference gave it no *locus* to discuss the political correctness or inwardness of the embargo in the first place. The report was never adopted so effectively there is no jurisprudence.

Pieter J. Kuijper:

I would just like merely to recall to Michael that when the Commission made proposals to engage cases before the GATT about this and tried to get some good faith definition or even good faith self-definition of what national security was, our member states were less than anxious.

Adelheid Puttler:

If I understood Mr Sherman correctly, a foreign subsidiary of a US company is considered a foreign person in this respect whereas in export control law, for example, it is considered as a US person. It seems that the US bestows its nationality differently with respect to the different kind of jurisdiction.

Andreas F. Lowenfeld:

No! It is like father and son. They are related.

Adelheid Puttler:

Yes, but sometimes the father forgets his son and sometimes he remembers him.

Harold G. Maier:

But the law does that constantly. We use the same label for different things and you have to look at the purpose for which the label is used in order to understand what you are doing with it. All this says is that if the label reflects one kind of policy decision, you treat it as having one meaning and for purposes of another kind of policy decision you treat it as having another meaning. There is nothing wrong with that approach just because the same word is used to describe different policy results.

Adelheid Puttler:

On the other hand nationality is a concept that is used in public international law.

Philip Bovey:

It is simply a definitional issue as Hal said.

Sir Ian Sinclair:

Could I just try and restore order?

Rutsel S.J. Martha:

I wonder if the approach would be different if the test is not national security but simply protecting a domestic corporation from a hostile takeover. I pose this question because in 1991 the Netherlands Antilles enacted legislation to make void acquisition of shares in domestic corporations, to the extent that these shares are traded on foreign securities stock exchanges and to the extent that these acquisitions do not observe the rules of this particular legislation in the Netherlands Antilles. The way this is enforced is that if the shares are acquired over a certain percentage and they are not reported to the board of the corporation, then the rights attached to those shares, including voting rights will not be recognised by the board during the shareholders meetings and also proxies given by those holding such shares will not be recognised either. So what you see is, in effect, the Netherlands Antilles effectively controls the situation that happens extraterritorially by denying the legal effects within its corporation law. I wonder whether the effect of that legislation should influence our approach and judgment.

Sir Ian Sinclair:

But is not that a topic we will address tomorrow morning?

Rutsel S.J. Martha:

The point is that I think the same thing can be done in the case of national security because the same is an acquisition of shares in a US corporation and that is what the US President endeavours to stop with an extraterritorial measure.

Andreas F. Lowenfeld:

The Canadians, of course, did that in the Foreign Investment Review Act which they then repealed. In the US, it has been proposed, but the US says we accept foreign investment generally and we try to keep everybody on national MFN treatment and of course there are some narrow exceptions. It is true that the exception is not directly defined but it tends to be confined to high technology dual-use weapons, those kinds of areas. But I think that we should not draw a general principle of international law from the Exon-Florio Amendment.

Cynthia C. Lichtenstein:

Once again though, are we not somewhat off topic in that all of this is questioning domestic legislation affecting domestic persons and having an undue effect on incoming capital, but it does not involve the attempt of the home jurisdiction to have its law operate outside of the territory. This is once again like the Tuna Reports, the actor coming in to the jurisdiction and having to respond to the jurisdiction's law in order to enter? It may be a violation of MFN but it is not a question of extraterritoriality.

Karl M. Meessen:

If I may venture to answer your question. It very much depends on what approach we are going to take, Cynthia. If we did it the traditional way and after finding a territorial or personal basis for jurisdiction stopped thinking, well then it would be the end of the matter, but if we followed, I think, that very pertinent question raised by Andy Lowenfeld, i.e. to look for where conflicts are caused, I then think that we might find it premature to stop thinking.

Andreas Weitbrecht:

Just assume the US likes that merger.

Karl M. Meessen:

Yes for employment reasons. So, therefore, I do not think we should prematurely define too narrowly our scope of investigation. It is a borderline issue and I think the way you raised the question was very precise and very much to the point but I hesitate to remove it from the agenda *a priori*.

Edward R. Sherman:

I agree. If one argues, and I think correctly so, that the significance of the territoriality presumption has been undermined or eroded by technological, economic and political changes[436] then that means both that extraterritorial regulation does not always necessitate a violation of international law and that

---

[436] See Born, 'A Reappraisal of the Extraterritorial Reach of the U.S. Law', 24 *Law and Policy in Intl Bus.*, No. 1, 1 (arguing that the territoriality presumption no longer reflects principles of public international law).

restricting a regulation to a state's territorial boundaries does not absolutely protect it from reproach. The US, for example, cannot have it both ways. It cannot claim that because of today's global economy and high degree of market interdependence, to effectuate the purpose of a given law, i.e. its antitrust laws, it is required to extend the reach of that law beyond its borders and thereafter assert that regulations limited to its borders are *a priori* outside the purview of international law. In asserting the former, the US subjects its laws, which are not extraterritorial in scope but which affect legitimate foreign interests, to review under international law. This is not to say that territoriality is not a factor, only that it is not dispositive of the issue. Thus, even in cases which do not involve extraterritoriality, we should ask whether the law interferes with the legitimate expectation of foreign interest. In the case of the Exon-Florio Amendment, the expectations cover a foreign interest in capital investment in the US. Whether those interests are legitimate, in light of various treaties, the US commitment to trade and capital liberalisation and especially GATT, is in my opinion questionable. Nevertheless, I agree with Professor Meessen that we must look to where conflict is and not limit our inquiry solely to acts of extraterritoriality.

Harold G. Maier:

But the other side of that is important too. Any proposal would become ineffective if it tried to take on too much. In fact, the definition of the territoriality issue that seems to be floating around could get us involved in designing principles for all international transactions. I do not think we want to do that – at least not now! I understand your point, Karl. I just wanted to make sure that the *caveat* on the other side is important too. I was more or less convinced by what Cynthia had said. Let's make sure we separate it out.

Sir Ian Sinclair:

Well, thank you all very much for your contributions to a lively discussion this afternoon. I will now bring it to an end and we will resume at 9 o'clock tomorrow morning. We will then take up the issue of extraterritorial rules in securities and then we will go on to discuss drafting rules of extraterritorial jurisdiction, a possible contour of something we might propose to the International Law Association. We do not propose to actually draft a resolution of this kind but I think it will be useful to have a discussion of what such a resolution would entail. I thank you all very much for your contributions. It has been a long day and I wish you all a nice night.

Chapter X

Extraterritorial Rules on Banking and Securities

Ulrich Bosch

Sir Ian Sinclair:

I think at this point we could perhaps begin. This morning is a kind of holdover from yesterday's programme. We have the topic of extraterritorial rules on banking and securities. We are privileged at this stage to call upon Ulrich Bosch from Deutsche Bank in Frankfurt am Main to talk about this. It is obvious from the position that he holds that he has a great deal of experience in the practical problems that arise in this field and no doubt his contribution will be heard.

Ulrich Bosch:

Thank you, Sir Ian. My introductory statement cannot constitute a comprehensive overview. It is no more than a selection of topics. I have chosen some which I have actually come across, either occasionally or quite regularly, and which appear to have particular relevance in practice.

Extraterritorial discovery orders against banks in civil or criminal litigation will be outside the scope of my presentation because many of the legal issues that arise in such a context are not peculiar to banks. The special aspects that do arise are that the bank becomes mostly involved not as a party, but in a witness-like function, and that it has a duty of confidentiality, which can conflict with the discovery order. Elaborating on this could be a subject on its own.

For another reason, I should like not to cover banking regulations in the sense of supervision regarding capital adequacy, responsible management and business practices. In this respect, some well defined extraterritoriality is the rule and the desired goal. It is universally expected and agreed nowadays that a bank and its group should be globally supervised by its home regulator. Any inefficiency in this regard is considered a failure, as the BCCI disaster has shown. All this means that the supervision of a regulated industry involves peculiar and unique aspects. In the banking area, these have been addressed in the form of common principles developed, particularly, by the Basle committee of banking regulators formed at the Bank for International Settlements.

The subjects which I wish to cover are:

(1) attachments of, or injunctions relating to, foreign deposits;
(2) attachments or injunctions regarding other assets maintained abroad;
(3) money laundering legislation;
(4) information requirements regarding substantial shareholdings in publicly traded companies;
(5) securities and tax law provisions restricting public offerings of securities; and
(6) other securities law requirements, including 'trading rules' relating to market manipulation and stabilisation.

1. Attachments/Injunctions Regarding Foreign Deposits

As this subject has already been discussed in this symposion, I can limit myself to a few observations, primarily from a German law perspective: first, where a person pursues a money claim, the injunction is not available under German procedural law, neither against the defendant nor against third parties who hold assets of, or owe something to, the defendant. Instead, the attachment of assets of the defendant is the appropriate remedy.

Secondly, an attachment order regarding a deposit maintained with a foreign office of a foreign bank (whether or not that bank has an office in Germany) can theoretically be issued by a German court. The court's jurisdiction depends on whether the depositor is subject to its jurisdiction, e.g. as a German resident (s. 828 para. 2 Code of Civil Procedure – 'ZPO'). However, the order takes effect only if it is properly served on the bank abroad (s. 829 para. 3 ZPO). For this purpose, the German court must request the competent foreign authority, through the appropriate channels, to effect the service abroad. The German judicial authorities normally do not even pass on a relevant request, as they would not themselves, for reasons of judicial sovereignty, grant reciprocity. Even if the request is passed on, it would have little chance of success. It would generally be turned down because the German court order would not be capable of being recognised in the foreign country: There are rules of international and domestic law on the recognition of foreign judgments, but normally no equivalent rules regarding foreign attachment orders. In summary, the foreign authority would generally not effect the service.

Karl M. Meessen:

The US would.

Ulrich Bosch:

I am not sure, but what I describe is the general rule: in most cases one would have to expect that service would not be effected.

Andreas F. Lowenfeld:

Even under the Hague Service Convention?

Ulrich Bosch:

The Hague Service Convention is concerned with the service of a complaint for the purpose of beginning a legal action, but not with execution proceedings.

Thirdly, even with regard to an attachment by a German court of a deposit maintained with a foreign branch of a German bank, served on the bank's domestic head office, it has been argued in legal texts that the attachment order would be invalid due to a lack of jurisdiction, because it would result in the exercise of compulsory power in a foreign territory.[437] That theory has not yet, however, been affirmed by the German courts.

Fourthly, assuming that a German court, disagreeing with that theory, does attach such a foreign deposit, and subsequently purports to transfer it to the creditor, the creditor may still have a long way to go before having his claim satisfied. When claiming payment from the bank, he will generally find out that the deposit is subject to the law and jurisdiction of the branch country and that the courts of that country do not recognise German attachment and execution orders. And that can be the end of the story, particularly if the jurisdiction of the branch country is exclusive.

Finally, whenever a German court or, for that matter, any court not located in the branch country, orders the bank to repay the deposit to a person other than the depositor (e.g. to a plaintiff having attached the deposit), this would effectively amount to requiring the bank to repay the deposit twice: as the order would not be recognised in the branch country, the bank would continue to be liable, unconditionally, to its depositor. This unfair result should, I believe, be recognised by the German courts as a valid defence in its own right against the effectiveness of such an attachment.

Based on this last consideration, the following should, in my view, be generally accepted as a jurisdictional principle. A court should not claim, or not exercise, jurisdiction to attach a foreign deposit (as described above) unless it has

---

[437] See Mülhausen, 'Zwangsvollstreckungsmaßnahmen deutscher Gerichte in Bankguthaben von Inländern bei Auslandsfilialen', *Wertpapier-Mitteilungen* 1986 p. 957 *et seq.*, 985 *et seq.*, 989.

ascertained that its attachment order would be recognised in the country where the bank is located and under the law to which the deposit is subject; such recognition cannot normally be expected. Failing such jurisdictional restraint, the bank would be exposed to the risk of effectively repaying the deposit twice. An order creating the risk of such an unjustifiable result should be regarded as an improper extraterritorial exercise of jurisdiction.

2. Attachments/Injunctions Regarding Other Assets Held Abroad

Occasionally, restraining orders or injunctions are issued with regard to assets other than deposits, such as cheques, securities, etc. held with bank offices in a country outside the court's jurisdiction. Generally, my comments on the necessity of jurisdictional self-restraint in connection with foreign deposits apply also to these situations.

The following is an example of such a situation. It is a true story about a German bank that became a party to divorce proceedings in the US. Were I not obliged to omit a few confidential details, the story would appear still more lively. A customer, the defendant (as it turned out later) in divorce proceedings pending before a US court, had deposited two US bank cheques (drawn by and on a US bank) with a German branch of a German bank for collection. The cheques had been issued to him as custodian for his children. While the cheques were still in the possession of the German bank, the US court issued two orders, which were served on the German bank's New York branch, to the effect that:

(1) the German bank might be named as a party to the proceedings;
(2) it may not release to the customer any funds received by way of the checks, and the customer may not dispose of those funds;
(3) the checks were to be returned to the issuing bank in the US, and the customer and his wife were directed to sign an authorisation to the German bank to do so.

(The background was unknown to the German bank. Conceivably, the wife suspected that the funds might be misappropriated.)

The authorisation was initially difficult to obtain from the customer. What should the German bank do to dispose of the unwanted cheques? Return them? That might make it liable in Germany because it would be disregarding its customer's instructions; the US court order as such had no effect within Germany. Keep the cheques? This might be regarded as contempt of court, although the bank could have argued that it had not been instructed to return the cheques without the customer's consent. Deposit the cheques with the appropriate German 'Amtsgericht' because of uncertainty as to who was entitled to them? That could make the contempt risk worse. The bank decided that to keep the cheques (or in other words do nothing) was the least risky alternative, but it could be anticipated that this was no more than an interim solution, which could not ultimately satisfy the US court.

A simple idea finally helped: the German bank explained to the customer that it would be compelled to communicate the full story to the US court, and that a persistent refusal could make him liable to contempt sanctions. As the customer was a US resident, that convinced him. The consent was given, and a jurisdictional conflict thus avoided. However, the situation had appeared critical at some points and could have become unresolvable in view of the conflicting demands of US and German law. In my view, the US court order issued in this case should be considered an improper exercise of jurisdiction. The appropriate remedy would have been an attachment of the cheques, and the funds received, in Germany upon demand of the customer's wife.

3.   Money Laundering Legislation

Money laundering laws, including the pertinent German statute which just passed Parliament, impose certain compliance obligations on banks. If these obligations, particularly reporting requirements, are extended to foreign branches and subsidiaries, this can result in a jurisdictional conflict. The rules imposed on the bank may be inconsistent with, or even contrary to, requirements of local law, including local money laundering statutes and bank secrecy in the country of the branch or subsidiary.

My proposal as to a jurisdictional rule in this context is as follows. An obligation imposed on domestic banks by their home state to ensure that foreign branches and subsidiaries identify customers and keep records in certain circumstances (e.g. as in the recently enacted German Money Laundering Act, cash payments exceeding DM20,000) should prove acceptable as a principle.

Andreas F. Lowenfeld:

But if I come to you and I say: Do you have an account for Mr Schultz, will you tell me?

Ulrich Bosch:

No. What the statute requires is that the bank makes sure it knows the customer, and there must be records about him. That may be burdensome, if the rules are different in the two countries concerned, but we think that is manageable. Information about the records will be available to prosecuting authorities, but not to private individuals.

Coming back now to the proposed jurisdictional rule, a requirement to report doubtful transactions to criminal prosecution authorities can only be imposed and enforced by local statute and local authorities in the country in which the relevant branch or subsidiary is located; a reporting requirement imposed by the home state of the bank on its foreign branches or subsidiaries would not be practicable. Reporting to 'home state' authorities would usually not be allowed by the local law applicable to the branch or subsidiary, and an obligation to report to local authorities can be meaningless if there is no such authority designated by local law for that purpose. For example, what would be the appropriate authority in a country that is a major narcotic drug producer?

Andreas F. Lowenfeld:

What are you doing there anyway?

Ulrich Bosch:

My example is a hypothetical one. In summary and more generally, I suggest that whenever compliance is factually or legally impossible, a state should refrain from extraterritorially exercising (or attempting to exercise) jurisdiction to prescribe.

4. Information Regarding Substantial Shareholdings

Banks in all jurisdictions can face foreign information requirements regarding substantial shareholdings in publicly traded companies, under corporation and/or securities laws. As custodians of securities, they can be requested by foreign securities authorities or foreign corporations to report on securities held by them for the account of customers, including in some instances on the customers' names. This can conflict with domestic law, particularly bank secrecy principles.

Examples for this type of disclosure statute are s. 212 of the UK Companies Act 1985 and s. 261 of the Australian Companies Act 1981 and Codes. Banks, in Germany and elsewhere, receive disclosure requests from companies in those countries from time to time, but also from, for example, France, the US, Sweden and Norway. I believe that banks in Germany have generally been able to satisfy such requests by giving information in generalised form (total number of customers holding the relevant class of shares, highest single holding, etc.). Requests to disclose names, when originally made, were withdrawn or not pursued after the legal impediments were explained. There may, however, be situations where one or more customer names are essential, and where the company, or a foreign authority conducting an investigation, may not yield.

For such situations, let me suggest the following guidelines. Information requests of this type should be made and enforced by the courts only to the extent necessary or legitimate in order to reach the goal prescribed or permitted by law, e.g. to determine substantial shareholdings, and taking into account bank and other professional secrecy principles in other jurisdictions. Where the disclosure of account details, including customer names, is necessary or legitimate for such purposes the bank should, in its home jurisdiction, be considered to be authorised to make such disclosures. The basis for this is that the customer, by buying foreign shares, should be regarded as having implicitly accepted becoming subject to applicable foreign corporate and/or securities law rules.

Andreas F. Lowenfeld:

We used to call that waiver by conduct.

Ulrich Bosch:

We come close to that concept, at least. The first question is: does a person who acquires shares in a company become subject to the rules of the applicable company law, including pertinent disclosure rules? I think that the answer would be yes in almost every country of the world. The problem with the waiver-by-conduct approach was that even the intermediary who, as a matter of routine, passed on an order to, say, a US broker, should be deemed to have waived, by conduct, its domestic secrecy requirements, which it cannot do because it has no power to dispose of these rules of law.

Andreas F. Lowenfeld:

Well then how does your proposal work with respect to intermediaries?

Ulrich Bosch:

What I am suggesting is a proposed, not an already established, jurisdictional principle: the 'waiver-by-conduct' theory is by no means a generally recognised rule of law. However, at least in certain cases, the courts in the bank's home jurisdiction could solve a conflict on that basis.

5. Restrictions on Public Offerings of Securities

I wish to make a few comments on some securities and tax laws and regulations restricting offerings of securities

- (1) in the US and Germany; and
- (2) to US nationals residing outside the US.

I mean s. 5 of, and Reg. S under, the US Securities Act 1933 and Treasury Regulations ss. 1.163–5(c)(2)(i)(D) (the 'D Rules') under the US Tax Equity and Fiscal Responsibility Act (TEFRA) 1984 on the one hand and the relevant aspects of the German Offering Prospectus Act 1990 on the other.

The securities law aspect is this: most countries having developed capital markets prohibit, with certain exceptions, the public offering of securities unless a prospectus in a format prescribed by their national law is published. The motivation is investor protection.

The tax law aspect is entirely different and peculiar to the US: US tax law has imposed a sort of ban on debt securities in bearer form (bearer bonds) because these are viewed as instruments favouring anonymity and, allegedly, tax fraud. As the US tax authorities are concerned with potential effects on US taxpayers, and these include US nationals residing abroad, the restrictions on sales of bearer bonds under TEFRA, as implemented by, in particular, the D Rules, relate to sales both into the US and to US nationals abroad.

In relation to securities laws, too, the following question arises, does the prohibition apply extraterritorially, and if so, under which circumstances? Most pertinent statutes fail to address the issue expressly, and that is true also with regard to the US Securities Act 1933 and the German Offering Prospectus Act 1990.

Let me address the latter first. Following traditional rules of interpretation, I am of the opinion that the Act applies within the German territory, that is, broadly, in the case of sales to German residents. It should not apply to offers made abroad, neither because non-resident Germans could be the buyers nor because any securities sold abroad could later find their way to Germany. If the latter were the case, then the person actually offering the securities across the border into Germany would potentially violate German law, but not the persons further up in the chain of offers and sales, including the issuer of the securities. That analysis can be different, I believe, only where an offer abroad is made with the intention, knowledge or expectation that the paper would be sold on into Germany.

The US approach has been somewhat different: in the so-called Foreign Offerings Release (SEC Release No. 33–4708, also referred to as 'Release 4708') in 1964, and later, in the *Singer* ruling (1974) and further rulings, it was conceded by the Securities and Exchange Commission (SEC) that the Securities Act 1933 was 'primarily intended to protect American investors'. These were meant to include US residents, and also US nationals residing abroad. The formula developed by the SEC was that a foreign offering of debt securities can be made by a US company if 'the offering is made under circumstances reasonably designed to preclude distribution or redistribution of the securities within, or to nationals of, the United States', or in circumstances that would result in the securities 'coming to rest' with foreign investors abroad. Participants in a foreign offering were expected to actively take measures to prevent sales into the US and to US nationals outside the US, including a whole series of contractual restrictions, confirmations, warnings and delivery restrictions. As against that former practice, Regulation S, issued in 1990, took what the SEC called a territorial approach. The restrictions regarding offers to US nationals outside the US were eliminated. For the rest, the regime was slightly liberalised, but the principle remains that where US investors may have an interest in buying the securities, the participants in the foreign offering must do their best to frustrate that demand.

Sir Ian Sinclair:

How do you do that?

Ulrich Bosch:

As I said, there is this whole scheme of contractual restrictions which you have to comply with and the purpose of which is actually to prevent sales to US investors.

I do not think that the desire of a state to protect its nationals abroad (based on some kind of passive nationality principle) or to prevent them from avoiding taxes should permit that state to prescribe specific actions (or their omission) by foreign persons (issuers or underwriters) engaged in an offer of securities abroad without a territorial link to that state. The 'passive nationality principle' has been developed in relation to crimes like terrorism, and treating offers of securities similarly under jurisdictional aspects would be, to say the least, surprising and, I believe, excessive. Likewise, there is no internationally recognised jurisdictional principle permitting a state to regulate conduct (like the sale of bearer bonds) by foreigners abroad in order to compel compliance by its nationals with its tax laws.

Finally, and more importantly, the hypothetical possibility that securities offered abroad might later on end up in the hands of investors of a particular state does not, in my opinion, provide a sufficient basis for that state to exercise jurisdiction over the participants in the foreign offering. The actual sale of securities into the territory of that state, even if made from abroad, constitutes an effect in that state which provides a jurisdictional basis, but the mere possibility of such a sale should not be regarded as such a basis. There is no 'potential effects doctrine' in international law, and there should not be one in the area of national securities laws. Otherwise, the consequence would be that dozens of foreign regulatory regimes would have to be taken into account in any securities offering, so that such offerings would no longer be reasonably practicable.

6.   Other Securities Law Requirements

Extraterritoriality issues arise with respect to a number of other aspects of securities laws and regulations. I shall deal with three of them.

A.   *Accounting Requirements*

One could raise the question of whether the requirement by the SEC that foreign companies publish accounts, different from their home country accounts, pursuant to US accounting principles as a condition for a public offering or stock exchange listing in the US is an extraterritorial exercise of jurisdiction. It is true that such a requirement may appear unreasonably restrictive. It does not exist in other developed securities markets, and it reduces substantially the attractiveness of the US market. Accordingly, the number of non-US companies whose shares are listed on the New York Stock Exchange, for instance, namely 120, corresponds to only about a third and somewhat less than a quarter, respectively, of the number of foreign companies that have their shares listed on the stock exchanges in Frankfurt (356) and London (514). In addition, the non-US companies listed in New York are predominantly Canadian.[438]

However, this is a political and business judgment. Legally, I do not think that we are facing here an extraterritoriality issue. In my view, statutory or regulatory rules of a state requiring, as a condition for the public offering or the stock exchange listing of foreign securities in that state, that accounts are published according to, or adjusted to, standards prevailing in that state should not be regarded as an exercise of extraterritorial jurisdiction because they regulate conduct by the issuer or offeror of the securities in the relevant state.

B. Insider Trading

One may wonder whether the application of insider trading rules by a state to non-resident buyers or sellers of securities is an exercise of extraterritorial jurisdiction if the buy or sell order is executed within the territory of that state. One might argue that in such a case the state is essentially regulating conduct within its territory. In any event, whatever the conceptual approach may be, it is hardly contested that the exercise of jurisdiction by the state in question is legitimate and necessary in such circumstances.

The issue becomes more complex if the trade was executed outside the state claiming jurisdiction, the issuer is not a resident of that state and the only link to the relevant state is the fact that the securities bought or sold are tradeable on a regulated or unregulated market (e.g. officially listed or traded over the counter) in the said state.

Andreas F. Lowenfeld:

That's the market, you see. Daimler isn't going to go up in Frankfurt and down in New York on the same day.

Ulrich Bosch:

Indeed, the insider trading statutes of many states claim jurisdiction over those cases, and that is true also for the proposed German insider legislation.[439] This can result in a difficult jurisdictional problem if, for instance, the giving of the order does not constitute insider trading under the laws of the main trading market of the securities or the home country of either the issuer or the buyer or seller, but does violate the insider trading laws of another country (e.g. because

---

[438] See Loehr, 'Börsenzulassung in den USA für deutsche Unternehmen', *Wertpapier-Mitteilungen* 1994, p. 148.

[439] Section 12(1) No. 1 of the proposed Securities Trading Act (Wertpapierhandelsgesetz).

of different definitions of 'insider' or of 'unpublished price sensitive information'). I think that reasonable jurisdictional guidelines have yet to be developed for those cases. There seems to be no obvious answer.

C. *'Trading Rules' Regarding Market Manipulation and Stabilisation*

A peculiar phenomenon can often be observed in connection with international offerings of equity securities if the offer extends also to the US market. Whether or not the issuer of the securities is a US company, the underwriting and distribution agreements typically require that all financial institutions that participate in the offering comply with certain rules under the US securities laws. Quite frequently, the agreements simply state that the signatories, whether located and acting in or outside the US, must observe, in connection with the offering, all US securities laws and regulations. Those, however, comprise thousands of pages, and there cannot, accordingly, be any realistic expectation that foreign banks and financial institutions have a system in place according to which their trading, sales and syndicate staff are familiar with all those rules and comply with them.

Andreas F. Lowenfeld:

If you are an underwriter?

Ulrich Bosch:

Yes, in a public offering which also extends to the US.

The background of such contractual provisions is interpretations from SEC staff to the effect that US rules must be complied with worldwide if a significant portion of the securities is offered in the US. In addition, US lawyers are generally of the opinion that the regulatory restrictions must, or should, in addition to their applying by operation of law, also be made contractually binding. The type of all-encompassing contractual compliance undertakings referred to above reflects a dilemma: as those who draft the agreements feel unable to describe the extraterritorial impact of the US rules in the form of a few clear-cut guidelines, they resort to broad but unrealistic clauses.

Of some importance in this context are certain rules issued by the National Association of Securities Dealers (NASD), e.g. strictly observing the published offering price (which means selling neither below nor above that price) during a certain period (the so-called 'Papilsky rules'), and actually offering the securities purchased as underwriter, rather than keeping them for the underwriter's own portfolio (the 'free-riding and withholding rules'). Although the customs in other securities markets may be less restrictive, I am not aware of actual problems having arisen with respect to those rules.

This is not so with regard to the so-called 'Trading Rules', i.e. rules 10b-6, 10b-7 and 10b-8 under the US Securities and Exchange Act 1934. These considerably limit own-account trading (including market making), and stabilisation and risk management activities of financial institutions participating in an offering of securities. For example, financial institutions which, directly or through affiliates, usually trade and make a market in securities outside the US would be unable to purchase the securities during the period of their distribution and for a period of at least two business days prior to the commencement of the distribution. In a capital increase by way of a rights issue of a German company, this could mean in practice that all major German banks, which are normally members of the issuing syndicate, and thus all major market makers in the relevant securities, would be precluded from engaging in purchases of the securities during a period of up to 30 days. (The period could be that long because, among other things, the subscription period (Bezugsfrist) of at least two weeks would be regarded as part of the distribution period.)

Already in the past, global distributions of equity securities had been hampered by the Trading Rules. In the case of German companies, the risk of a collapse of the market due to the exclusion of its main participants for a considerable period of time would have been particularly relevant. This was explained to the SEC during the preparation of the Daimler Benz AG listing on the New York Stock Exchange, which took place on 5 October 1993. Shortly before that, significant problems had arisen in connection with the international distribution of shares of ZENECA, a UK company.

On 6 October 1993, the SEC formally decided on a far-reaching revision of its policy, which is considerably reducing the extraterritorial effect of the Trading Rules. It formulated an exemption which applies to equity securities of certain German companies that have a broad and active home market.

In summary,[440] the exemption provides as follows:

(1) the Trading Rules must be observed for trades which take place in the US;
(2) for trading in Germany, it is sufficient that it takes place in compliance with German law;
(3) if the price at which the securities are offered is less than 10 per cent below their market price, trades must be reported to the Frankfurt Stock Exchange, or to the lead German underwriter's independant accountant if the Frankfurt Stock Exchange is unavailable (it should be noted that in the case of a rights issue, the offering price is generally considerably more than 10 per cent below the market price);

---

[440] For details see Roquette/Stanger, 'Das Engagement ausländischer Gesellschaften am US-amerikanischen Kapitalmarkt – Rechtliche Erwägungen für deutsche Gesellschaften, erläutert am Beispiel Daimler-Benz', *WM* 137/142 *et seq.* (1994).

(4) trades in certain significant markets other than Germany and the US must comply with the Trading Rules, but subject to exemptions granted by the SEC with respect to those markets;

(5) prospectus materials must contain a brief description of the trading and related activities that are proposed to be undertaken.

In an attempt to analyse the extraterritoriality aspect of the said Trading Rules, I should like to make the following comments. On the one hand, the extraterritorial application of those rules has a territorial basis when seen in the light of the 'effects doctrine': trading, market-making and exercising an influence on the price of the securities has an effect on the US market for the relevant securities. In addition, the Trading Rules, by limiting trading activities, do not typically create the problem of conflicting commands, as there is normally no obligation to trade. Nevertheless, from a business perspective these Rules are often impractical and in conflict with the realities of foreign markets. Furthermore, if applied outside the US, their effect can be substantially more restrictive than in a US domestic offering (for which they were originally developed). Finally, it should be realised that multijurisdictional offers of securities would be impracticable if the US approach became the general rule, so that the laws and regulations of all countries in which the securities are offered would have to be observed worldwide.

Andreas F. Lowenfeld:

But are they inconsistent? Does one say go up, the other says go down or are they overlapping?

Ulrich Bosch:

They can be inconsistent. My conclusion, therefore, is as follows: in an international offering of securities made simultaneously in various states, the rules of any of those states limiting own-account trading, stabilisation and risk management activities of financial institutions participating in the offering should not apply outside the territory of that state. The problem arising from the fact that such activities outside that state can influence the price in that state should be addressed by means of appropriate disclosure; in particular, the prospectus prepared for such offering can contain a notice warning that such activities may occur, and a brief general description of such potential activities.

Sir Ian Sinclair:

Well, I am grateful for that very interesting and absolutely fascinating account of the practical problems that may arise in this area. I would like now to call upon Cynthia Lichtenstein to comment.

Cynthia C. Lichtenstein:

Thank you, Sir Ian. Before turning to commenting specifically on Dr Bosch's talk, and by the way, I largely agree with what Dr Bosch has said, I would like to make a few general observations on the last days' discussion and give my reflections on the discussion. Those general observations have to do with the balancing test and, specifically, the 'balancing test' in the Restatement. I would like to suggest that in thinking about the balancing test as required by the Restatement we worry about the focus of the balancing test. The Restatement by and large speaks of taking the interests of two states, the states whose law conflicts, into account. The Restatement does say in s. 403(2)(c) that the judge shall consider, and the language was quoted in the *Hartford* case, the extent to which other states regulate such activity and the degree to which the desirability of such regulation is generally accepted. But when the factors come down to being listed in *Mannington Mills,* for instance, that issue of international practice is not even mentioned. There is nothing explicit in the Restatement. There is no explicit direction to a court to consider the interest in the subject matter of the international community. It is only focusing on the interests of the two states.

Andreas F. Lowenfeld:

That is not true. That is unfair. Look at s. 403(e). It says exactly what you say it does not say. Do you have it there?

Cynthia C. Lichtenstein:

No.

Andreas F. Lowenfeld:

It mentions the importance of the regulation to the international, political, legal and economic systems. That is exactly what is says. How can you say that it does not say that?

Sir Ian Sinclair:

I would rather it said the importance of the regulation on one regulation.

Andreas F. Lowenfeld:

Well, that one can say.

Cynthia C. Lichtenstein:

When it comes down to talking about the test as it appears in *Mannington Mills, Mannington Mills* does not say this. It may be the Restatement does say it, but I am suggesting, however, that in thinking about these problems, as we go through the criteria, we re-emphasise the interests of the international community in the form of regulation. A good example of this, although I do not think that it involves extraterritoriality, is the 'Tuna' case, the discussion of which came up yesterday, where you had a series of international rules coming out of GATT and balanced against that, you had unilateral regulation by the US under the Marine Mammals Act. I suggest to you that if, in fact, there was an international treaty addressed to drift net fishing and prohibiting drift net fishing, you would have had a completely different result.

Andreas F. Lowenfeld:

If it were whales instead of tuna, for instance.

Cynthia C. Lichtenstein:

Yes. Yes. But there is for the moment no clearly articulated international norm with respect to drift net fishing. There is no international agreement. There is no international consensus.

Sir Ian Sinclair:

If I could just interrupt for a minute, Cynthia. The same thing applies right across the board. For example, look at the whole area of US export control measures, where there is international agreement, as for example reflected in resolutions of the Security Council, as regards sanctions to be taken with respect to certain countries, each country then applies its own measure and you have a total ban but you have no real conflict of extraterritoriality.

Cynthia C. Lichtenstein:

Absolutely.

Andreas F. Lowenfeld:

It has to go beyond that because, for instance, the Rhodesia regulations, only the US and Britain enforced them and they did enforce them extraterritorially.

Cynthia C. Lichtenstein:

Perhaps we could debate this after I finish my presentation. In other words, I am stating a general thesis that in judging the appropriateness of an extraterritorial assertion of jurisdiction, the interests of the international community in the scheme of regulation ought to be taken into account. Specifically, to try to apply this to the areas of international bank deposits and securities law, I agree completely with what Dr Bosch has said about bank deposits and I would go further. I would say, with due respect, Campbell, . . .

Campbell McLachlan:

That is usually a preface to a disrespectful remark.

Cynthia C. Lichtenstein:

... I would suggest that in considering *ex parte* orders affecting bank deposits 'sited' in a foreign jurisdiction, in a branch, simply because there is personal jurisdiction over a head office or branch of a bank, to say that such orders only involve legal process, is, I think, disingenuous. International banks invariably get tangled up in the domestic legal process because the malefactors have to keep their ill-gotten gains somewhere. And where else than in a bank or a head office in a jurisdiction with secrecy laws and strong rules of confidentiality of customers' accounts. In these situations, there is bound to be a conflict between the *ex parte* orders and/or the disclosure or reporting requirements and the law of the country where the deposit is on the books of the banks. It is simply no answer to the problem to say that if banks want to avoid the problem, they should incorporate their branches, and then international law would curtail the excessive application of jurisdiction based on the nationality principle. That's just no answer, because local incorporation involves a host of other issues, including the necessity of endowing the separately incorporated bank with adequate capital. I would suggest that the inquiry be made in these conflicts arising between the country having jurisdiction over the person and the bank and the country having jurisdiction over the *situs* of the deposit as to what resolution best serves the interests of the international community.

Andreas F. Lowenfeld:

So if the depositor is a drug lord it is one thing, and if he is just a refugee it is something else?

Cynthia C. Lichtenstein:

I am talking about seizure of deposits which could happen with a drug lord. I am not talking about the Restatement which is very clear that where a bank would have to pay twice, that goes to the argument against the exercise of jurisdiction. But what I'm suggesting is that the international community's large interest is in the health of multinational banks. We have an emerging international regime of internationally significant bank regulation. This is the only way I will talk about the Basle Accord. The whole point of the Basle regime is to protect the health and safety of internationally active banks and it is fundamentally grounded in the sense of importance to the global financial system of the stability of these sorts of banks.

Andreas F. Lowenfeld:

It is also the integrity of the bank. Think of BCCI.

Cynthia C. Lichtenstein:

That is another scheme, however. That involves the division of jurisdiction among regulators. The regulators have now taken care of that by themselves insisting on a mutually applied scheme of minimum standards of supervision. I am addressing now the emerging international regime for safety and soundness. There is a norm developing here, which is to say, our international payments system is effectuated through these international banks and the interlocking deposits, and in that you can find considerable 'interest' here of the international community. I think that this principle would have solved the problem for Standard and Chartered. There is a description in Collins' book, a book which was cited by Campbell McLachlan. I am referring to Dr Lawson Collins' Hague lectures on provisional and protective measures in international litigation. You will find in there a complete description of *Securities and Exchange Commission v Wang and Lee* which Professor Lowenfeld also includes in his wonderful teaching materials on international litigation. In this situation, the SEC wanted to ensure that it would have a fund in the US should it win in its accusations against Mr Lee, a Hong Kong resident, concerning insider trading. The details are highly complicated in terms of who was the moving party.

Andreas F. Lowenfeld:

But he had an informant in Morgan in New York so the accusation was quite credible.

Cynthia C. Lichtenstein:

... but the essential story is that the SEC got a New York court to order Standard and Chartered and the Court had personal jurisdiction over Standard and Chartered because of Standard and Chartered's branch in New York. The New York Court ordered Standard and Chartered to take Mr Lee's deposits in its branch in Hong Kong, denominated in Hong Kong dollars, convert them at its own loss into US dollars and put a fund back in New York. Standard and Chartered did so at considerable loss, protesting all the while that, under the law of Hong Kong, Mr Lee meantime was applying to the Hong Kong Court asking Standard and Chartered to give him back his deposits. The results would have been that Standard and Chartered would have had to pay twice except the Hong Kong Court was quite clever. The Hong Kong Court saw the difficulty and did not try to apply international law or anything else, but rather used a legal device. They said it is true, normally you have to repay a deposit booked under our law, however, there is a constructive trust here over these deposits in favour of the defrauded purchasers. Thus Standard and Chartered by transferring the deposit booked to New York had complied with Hong Kong laws.

Campbell McLachlan:

There might be!

Cynthia C. Lichtenstein:

So they refused to order the Hong Kong branch to give Mr Lee back his deposits. But I would suggest that in this situation, the New York court should have been advised that the interest of the international community was in not putting the bank in a situation where it would have to be saved by the grace of the Hong Kong court.

Ulrich Bosch:

May I suggest that we disregard, for a moment, aspects like drug dealing or insider trading in order to avoid the impression that we are always facing, in this context, a struggle between the good and the evil. Take the situation of a lawsuit between two private parties, instead. The plaintiff, a New York resident, enforces a judgment, obtained in New York, against the defendant, a Hong Kong resident, by obtaining an order from the court in New York requiring the defendant's bank in Hong Kong to pay to the plaintiff the amount of the judgment out of a deposit maintained by the defendant in Hong Kong. There would be no basis for a 'constructive trust' or the like that could serve as a defence to the Hong Kong bank when requested to repay the amount of the deposit (for a second time) in Hong Kong. The parties could be quite happy about that result. They would not have lost any money. The bank would have paid, and made a loss, instead.

Andreas F. Lowenfeld:

Take a deserted wife who seeks from her absconding husband the assets with her so she comes to Standard Bank and says, 'I want to win'. Let's say they were living together in New York, I think the New York court might do what Cynthia describes. At least a temporary injunction.

Cynthia C. Lichtenstein:

I suggest to you that given the international norm of the health of these actors, the multinational bonus, that is the wrong solution by the New York court.

As to applying this to securities law, there [i.e. New York], there's a great difficulty, I think, simply because in the area of securities law the international regulatory norms are only beginning to be worked out. We are starting to get some more general agreement on the shape of securities law. For example, Germany has now enacted a scheme that looks much more like the US scheme of regulation. There is a very strong reason to harmonise these rules, which is to cease impeding capital flows with different rules in 50 states. The difficulties that Dr Bosch has described are a drag on the international, global, financial markets. But the way in which we deal with these impediments to the full flow of international capital will come slowly, I think, with harmonisation through an organisation, for instance, called the International Organization of Securities Commissions (IOSCO). But the regime growing up in IOSCO is presently far less articulated. It is not working out as well in the securities field as it has in the banking field where the Basle Committee is beginning to articulate truly harmonised rules so that your national enactments really do resemble. Basle, in effect, is creating on the international level what the European Community creates for the member states. The central banks that had worked out the Basle regime do not label what they are achieving with the label 'international agreement', but they have reached such an agreement on certain basic prudential standards. In the securities field, however, it is much more difficult to say that we have an agreed upon international standard. Perhaps this could be said in the area of co-operation in enforcement, so that in the case of conflict between a state's bank secrecy laws and a securities regulator's request for information concerning suspected insider trading, the co-operation norm would probably outweigh the protection of secrecy if the judge will take this into account. I suspect. On your Reg. S suggestion that it is improper for the US to insist that foreign offerings come to rest abroad, I don't think we have developed any agreement as to the necessity for protection of investors. There, you say, the exercise of jurisdiction is based upon potential effect and not actual effect. But the SEC will continue to insist upon jurisdiction so long as these are US citizens in the markets. And the judge will not have an international norm to balance.

Andreas F. Lowenfeld:

The fraud case will go back to issuer case, I mean *Bersch* is the perfect example, when you look at the US nationals abroad like the servicemen, non-US nationals abroad and so on.

Cynthia C. Lichtenstein:

But the fraud case is being brought under rule 10b–5 under the 1934 Act. And you said, yourself, there's considerable agreement on anti-fraud. That is not a case of violation of the 1933 Act.

Andreas F. Lowenfeld:

I understand but if you have a fraudulent prospectus and it doesn't comply, you can get . . . you'll see.

Cynthia C. Lichtenstein:

But not under the 1933 Act rules. It's going to be under rule 10b–5 because the time period for rescission under the 1933 Act is so short that no one uses it, so the case will come up in the fraud context and not on the violation of . . .

Campbell McLachlan:

Cynthia is going much wider that genuine fraud. The others are misrepresentation.

Cynthia C. Lichtenstein:

But I did not hear Dr Bosch addressing the SEC's assertion of extraterritorial jurisdiction, or rather plaintiffs' assertions of extraterritorial jurisdiction under rule 10b–5. What we were discussing was the Offering Rules.

Pieter J. Kuijper:

... the Trading Rules that Mr Bosch was talking about?

Cynthia C. Lichtenstein:

I was addressing first his question of the disclosure. What we are going to find here, with respect to the Trading Rules, there are rules 10b–6, 10b–7 and 10b–8. And they are the rules that are aimed against the participants in a public offering during the commencement of the distribution manipulating the markets.

Sir Ian Sinclair:

Misrepresentation?

Cynthia C. Lichtenstein:

No!

Ulrich Bosch:

I think manipulating, in this context, means certain ways of influencing the market by being active in the market as a buyer or seller.

Cynthia C. Lichtenstein:

I think you have to distinguish these issues from the fraud issues because these are questions of the process by which public offerings reach the public market. It is an ideal area for harmonisation of the law. That is what I think the SEC is realising when it listens and gives the exemption. It is saying, yes, a qualified German security. The exemption was given by the SEC, I suspect, because the particular security was also fully subject to German regulation and it was so argued in applying for the exemption to allow a US distribution of a German security of Daimler Benz which meets the SEC requirements for particular forms.

Andreas F. Lowenfeld:

This is an exemption from the Trading Rules, but suppose that the prospectus had a misleading statement ... it is a partial exemption. It is not a decline of jurisdiction. It is a substantive exemption from a certain rule that is burdensome because it is overlapping.

Cynthia C. Lichtenstein:

Yes, and the exemption really was speaking to market participants. Those who were participating in the distribution. It was not speaking to the information requirements with respect to the issue. Okay?

Sir Ian Sinclair:

Well I am most grateful to you, Cynthia, for your contribution.

Campbell McLachlan:

If I may be permitted, Chairman. Can I just say that I agree totally with Cynthia's general thesis. In fact, it is one in which I believe passionately in terms of its application to private international law generally and I have written about this in other contexts, the idea that private international rules generally, including jurisdiction and choice of law rules, have an international context as well as being ... law. But what I find a bit difficult to accept is the notion that the international rule here is the health of the international banking system and that actually provides an answer as to when you should make orders or not. Because the health of the international banking system is only there to protect customers and depositors of banks. It is not there just for the sake of the banks. The aim, if there is a policy at all, is to protect customers. An the logical implication of what Cynthia has said would be to lead to the rule which never imposed on a local branch or head office of a bank any obligation to do anything *vis-à-vis* a deposit abroad. Now that may be the right rule but I am not sure it is so easy to say that that is the right rule simply because you want to preserve the health of the international banking system. After all, we are very often talking about what I might call unhealthy deposits. We are talking about cases often of abuse by depositors of the international banking system and where you may not have an effective local remedy and I am not sure that it is easy. The result of Cynthia's rule would be that Barclays, for instance, could simply sit back and, in the *Pantell* litigation, could have done nothing whatsoever about removal of deposits from its Guernsey branch. Maybe that is the right rule but it leaves me with an uncomfortable feeling.

Andreas F. Lowenfeld:

How about the Manufacturer's Hanover, where transfers of billions of dollars from Italy on their way to Columbia were grabbed in New York, a momentary electric clip, you are not opposed to that?

Karl M. Meessen:

I just wonder to what extent the right answer in this kind of dispute would depend on what the transaction costs are for the foreign bank. Once you make this a regular business. There are plenty of Mareva injunctions but I guess there is not plenty of enforcement of Mareva injunctions. But once it becomes a common feature of the banking business we have the risk of double payment, we have the need for the foreign bank to find out to what extent they are covered or not covered by the *Babanaft* proviso and I think that this is a nuisance also for the banking system since it makes holding deposits for non-residents more expensive than holding deposits for resident customers.

Sir Ian Sinclair:

Is there a risk in that to a certain extent?

Karl M. Meessen:

If it becomes a standard feature of enforcement of claims, I think that the banks will have to calculate that risk and this will translate somehow into some fees which are terribly high.

Andreas F. Lowenfeld:

Even lower interest rates?

Ulrich Bosch:

Theoretically yes, but when charging high fees or paying low interest rates, the relevant banks would not be competitive. They would rather have to close down their foreign offices. But, coming back to the risks, I really think, as already stated, that the issues become clearer if we do not focus only on dirty money cases, but also on day-to-day private litigations. I imagine the debtor who says to his creditor: 'You have a claim against me; so you attach my Hong Kong deposit in New York and then make sure you get paid in New York and I will get paid in Hong Kong.' And they make money out of that scheme. This may be an extreme case, but whether or not there are such types of conspiracy, the risk of double payment is always there. Now, looking for a possible resolution of the conflict, let me get to a more theoretical point. There must be, I believe, some kind of balancing, with the result that either one or the other jurisdiction has the right to command. Now what is the problem with balancing? Quite often, the court balances the interest of its home state (say, the US) to enforce its securities, antitrust or criminal laws or its rules of jurisdiction against interests of a private party. I remember a US lawyer's comparison with a sports event: the US always wins.

Andreas F. Lowenfeld:

Can I follow this up? I want to know whether German law has changed. The key in the banking area was the *Quinine Cartel* case in 1968 in which the US had a federal grand jury investigating a guy who was accused of raising the price of quinine. Remember, we had a half a million soldiers in Vietnam, and whether that was right or wrong you did not want them to get malaria and die. The accusation was that the target was maintaining accounts in the Frankfurt branch of Citibank, but I do not think it matters whether it was Citibank or Deutsche Bank because both are in New York and Frankfurt and the US court, you may know the case but others said, well, Germany's interest, it's civil, not criminal. Switzerland is different from Germany, there are specific laws against priests and doctors giving disclosure, but not banks and it was not private, the holding right or wrong was that the German interest was not very great. Now has that changed?

Ulrich Bosch:

Well, I have not yet come to the point that I wanted to make. I said there is a problem in that the interest of the state is balanced against the interest of a private party. First of all, I think that the test should rather be the interests of the two states balanced against each other. The next question is: Should the judge determine which is the 'better' or stronger interest or shouldn't he rather apply a slightly more objective test and ask which jurisdiction has the closest link?

Andreas R. Lowenfeld:

I am not so sure that would be more objective. You can have a test based on the closest link with the transaction, but in fact even that is not totally objective.

Sir Ian Sinclair:

I just want to call on Cynthia and then Philip and then after that we will break and have our coffee. And then the next discussion follows and in the general discussion if any one wants to say something else about securities law, let him do so. I would like to say something myself and would have an opportunity of doing so. Would that be acceptable?

Cynthia C. Lichtenstein:

The difficulty I have with utilising the closest link as the deciding factor is that now under the Rome Convention and in the proposed draft OAS Convention on applicable law, the closest link is the standard for choice of law except when the judge determines to use the mandatory law of one of the jurisdictions and, since securities law is going to end up being a mandatory law within that definition, the closest link is out the window, unfortunately.

Philip Bovey:

I think another problem with this and one of the reasons why I think the *Lee* decision was right is that, if you put it into a common law interpretation, that was money which the US courts were entitled to say, having been taken in the US, belonged as a matter of proprietary interests to a fund held on behalf of the investors, and to which those proprietary interests already attached by the time it went to Hong Kong. The difficulty is that this proprietary tracing thing, which is so fundamental apart from common law attitudes towards it, does not fit in with civil law concepts. We have a clash between the two different sets of thinking which produces different results in different cases and a closest connection test is not going to resolve that dichotomy between common and civil law analysis. In that particular case, in the *Hong Kong* case, we had three countries with the same common law analysis and that is why our efforts in that case were devoted toward getting the SEC to apply to the Hong Kong courts which faced an awful problem. They said that this would be surrendering to a foreign power. It was relatively easy to produce a common analysis. What was difficult about it, was that when you carry it across into a civil law jurisdiction there is a wholly different set of principles which are not compatible.

Sir Ian Sinclair:

Is it really in this area not compatible?

Philip Bovey:

He is going on attachment. You see we held that that was subject, that we and the Hong Kong attorney general were content to allow it to be argued that those assets were subject to a constructive trust in the hands of Lee when he received them in the US and then when he put them into the bank he was a trustee already acting for somebody else's money. Now I do not know enough about civil law to know whether you could produce the same ...

Campbell McLachlan:

Arguably you could get it through the restitutionary route under the civil law systems but there may be a problem as to when that restitutionary right comes into being. In the *Lee* case it could have already been a civil law matter come into being in New York or if it has not come into being then you assert your claim for restitution in the place where the assets are found.

Andreas F. Lowenfeld:

Not until the end in two respects. Part of it was applied and part of it was restitution, the assets that they could find. It was both penal and restitution.

Sir Ian Sinclair:

At the very least you can get different ways of working it out but if the end result is the same and basically right then it does not matter all that much.

Philip Bovey:

Your immediate reaction was to the Hong Kong court, but I think that without the proprietary interest so would ours be, so that if the proprietary interests arise at a different stage in the analysis you get a different result according to . . .

Cynthia C. Lichtenstein:

And that interest only arose because of particular facts in this case.

Sir Ian Sinclair:

Well I think at this stage we will break for coffee and we will resume at a quarter to two when Karl Meessen will give his short introductory statement on the drafting of rules of jurisdiction.

Chapter XI

Drafting Rules on Extraterritorial Jurisdiction

Karl M. Meessen

Sir Ian Sinclair:

I will call upon Karl to make an introductory statement about drafting rules of jurisdiction. I am not sure what title we should give to it but the point is that the International Committee of the International Law Association on Extraterritorial Jurisdiction does have a mandate to study the legal aspects of extraterritorial jurisdiction.

Karl M. Meessen:

Having listened to a series of excellent papers, I can only try to highlight some of the points made and to do this in more abstract terms than is actually appropriate regarding the sometimes very technical subject matter. The title of what I am going to say – Drafting Rules on Extraterritorial Jurisdiction – is open-ended indeed and it will be for the discussion to give it a more precise meaning.

1. The Exercise of Extraterritorial Jurisdiction

If Zahnradfabrik Friedrichshafen (ZF) is prohibited by the Federal Cartel Office from acquiring Allison, a division of GM, such decision may annoy Allison, that is, GM. In addition, it may annoy the US and the state where the premises are located if, for instance, preventing the merger interferes with plans to rescue an ailing company. I have no knowledge of the details of this particular transaction but rescue operations of that kind are common practice. The question then is the one put before us by Cynthia: are we really confronted with an exercise of extraterritorial jurisdiction?

If ZF handled the acquisition through its subsidiary 'ZF Incorporated, USA', would a prohibition order then be outside the jurisdictional reach of the Federal Cartel Office? If so, should the effect of the order be confined to Germany? How could this be done? Would the part of Allison operating in Germany constitute a viable business to be sold separately? Would anyone purchase such a unit in a global market?

It may stretch, maybe overstretch, our subject matter if we also look at cases where there is a clear basis of personal jurisdiction. Some of the most fiercely contested conflicts of jurisdiction, however, were cases where there was a perfect basis for territorial jurisdiction, the *Shipping* cases, for instance. The US was by no means generally prevented from examining freight rates applicable to and from US ports, and yet objections against US enforcement do not seem to have been totally unfounded. Even territorial jurisdiction, therefore, sometimes stands to be scrutinised under the jurisdictional rules of international law.

The jurisdictional issue has often been split up into legislative (or prescriptive), adjudicative, and enforcement jurisdiction. The Restatement makes that distinction but whether it has more than a descriptive value and actually contributes to settling and defining the law from an international perspective, I do not know. At least there is no reason for us to single out just the one or other aspect.

The Committee, which has initiated this conference, ventured to distinguish direct from indirect extraterritoriality in the field of export control law. Direct extraterritoriality refers to orders to be observed abroad whereas indirect extraterritoriality is involved when parties to a private contract are ordered to make performance abroad subject to domestic embargo law. Whether that distinction makes much sense outside export control is an issue which, I believe, should not *a limine* be excluded from our considerations.

Referring to Andrea Bianchi's paper, I agree it is the intensity of exercising jurisdiction that really matters in international law. The exercise of jurisdiction by the legislature has a lesser intensity. No one really cares before the law is implemented, at which point there is still occasion to call for restraint. Only enforcement and adjudication bring matters to a head. It is then when interference with foreign sovereignty assumes an authoritative character. The more pinpointed the exercise of jurisdiction gets, the more likely is an infringement of the sovereignty of the foreign states involved. Both aspects have to be included in our study but there is at least a difference of degree that we should keep in mind.

2.   National Conflicts Law and Customary International Law

National conflicts law and customary international law have to be distinguished. The main point is: customary international law cannot be altered unilaterally by a single state. Thus we should not expect the Department of State to be particularly keen on contributing to the making of binding rules of international law. If they did, they would have voluntarily reduced their scope of action whereas conflicts law can be changed any time.

Furthermore, if international law is to be applicable before national courts, the way of making it applicable differs from state to state. This again affects the readiness of courts to rely on international law when giving the reasons for a decision in a particular case. They prefer rules of conflict of laws since rules of conflict of laws need no *Charming Betsy* to become applicable. They are an integral part of national law and can be developed under notions of law-finding familiar to the judges whereas rules of customary international law constitute a strange and unruly species to most national judges. Hence what is stated in terms of national conflicts law may sometimes in fact reflect an *opinio iuris* of international law.

Finally, national conflicts law, since it determines the final outcome of cases, has to be more precise. It is striving for the optimal rule making, whereas, as I tried to formulate this many years ago in a contribution to the Festschrift in the honour of a late friend of many of us, Francis Mann, international law only has the function of setting up a minimum order. Yet the resulting rules have an overlapping content which makes it hard to tell the ones from the others. Even the Restatement combines comity with international law in a way which is bound to leave many an observer in doubt as to what is what.

3. The Role of International Agreements

Intergovernmental agreements have their constitutional limitations. I wonder, for instance, to what extent positive comity could impose alterations of rules of national law. After all, offering positive comity as a result of an intergovernmental agreement would extend the scope of application of national law *vis-à-vis* those covered by national law. If executive agreements are left aside, actual treaty commitments on jurisdictional matters are rare and art. VIII of the IMF Articles of Agreement is the exception proving the rule.

What are the prospects for future development? I agree with Andreas Weitbrecht that harmonisation by treaty law will reduce the occasion for conflict. But small differences are likely to remain unless we propose to have uniform law which might be a good idea for the issuance of equities in view of the global trading of equities but, in antitrust, the introduction of much uniform law is neither likely to happen nor, apart from basic principles, desirable. Even within the EC the odds are against uniformity. It was recently decided not to extend the scope of application of the Merger Control Regulation because some still prefer, perhaps Dr Stoephasius will agree, their national law.

Peter von Stoephasius:

No, not at all!

Karl M. Meessen:

But the German government was reported to have objected to extending the applicability of the Merger Control Regulation of the EC. Above all, a national focus is likely to remain even if the law is harmonised unless we all strive for global welfare instead of national welfare.

4.   Criteria Reflecting Territorial Links

It is the territoriality of government responsibility that characterises the political system of our time, with territorially divided territories, and territorially responsible government and national welfare as a primary policy goal – and a possible offshoot of all this is Gary Born's presumption in favour of territoriality.

The concept of territoriality is more elusive than it seems. It includes, of course, place of action and place of effect, the latter, in the case of constituent effects, being called 'objective territoriality' and, with regard to effects on nationals, 'passive personality'. A less obvious variant of territorial links is provided by the persons actively involved since the notion of the nationality of corporations – the seat theory or the law of incorporation theory – refers to formalised territorial links. With regard to natural persons, it is not only the *jus soli* that in the end attaches people to territory but also the *jus sanguinis* principle. Even German bureaucrats give up at some point when establishing the nationality of ancestors and simply rely on the presumption that those ancestors, having lived in Germany, must be considered to have been of German nationality. Thus nationality under the *jus sanguinis* principle also has to be perceived as a formalised territorial link making 'universality', i.e. links to every state at the same time, the real antonym.

Establishing territorial links is how national conflicts law seeks to avoid conflicts with foreign laws and policies. It usually works. It is on the small fraction of cases where it does not work that we have to focus. We are then tempted to turn to international law and even conflicts lawyers have no objections. What are those rules? Should they be defined by the field of law as is suggested by the choice of subjects in the programme of this conference?

With regard to tax law, for instance, I have not heard anyone saying: 'this particular tax, levied in practice, is illegal under international law'. Even unitary taxation was considered legal unless it is abusive. Open-ended statements of that kind may be all we can realistically achieve.

Regarding procedural law, I appreciate Campbell McLachlan's approach which was to give the Mareva injunctions a territorially reduced interpretation and to tell foreign banks that they are not subject to contempt of court, with the term 'foreign' applying only to those banks over which England does not have jurisdiction.

Campbell McLachlan:

There are not many of them.

Karl M. Meessen:

Indeed, that is the reason why I find that reservation to lack real meaning.

Regarding export control, the Committee stated that export control is not permitted if the only link is the origin of goods or technology. The question is whether contracts making foreign partners subject to domestic law are to be covered by that rule as well.

In the case of disclosure rules, we heard from Ulrich Bosch, that there is no problem if they are made a condition of the listing. The logic is: if a company wants to take advantage of a certain market, it has to abide by its particular rules.

In competition law, the effects doctrine, referring to effects that are direct, substantial and foreseeable, dominates practice and only meets with occasional opposition as a matter of principle rather than genuine concern. A new problem arises, as was pointed out by Yoshio Ohara last night, when the doctrine is made applicable the other way. Would an indirect impairment of domestic exporters by tolerating or even encouraging restrictive practices in a foreign territory constitute a sufficient link under the old effects doctrine? The connection between competition and trade becomes obvious at that point: the extraterritorial application transforms a problem of competition law to one of fair trade.

Andreas F. Lowenfeld:

That's right – including the problems with the GATT. The Americans are saying that there is a new non-tariff barrier which is not enforcement of competition law. That is really the American government's position.

Karl M. Meessen:

Yes, that puts it nicely but, under jurisdictional scrutiny, I have grave doubts and for a non-tariff barrier it still lacks international agreement.

Andreas F. Lowenfeld:

You and I agree.

Karl M. Meessen:

As I mentioned before, private agreement can serve as a substitute for a territorial link. The question is: does contractual acceptance remove all the jurisdictional problems? The US could run its pipeline type of export control regulation simply on the basis of making it an obligation under domestic law, binding upon all exporters of technology and goods, to include in their contracts a clause to the effect that the contracts are subject to the export control law of the US as it may stand at any point in the future and that that obligation has to be passed on to every future purchaser of the goods. Should the means of private contract law justify their public law ends? There will be policy conflicts as between states, and such conflicts, in my opinion, call for international law scrutiny, even though the territorial reach of the law may be impeccable.

Harold G. Maier:

Would you put into that same category an order by a US court to a foreign corporation before it to bring documents from its home country in violation of a blocking order? And if not, what is the difference?

Karl M. Meessen:

There is an additional problem in that case. It is the aspect of violating a foreign state's legislation. Furthermore, I miss the element I am discussing at the moment: the relevance of a private agreement.

Harold G. Maier:

I do not understand the difference though because assume, in fact, there was an implicit agreement that the court will not prosecute a corporation for contempt which, in fact, puts the documents on the desk, and the corporation says the documents are in France. Let us assume that France permitted the documents to be brought, I do not have to go and get them. The court then says, you are right, you do not have to go and get them but you have a bank account here and it is going to cost you. Now, I really do not understand the difference between the effect of that and the effect of the US government saying that if you want this contract you have got to promise that you will do certain kinds of things. I am not arguing that one is right and the other is wrong. I guess I don't see much difference in the jurisdictional issue.

Karl M. Meessen:

I guess I now see your point, in both cases foreign conduct is induced, and yet there is more of an authoritative element in your case which I would therefore see in an even more critical light.

As to what is voluntary, let me come back to a seemingly different matter – the tax matter. Gary Born tells us that the companies can choose where to operate. The companies will be agreeable to this if they are allowed to opt out of unitary taxation, but whether the foreign state, which faces a loss of revenue, is also agreeable to this, I doubt it.

Paul Peters:

Many companies would not agree.

Karl M. Meessen:

But, if they can choose, what else can you expect?

Paul Peters:

The company affected can go to its government and seek diplomatic protection. The home government may take the position that, irrespective of what the company has agreed with a foreign government, this cannot diminish any right or interest which the home government has under international law. This is the position adopted by many governments and arbitrators *vis-à-vis* the Calvo clause by which companies are 'persuaded' to sign away the right to invoke diplomatic protection or to submit disputes to international arbitration.

Karl M. Meessen:

Indeed, it is the home government's view that matters from an international law perspective in addition to the one of the company.

5. Criteria Taking Account of the Attitudes of Foreign States

So far we have proceeded the traditional way, looking for rules establishing criteria derived from the facts of the case and then relating the case to a certain law. I now propose not only to look at the facts of the case but, in addition, to take into account the reaction of foreign states involved in the particular case.

Private international law does that when, disenchanted with the results of applying the applicable foreign law, domestic law comes in under the public policy exception. The same technique, possibly with contrary results, is employed when the application of foreign mandatory rules of law is considered. It is a sensitive, delicate matter. The point I want to make right at the outset is not meant to be a substitute for criteria permanently established by territorial links. It is a last resort, albeit sometimes the only resort.

Consent given by the foreign states can remove the basis for a jurisdictional complaint. If a British company approaches its government to raise objections on jurisdictional grounds to the application of a foreign law or regulation and if HM government, agreeing to or not caring for the foreign proceedings, chooses not to defend its sovereignty on this particular occasion, the company might find its efforts to fight the application of, say, US rules frustrated.

Contrary positions of foreign states are of greater interest. National law prescriptions to respect them takes us into the midst of comity. Its record may not be flawless, considering *Hartford*, for instance. There are plenty of recent decisions, I am not so sure whether many of them were wrongly decided on the basis of comity. The record of judicial case law is not as poor as Francis Mann used to tell us. In addition, there is comity as applied by the executive branch of government. For fear of international implications, the Federal Cartel Office, for instance, sometimes simply omitted to bring a case against foreign parties, or it developed some compromise accommodating foreign state interests. Where there is not much private litigation of competition laws, the fact that an administrative agency declines to take up an internationally sensitive case is usually the end of the matter whereas, in the US, lawyers, acting on a contingency fee basis and striving for treble damages, will still bring their case.

Andreas F. Lowenfeld:

Hartford was not a contingency fee case. It was government connected.

Karl M. Meessen:

I was thinking of *Laker*, for instance.

Is there a rule of international law making deference to foreign state interests mandatory? We will easily agree on the scope of the procedural obligation to consult, share information, etc. Paul Peters reminded us of the OECD Rules, and Philip Bovey and Michael Johnson told us about the extended practice of applying those rules and other more detailed bilateral agreements.

The critical point relates to substantive law. Is there a substantive law obligation to defer to clearly greater interests of foreign states? Such a rule, more difficult to handle by national courts than by the executive branch, seems to reflect the moderate final outcome of most jurisdiction cases. I am pleased to note that a recent resolution of the Institut de Droit International includes a reference to such balancing of interests.

Sir Ian Sinclair:

I was absent from the Milan session.

Andreas F. Lowenfeld:

I went to the museum that day.

Karl M. Meessen:

As a final point let me say a few words on the impact internationally agreed policies can have on state jurisdiction.

6.   Internationally Agreed Policies

The International Law Association Committee made internationally agreed policies an element of its 1990 Resolution on Export Control. During this

Symposion, they have been mentioned by our Chairman, on several occasions by Andy Lowenfeld, Andrea Bianchi, by Francesco Francioni, and sometimes the reference to them took the form of saying, well, let us not forget about the rest of international law, there are general principles available, let us try to apply them in the jurisdictional context. That is how human rights come in, dolphin rights come in.

Cynthia C. Lichtenstein:

Banking rights.

Karl M. Meessen:

Mentioning them may show possible pitfalls. I would like to mention two of them:

(1) At what point could we consider a shared policy to justify an extension of jurisdiction? Is it not the differences on details that matter? We discussed drugs, arms control, environment, and competition law. Can we really extrapolate emerging agreement on substance to a licence to legislate and enforce extraterritorially? Positive comity, in the context described by Yoshio Ohara, can be made part of a treaty. It is not a rule of customary international law.

(2) How will agreement, consensus, be established? Ian is right when he refers to binding resolutions of the Security Council. Only a few of them have been adopted, and the future may or may not allow the Security Council to live up to the role it was given in the Charter. But when we do not have such authoritative coverage, what about treaties that clearly reflect public opinion but have not yet become binding? One has to be very careful, even in the environmental field, and not go beyond what was actually agreed or start enforcement before the treaty has actually entered into force.

Sir Ian Sinclair:

One must not leave out of account, I would have thought, the kind of situation in which there may have been a veto in the Security Council, or a threatened veto preventing the adoption of a resolution, but where a group of like-minded states nonetheless wishes to pursue a common policy involving, for example, some kind of limited economic sanctions, in order to counter a blatant breach of international law. In fact they may have agreed upon such measures within another framework, not necessarily the Security Council, and that has happened.

Karl M. Meessen:

There may be a kind of informal consensus and yet, while agreeing on condemning violations of human rights, one may well disagree on the nature and timing of individual measures and how to enforce them. I would say a grave concern of public opinion is an insufficient basis for an exercise of extraterritorial jurisdiction by reference to an internationally agreed policy.

Sir Ian Sinclair:

I am very grateful to you, Karl. That was very useful. I think I explained right at the outset what the aim and purpose of this meeting was, and I think that your outline certainly is one way of tackling this in seeking to formulate possible rules or elements that have to be taken into account in assessing jurisdiction. There clearly is a major problem in trying to draft some kind of generalised resolution on this topic which covers an enormous range of international law problems and where the actual substantive international law provisions are unsettled or controversial. Certainly, there may be particular aspects which render the solution of the jurisdictional problem more difficult or, in fact, more easy. I must confess that one of the impressions that I have formed in listening to the discussion over the last two days is that there are certain areas in which there may still be considerable differences among us as to the actual jurisdictional rule or rules that may be applicable in that particular area, but where, in fact, little conflict arises. I just wonder whether we ought not to seek to concentrate our efforts on what the problems areas are.

Campbell McLachlan:

Can I speak in support of that? Because although my paper talked about a particular aspect of civil enforcement jurisdiction, what I intended to say with regard to original jurisdiction was that on one view an awful lot of it is extraterritorial. It is all about taking jurisdiction over foreigners, and yet there is very little evidence to suggest that any of that actually gives rise to conflicts between jurisdictions in the sense that one state says, 'no, absolutely not, you must not exercise jurisdiction over this person', so that when you then boil it all down to the actual cases where there really is a real live conflict, you are talking about a very much narrower field. It just strikes me that we may make more progress if we focus on that than if we try and talk about the field of the public international law of jurisdiction generally as being rules which deal with the non-conflict situation, i.e. the core situation, if you like, as well as the hard cases.

Pieter J. Kuijper:

One should be in promulgation of the others. I mean it is certainly impossible, it seems to me, to talk about the conflicts in isolation. You have to have some basic rules which cover day-to-day life and also times when there is no conflict and which also inform your solution in conflict situations which guide you in conflict situations.

Andreas F. Lowenfeld:

I had several points and maybe I will get back to the general response to Karl, but on this point I think that we can make a contribution by saying where the substantive solution is the same. For example, we see this just recently in the *Maxwell Bankruptcy* cases, where we have had a shift in the English courts in about two years. Both the English and the American courts now combine; instead of saying well the money is here, we are not going to let it go which happened in the *Dock* case. So I think that is the kind of thing that the International Law Association can point out and the way it can point it out is to say that in situation X, you are not giving away everything else, that we do concurrent and not conflicting exercise of jurisdiction in bankruptcy without prejudice to what might happen to a securities issue or we do a securities issue without prejudice as to what may happen in insurance and so on. I think that that is the kind of contribution that an association like the International Law Association can make.

Karl M. Meessen:

Joint enforcement?

Andreas F. Lowenfeld:

Well it is not necessarily enforcement. You enforce it but we will not object because our genuine interests as compared to some worry about . . .

Campbell McLachlan:

Maxwell is joint enforcement.

Andreas F. Lowenfeld:

Yes, it happens to be but some might simply be, you take care of it and we do not mind.

Harold G. Maier:

I just want to say that this makes a great deal of sense to me because, in fact, one of the problems in this field is to take generalised statements and then from those statements abstract rules of international law which do not reflect the policies that are present in some kinds of decision making and resolution and not in others. What Andy is suggesting, as I understand it, is to identify those areas where the policies which inform the question as to what the nations are to do are sufficiently acceptable so that in fact the International Law Association could say, look here is a situation. There will not be a precedent created for others which are more difficult but in these kinds of circumstances, like those you suggested, there is consensus and that agreement . . .

Cynthia C. Lichtenstein:

Are you suggesting that this might take the form of say guidelines for Mr Bovey's office as to when they would want to intervene and not want to intervene? You suggested yesterday, when I asked you a question and then you said it is very difficult. We look at the reasons why the private plaintiff is making the claim.

Andreas F. Lowenfeld:

Karl was talking about shipping, for instance. The British in the 1960s went wild about the idea that the Americans were looking into the shipping rates without asking themselves really, are we benefiting from these private cartels? They never asked themselves that question. You reminded me of this.

Paul Peters:

The way we are trying to deal with particular situations that have turned out to be controversial is difficult. We ought to discuss general rules or principles, irrespective whether the practices in question have raised controversy. So far we have been concerned mostly with American infringements of alleged rules on extraterritorial jurisdiction, as though the US were the only culprit. I also want to draw attention to the Arab boycott of Israel which went on for years, even decades, without creating many problems until the blocking statutes came about in the 1970s. We should think about rules and principles applicable to all cases of extraterritorial jurisdiction. Such rules and principles could be formulated as guidelines or as a code of conduct addressed to states generally.

Sir Ian Sinclair:

This is a problem. The question is should we be trying to look to the future or should we start where we are now in the light of a convoluted history? I am reminded of a story, that I repeat now and then, of two American tourists who hired a car in Dublin, and they got out into the countryside and they lost their way. They stopped an Irish farmer and asked what is the quickest way back to Dublin and he scratched his head and said: 'Sir, if I were you, I would not start from here'. I frankly don't like to start preparing a draft of rules on extraterritorial jurisdiction based on where we are now.

Andreas F. Lowenfeld:

Could I respond to that if I might? A good deal of reference has been made here to the Restatement, and in particular, to s. 403(3) and Comment e which raised the question of what happens when more than one state has a reasonable basis for exercising jurisdiction. After some debate, and Karl was present for a good part of it, the American Law Institute was prepared to say that each state is required by international law to evaluate the other state's interests. An amendment was suggested from the floor (and it had been previously suggested actually among the reporters but then we did not manage this debate) which said, let us go further and say the state with the lesser interest 'shall' defer to the state with the greater interest. Well, the amendment was 'shall' and that was defeated and the most it could get through was 'should' and 'should' in the comment, not in black letter. I am suggesting that an association like this might do that. I made the same proposal to the Institute of International Law but in a more limited context, having to do with the liability of multinational corporations but, of course, that is an aspect of what we are talking about here. It seems to me that if the International Law Association were prepared to move that extra step – of course, by itself it is not sufficient – we still need to define conflict, we still need to define what we mean by a territorial preference or a greater interest, but it would be a step forward and not asking, how the hell do you get to that building in Ireland?

Cynthia C. Lichtenstein:

If the International Law Association is to move toward propositions of what states and courts shall do, this is exactly where I would like to have the statement 'and shall consider the impact of internationally agreed policies'.

Harold G. Maier:

What does that mean? Where do you find the agreement?

Cynthia C. Lichtenstein:

That is what we have to find. That is what we have to talk about and I suspect that exactly is Sir Ian's problem. You cannot get there from here. We have the same joke but from Maine.

Pieter J. Kuijper:

I think that there is another issue which ought to be decided as far as the scope of our work is concerned. Over the past two days there have been issues raised, which I touched upon and which Francesco also touched upon in his discussion on environmental extraterritoriality, and those are issues which do not involve extraterritoriality in the classic sense of the word although they are comparable to it. These are rather mechanisms. One has to say again, unfortunately, it is mainly the US using them. Mechanisms to force others into mirror image legislation or mirror image behaviour and there is a continuum there from extraterritoriality to other areas. If you look at the intervention in the pipeline question, the intervention was directed so as to make the European countries change their stance which was restricting imports from the Soviet Union rather than restricting exports. That is the devil of the implementation, even if you have a common policy which was still very important to us. Further on the continuum you have the Cuban Democracy Act, which arguably has extraterritorial aspects to it and that adds certain sanctions on transport in order to bring that home. A step further again is 'tuna/dolphin' where there is no serious extraterritoriality except that the US lays down certain rules for the high seas but others can only fish in that part of the high seas if they follow the same rules or otherwise they lose trading rights. That is something that, perhaps, you can exclude from extraterritoriality altogether. But I just wanted to point out that there is a certain continuum there and where do we draw the line?

Andreas F. Lowenfeld:

It is attempting to force a decision in another state.

Andreas Weitbrecht:

I very much agree with what has been said here but are we not in danger now of discussing the possible content of our product? I think first the question was put, what kind of product should we aim for, should we aim for something that is similar to the American Law Institute's Restatement or the book recently published by the Institut du Droit International? Are we agreed that we are trying to do something which would purport to cover both the normal case and try to inform the difficult case?

Karl M. Meessen:

The idea is to present practice, to explain it and then to show where the more promising trends and where the less helpful ones can be found in order to show how to move on without necessarily pretending to reach a final goal. Starting from that proposition, I would like to react to what Andreas Weitbrecht has said just now. I wonder whether 'rules' is the right heading. I think that we should, perhaps, consider 'guidelines on solving', 'guidelines on how to solve, how to handle conflicts of extraterritorial jurisdiction'. Maybe only a small portion of my statement was to suggest rules, more was on how to structure the discussion and thereby give an idea of how to move on in this field.

Andrea Bianchi:

If I may say a word on what Professor Meessen has said. Yesterday, after all, I used this idea of standards to be traced to specific areas. So how do we go about it? Do we provide guidelines or do we evaluate standards applicable not to specific areas, or rather should we focus on some more general guidelines? I think this is not a detail. If we are to go about it the way I suggested yesterday – by specific areas, then I think that that is going to be quite helpful to issue . . . . It is a good service which we might do for the international community to draw these kinds of standards. In that respect, you should not feel unduly constrained by the deadline of the Buenos Aires conference because, after all, the service is worth the effort, I think. If we are to draw standards or guidelines then my suggestion is to go by subject matter and then go back to it once again. That would be very helpful, I think, to practitioners as well and that, after all, is what people expect.

Peter von Stoephasius:

I have doubts if a general statement would be helpful in the field of competition law. I was wondering that this idea still exists because I still remember listening to Professor Lowenfeld at the Salzburg Seminar almost 20 years ago, we then discussed the *Timberlane* case, and now we are at it again. So I think the idea of establishing general rules or international rules has been overruled by the tendency of other states to conclude international treaties such as the treaty made by the EC Commission, which was attacked last year by France, the Netherlands and Spain so it is not yet in validity.

Pieter J. Kuijper:

It is in operation. It has not been suspended by the Court.

Peter von Stoephasius:

That leads me to another point, which has not yet been covered by the discussion today. We have another extraterritorial aspect. This is a more decentralised application of European law by the member states, so that leads to the question whether a member state has the right to make a decision which would act in the whole territory. So this will have effect also on the territories of the member states. But, of course, this is a question of more concern to the EC Commission.

Sir Ian Sinclair:

Here you have the feature of the application of the European Convention on the Recognition and Enforcement of Judgments.

Andreas F. Lowenfeld:

If it is a civil case.

Peter von Stoephasius:

Yes, but these are authoritative decisions. So I think that this is more interesting for the practitioners in the Federal Cartel Office. And also, to answer the question you raised, it is necessary to harmonise our law. I think it is necessary because Germany, for instance, will be in the next years only in one corner of the EC because all the other member states will by then have adopted the wording of 85 and 86 and Germany will be the only country which has a different law. So we have to harmonise. Maybe we take over the wording or we have another but with the same sense and I think that we will have the solution maybe in five or ten years.

Sir Ian Sinclair:

Leaving that last point aside, I accept what you say but I wonder whether we could find a possible halfway house between what Andrea Bianchi was saying about concentrating on specific subject matter areas and the idea of generalised guidelines. Maybe we can codify the halfway house in the sense of trying to draw up a few generalised guidelines but in addition seeking to explain and elaborate on how these guidelines might be applicable to particular subject matter areas with any qualification that would be necessary.

Andreas F. Lowenfeld:

That is what the Restatement did, just to make your point. We drew general guidelines, I think this will be helpful, this is the famous s. 402(3) and then we said, well, what do we do about illustrating specifically and we concluded that in the tax area we could make specific illustrations pretty much universally applicable. I would say I had an adviser on that as I am not exactly an expert, but when it came to antitrust, securities and control over exports and control over foreign corporations we had to, we did not start out that way, but we had to label them US applications. If valid, another half decade has happened, you can move beyond that and make the illustrations more universal then, again, you have made progress.

Andreas Weitbrecht:

Given the fact that we are not aiming for hard and fast rules but rather for guidelines, we may have a chance.

Andreas F. Lowenfeld:

The black pen is dangerous.

Andreas Weitbrecht:

Just call it guidelines.

Campbell McLachlan:

It may be to the same effect. I just want to make another comment about this point about co-operation and co-existence and co-operation and all the rest of it which flows from the quote that I gave yesterday about the old rules are gone but the old rules remain. It is right to say as a very generalised proposition that what has happened to public international law generally over the last 20 years or so is that there has been a move away from a system of public international law which was all about co-existence between sovereign states, where the law of jurisdiction was the centrepiece of the regulation of that co-existence, towards a system of public international law which is much more generally speaking about co-operation between states and also which takes account of other actors in international law . . . as well as states. The logic of a notion of co-operation, of course, is that ultimately jurisdictional issues fall away because they become simply irrelevant if you have that degree of co-operation. Well, that may be happening in embryo in some fields and it seems to me that even the embryo is beginning to emerge in my field of civil jurisdiction and no doubt also in environmental and in many other fields and perhaps also in banking law; but the problem of course is that the full elements, the fully formed, the fully co-operative international law, has in no way yet been formed.

So we are standing at a watershed in that sense in terms of deciding what the continued relevance of the rules of jurisdiction is to be in light of a new system which seems to be partially emergent but which is by no means fully formed. And I would just say that it seems to me that we would do dangerous harm if we merely enshrine because we are focusing on really difficult areas of conflict where there does not seem to be much scope for co-operation, if we merely enshrine old rules which, in fact, are no longer of a general application for many other areas. And it seems to me, therefore, that what we should be looking for is certainly not rules, nor even simply factors, but defining an approach to the question of resolving jurisdictional problems. We could therefore give an endorsement, I think, to notions of joint enforcement and restraint which may resolve very many apparent jurisdictional problems. We could also endorse, in talking about an approach, an approach which does take account of the substantive content of the area and the international policies surrounding the particular area which has been being focused on without trying to draft now, because I doubt that we can, what result that might actually lead to in all the various specific cases.

Sir Ian Sinclair:

I think that that is very helpful, Campbell.

Michael D.C. Johnson:

Chairman, may I make a point on some of these issues from the perspective of a practitioner? I was struck and a bit worried by something Karl Meessen said when he implied, I think, that if in a particular case the British government took a decision not to intervene in support of a particular British citizen, who had a jurisdictional problem, that would in some way weaken or undermine the stance. I do not actually believe that to be the case. I described yesterday some of the ways in which we co-operate with the US authorities on the handling of specific issues that have come up, and indeed I very much agree with Campbell that the more you develop that co-operation the more outmoded one would hope these jurisdictional conflicts would become. Because we are not actually in the business of picking conflicts, at least I do not get fees for picking conflicts.

Andreas F. Lowenfeld:

Are you in the business of defending your turf?

Michael D.C. Johnson:

Oh, yes, I am in the business of helping British industry and commerce to operate smoothly and we do not do that by getting involved in conflicts and disputes. What we have to do is look for more practical methods, and I described yesterday some of the ways in which we handle specific cases. It is, if you like, a form of administrative balancing action, based very very closely on the facts of the particular cases. We may or may not decide at the end of the day that there is a case for the British government to move in on a particular issue. But I would submit that the act of studying or scrutinising the case in fact amounts to protecting our position on the underlying jurisdictional principles. I do not think that if we decide not to intervene on a particular case we have weakened our position of principle.

Cynthia C. Lichtenstein:

Campbell really stated it well, i.e. if you do go area by area, that approach does permit also writing about emerging international agreement with respect to the particular area.

Karl M. Meessen:

If I may just respond to what Michael has said. It is all on public record, so I can talk freely about it. I had the occasion to have a role in *Aerospatiale* and also to represent Volkswagen in the *Schlunk* case. In *Schlunk*, governments did not intervene, and this at least partially explains the difference in the outcome of the two cases both related to comity. The absence of governmental support in *Schlunk* did not disown Volkswagen in any serious manner but, after all, the issue of putting the Service Convention into play should have been taken seriously by governments. Whenever, therefore, rules incorporate positions of foreign governments, it is important to rely on a governmental position.

Andreas F. Lowenfeld:

I just want to add one word to that. I agree as a litigator with Karl but there is one more point which I think I want to add for Michael and Philip and that is, if a country is perceived as automatically, always taking its citizens side, after a while that gets devalued. For a while the Swiss had that reputation. For a while the Germans did too. ... that is why I made the statement about the automatic cranked-out brief. I think that genuine interests asserted only now and then become much more effective than a routine thing.

Adelheid Puttler:

You were talking about the litigator, I would like to focus attention on the courts. There are legal systems where procedural law does not provide for *amicus curiae* briefs. Should a court in such a situation infer consent from the absence of an *amicus curiae* brief? Perhaps the guidelines should be called to the attention of the courts.

Sir Ian Sinclair:

No.

Adelheid Puttler:

A country can do different things. It can file an *amicus curiae* brief if this possibility exists. It can lodge an official protest with the government.

Sir Ian Sinclair:

Which one would hope would get the attention of the court.

Andreas F. Lowenfeld:

But we have seen the opposite. We have seen litigants ask their embassy or government to come in and the embassy or government said, no thanks and the litigant says, 'See my adversarial tried and failed'.

Adelheid Puttler:

And if the litigant does not ask his government and the government does not come in, what should or may the court infer from that?

Sir Ian Sinclair:

It depends on the particular circumstances. I do not think that one can lay down any generalised rule. Going back to guidelines, I would suggest also that the guidelines ought to be called not only to the attention of the court as Adelheid has just said but also to the attention of the legislators. Because a lot of the problems that arise in this context come from faulty legislation.

Harold G. Maier:

I have a suggestion for a general guideline which we may not want to write down as such but one we may want to think about. It seems to reflect much of what has been said here and that is, and this is not perfectly stated but it is a start, 'no nation should assert the right to enforce its policies in a situation in which it itself would object to such enforcement by another nation if the situation were reversed'. That seems to me to be a very illustrative principle and it is one, in fact, with which you are all familiar.

Andreas F. Lowenfeld:

It is many years since I have been a government official. That aspect of reciprocity does not bother me – it is the other which says, 'I won't do it to you unless I am sure you won't do it to me'. I do not think, for instance, that the US should behave differently toward other countries. That is why I have been resisting reciprocity. I could go along with that guideline of Harold's.

Sir Ian Sinclair:

It is simply the Golden Rule.

Harold G. Maier:

That's exactly what it is, in fact; it is a description of international comity.

Adelheid Puttler:

What do you do if two countries pursue different policies? In environmental law, for example, country A may have a very strong policy about protecting the environment and country B, as Mr Hizon has shown us, may not be interested in environmental protection laws or rules because it cannot afford them and the country has other priorities. So country B, applying your guideline, could then say it did not consider A's rules as valid because it would never impose such harsh rules.

Harold G. Maier:

But this principle is not stated as a rule. That is why the word 'should' rather than 'shall' was used.

Andreas F. Lowenfeld:

But you see that is also why the second form of reciprocity is a bad idea. A is willing to observe B's rules of environment, but A will not do it because C will not.

Harold G. Maier:

It is the Golden Rule. It is pragmatic self-interest.

Sir Ian Sinclair:

It goes a certain way but it does not help in the kind of situation where state A may want to be active in a particular area and state B, frankly for a whole variety of other reasons, does not want to be active.

Harold G. Maier:

It provides a starting point.

Andreas F. Lowenfeld:

Francesco pointed out that unilateralism has moved . . . it is true in a lot of areas, antitrust, bank secrecy, human rights law, most of them have come about through one country pushing. Usually the US, but not always. In human rights, for instance, it was Europe.

Paul Peters:

If we are going to formulate guidelines, one principle to be included should be 'do as you would be done by'. This is the most basic principle governing the problem of extraterritorial jurisdiction. And, indeed, of law in general. It is recorded in the Bible: St. Matthew 7, 12; St. Luke 6, 31 (and as ye would that men should do to you, do ye also to them likewise); Tobit 4, 15 (do that to no man which thou hatest); and in the laws of King Alfred of around 900 (what you do not wish others to do to you, do not to other men).

Andreas F. Lowenfeld:

But do not start with an eye for an eye and a tooth for a tooth!

Rutsel S.J. Martha:

You were referring to the possibility of restricting the discussion to the areas of conflicts. I wonder, though, whether the experiences in those areas of extraterritorial jurisdiction that we have seen but which do not involve conflicts, contain lessons to be drawn in the pursuit of solutions in those areas involving conflicts. Mention was made of banking – what happened in the area of banking is that the relevant parties came together at Basle and agreed on how they would work together.

Sir Ian Sinclair:

Well that certainly would be a generalised guideline: the desirability of seeking to achieve either international agreement or internationally agreed policies, in respect of any area of activity in order to reduce or limit possible conflicts of jurisdiction. I am certainly in favour of that.

Philip Bovey:

I think that we ought also to recognise that some are much easier than others because there is universal agreement on the overriding health of the banking system as being a fundamental moral right.

Andreas F. Lowenfeld:

But it is interesting, you know the substantive agreement on banking, for instance the capital adequacy requirement, came later than the agreement that the old rules of whether it is the home country or the host country that exercises surveillance were obsolete, and the distinction between branches and subsidiaries was largely obsolete. So in that case it was the jurisdictional rules that fell before the substantive rules fell. Indeed, the substantive rules are still emerging as I understand them.

Philip Bovey:

But I do think that is because there is fundamental agreement as to what the objective of regulation is all about.

Andreas F. Lowenfeld:

It happened because two big banks crashed. That brought it to a head.

Philip Bovey:

You could have home state control.

Sir Ian Sinclair:

Any other comments at this stage? It is very difficult. We are having a very generalised discussion. One comment I would make, it is a rather negative one so I hesitate to make it, but it is in the area of export control, which, frankly, we have not discussed here because it was discussed beforehand in this committee. The problem is, I suppose, that since the end of the Cold War you may have a situation in which there is not the same community of interest, among western countries, to engage in some kind of concerted response to a particular act. I'm simply speaking off the top of my head. I just do not know what the position might be in particular circumstances. The principle still looks good – to the extent that there is a consensus of opinion that something should be done, then, fine go ahead.

Pieter J. Kuijper:

The consensus on target states is being exchanged for a consensus on the goods, which in any case are so vital they cannot be distributed at large.

Gary Born:

This is just a thought about what the work product might look like. In part, it could focus on areas where some progress has been made. Identify where co-operation has occurred, identify where views about jurisdictional principles have converged. Another part of it could be to focus on problem areas, areas where there is not agreement and where there are continuing jurisdictional disputes, and to suggest guidelines in those areas. Often the sorts of guidelines that come out of groups like ours are so vague as to mean different things to different people. Perhaps a way to go at this particular issue, which would be useful in bringing some convergence in the areas of disagreement, would be to take case examples in some areas of disagreement such as discovery, or a particular banking issue, or what have you, and to focus on how, if there is agreement about it, a balancing or reasonableness analysis would work as applied to that particular dispute. The problem, always, for those who have advocated balancing and rule of reason is that it is an evolutionary process; but the answer to those who object to it as being vague and ambiguous is that we have only just started down this path. Perhaps if this group were able to at least provide a start on how a reasonableness analysis would work in a discovery conflict or in an export control conflict, it might actually be of practical use to private companies, lawyers and government officials.

Sir Ian Sinclair:

I think that Karl and I are a little bit constrained by the practicalities of having to produce a report or a draft resolution for the conference in Buenos Aires next year. I believe our report will have to be brief. I do not think that, much as I would like to do it, I could engage in that kind of analysis at this stage, I mean within the framework of what we have to produce for the Buenos Aires International Law Association conference. I am not saying that the idea is not a good one.

Campbell McLachlan:

Well, I do not know that it has to be so exhaustive, Sir Ian. What I find attractive about Gary's suggestion is that, going back to your standing in Ireland analogy, that we would endorse, where we would be able to determine it, the areas in which progress had already been made and I think that that is an important function for an international body. That we would identify the areas where seemingly an irreducible conflict still remained and then we would show some sort of sense of vision about the direction that might be taken and whether that gets right down to actually providing concrete answers. I never read a resolution on this sort of area because they are so waffling that they are meaningless. I think it would be possible, and I have great confidence in the rapporteur in this sense, to identify with precision on the basis of the reports we all have prepared and submitted what the real issue is and what some tentative suggestion towards a resolution of it might be in particular areas. I do not think that any of us really seriously believes that we actually can draft anything right at the moment anyway and I would have thought that that could sensibly and still usefully be done within the compass of a few pages.

Andreas F. Lowenfeld:

I have two related remarks and one follows up on Gary and Campbell. I think that we can take the bankruptcy area as one where it is pretty well worked out and I think in most tax issues it is pretty well worked out, and, for example, we could build on the insurance and reinsurance cases that I talked about. And say now, what is the next step? The next step may well be that if the Community lays down some rules as to what kind of collaboration is possible among underwriters that in effect the US's assertion of unilateral pro-consumer protection may fade away. We can make that suggestion in a general way and point toward that. It is not so unreasonable to expect that to happen. That is my more specific point. My more general point, I wanted, Karl, to reply to your suggestion that many issues are best left to conflicts of laws or private international law. Well, the difficulty with that, in the traditional old rules, is that the conflict of laws tended to eliminate addressing public law issues like export controls. I have dedicated my life to saying, 'no, no the same kind of considerations are involved'. I said that in my Hague Lectures 15 years ago. I tried to instill that into the Restatement as I will in my Hague Lecture next year . . . I think that we can say that too: the issues of linkage, of reasonable expectations, of territorial preference, in sum the same kind of considerations do now also influence the public international law which takes some broader limits. The two subjects are really more and more coming together. I think that kind of statement, coming from our association would be a very useful introduction to the points that Gary, Campbell and I have suggested.

Andreas Weitbrecht:

There seems to be substantial agreement on what has been said by Campbell, Gary and others and that to do that would be a good thing. Then, of course, you remind us of Buenos Aires and the time constraints. Is there life after Buenos Aires?

Sir Ian Sinclair:

Absolutely.

Andreas Weitbrecht:

So, perhaps, we should aim for Buenos Aires as laying down the ground rules of what we intend to do rather than give a conclusive report, which has been suggested here and which everybody seems to agree would be a good thing.

Sir Ian Sinclair:

Well, I think then you had better leave that with us. We will have to see what we can do. But obviously as far as the problem of extraterritorial jurisdiction is concerned, irrespective of who does it, there is certainly life after Buenos Aires.

Michael D.C. Johnson:

If I might quickly say something about the environment because environmental law is a relative newcomer in this particular area but it has the capacity to confuse the debate. I do not want to go back over the 'Tuna/Dolphin' issue, because Pieter made the key point that it was not really an issue of assertion of extraterritorial jurisdiction at all and we heard a very clear description from Ernesto yesterday on how it infringed the GATT rules. Picking up on something Cynthia Lichtenstein said, indeed the case would have come out differently if there had been an international agreement in force. Of course, there are four paragraphs at the end of that Panel Report arguing very strongly that nations should get together and sort out these things by international agreement and I talked to the man in the GATT secretariat who drafted those paragraphs and put them in, in order to try and focus people's minds on the issue. Even though the report has not been adopted by GATT, it is influential. What I wanted to say, going on from that, was that essentially up to now, the whole issue presents itself as a trade policy problem, meaning action taken by means of trade measures to secure some objective in environmental policy. I do not think, however, that it needs much imagination to see that it will become a legal issue as well. Dr Puttler, I think, indicated that, but environmental action already appears in the NAFTA agreement as a matter that is justiciable between the parties in NAFTA. They are going to fine each other for infractions. It is going to be interesting to see how that works. There will also be the cross-border pollution problem too, where one country pollutes another. Thus, it does not need much imagination to see that it will become a legal issue. Moreover, I would hope, and I am speaking here as a trade specialist, that those who are deeply engaged in trying to work out what the boundaries should be within which trade measures can be used for the enforcement of environmental standards, should if possible get on with the work which is going on at the moment in the OECD, and GATT as well, before it becomes too enmeshed in issues of international jurisdiction.

Rutsel S.J. Martha:

I just have a suggestion for procedure. I think that we have covered all the issues already. I think that if it is possible for Professor Meessen to put together a text and then circulate it so that we can look at it . . .

Sir Ian Sinclair:

To be quite frank, this is, basically, the responsibility of the International Law Association Committee that is set up to study this problem.

Ulrich Drobnig:

I wanted to expand a little bit on Andy Lowenfeld's statement that the conflict of laws approach would be useful. I think, yes, and that is really the condition if you take into account public law, conflict of laws, but I think that it should be made very clear that the conflict of public laws is essentially quite different as distinct from private law conflicts. In the private law field, you look for one centre of gravity, so to speak, and apply the law of that place. Now that originally for the conflict of public laws does not work. There are several, at least, especially in the border crossing situation and the famous, or infamous, art. 7(1) of the Rome Treaty takes this into account and we have to take into account in each instance of extraterritorial legislation that there may be another centre of gravity in the local, or former law, affecting the target law. I think this is legitimate and it should be spelled out in those areas where no harmony of legislation or understanding exists, so that in such cases of conflict between the two centres of gravity the secondary, i.e. the territorial, prevails. That is my very strong view and at least if a bank has a branch there, nationality in my view does not constitute a true territorial link. It is residence of natural persons and companies' residence of a foreign branch which would be the point of attachment.

Yoshio Ohara:

At 178 RdC (1982-V) 247, Oscar Schachter stated as follows:

> An important difference between legislative and adjudicatory jurisdiction is that the latter may be exercised in civil cases when the parties agree, irrespective of their connection with the forum. Thus, contractual consent to jurisdiction appears to be sufficient as far as international law is concerned.

Restatement (Third) of the Foreign Relations Laws of the United States s. 421(3) also provides that 'A defense of lack of jurisdiction is generally waived by any appearance (equivalent to consent) by . . . a person . . . if the appearance is for a purpose that does not include a challenge to the exercise of jurisdiction'.

However, consent seems to provide the basis of legislative jurisdiction in the extraterritorial application of export control legislation. John Ellicott justified US re-export control by constructing a *de facto* consent between an American exporter and a final consignee because the latter would have noticed the warning against unauthorised re-export attached to goods made in the USA, concluded with the former (see 1984 *Private Investors Abroad* 16). In the *Siberian Pipeline* case of 1982, amended US Export Administration Regulations were applied to Alsthom-Atlantique as a foreign licensee which consented to observe US Export Administration Regulations. Against control based on a submission clause, the EC Commission stated in its comments that:

> Private agreements should not be used in this way as instruments of foreign policy. If a Government in law and in fact systematically encourages the inclusion of such submission clauses in private contracts, the freedom of contract is misused in order to circumvent the limits imposed on national jurisdiction by international law.

As I raised a question to Pieter J. Kuijper at this Symposion, submission clauses which US licensors, in fact, impose on foreign licensees, should not be condemned unlike those which a government in law encourages.

Sir Ian Sinclair:

Well, thank you. At this stage, I don't frankly think we have time to re-open discussion on a topic where there are a number of conflicting views. I think that at this stage, what I would like to do now is to call upon Karl here, as the rapporteur of the International Committee, to sum up. We, of course, have to assume our responsibilities, which we will do, but we will do it in the light of the extremely helpful discussion we've had this morning and, as this will probably be the last statement that I will make, I would like to thank everybody very much for coming here and making such a spirited contribution to our discussions. I have personally learned a good deal more in the last two days on a topic which I have not been able to follow all that closely in recent years.

Karl M. Meessen:

I would agree that there will be life after Buenos Aires. We are not particularly keen on extending the lifetime of the Committee but we have to give occasion to the International Law Association at large to give comment on our product and if we realise that those comments suggest further action, I think we have to do another round and then wind up during the conference after Buenos Aires.

The real difference between conflict of laws and international law is the different way of establishing the law. Conflict of laws is national law and judge made law. It is made by one legislature and one judiciary. Academia just has to develop bright ideas and, if they can sell them to the legislators or the judges, that is it. Whereas in international law scholars are bound to be meticulous fact finders and simply have to stick with practice as they find it.

Especially regarding matters in rapid transition, such as environmental law, it would be helpful to confine ourselves, just formulate the questions. Not to give the answers in every respect. I found the two papers we heard yesterday very helpful. On the other hand, I am also aware that we do not have indefinite time to spend on this matter and, therefore, I would personally favour the approach of sticking with the borderline issues also for the reason that, under customary international law, you have to find evidence for an *opinio juris*. When you have a pattern of rules which has not been disputed ever, it need not represent international law. It simply has not reached that level of exchange between nations. Parking prohibited – it is not a rule of international law even though it is a rule in every city of the world.

Finally, I would prefer to stick with the borderline issues maybe because they are the most interesting ones and it is just impossible to cover all the legal questions. Let me add to this that I will not in the afternoon sit down and draft the resolution and then it is done. Of course, I will not do that. I will take a careful look at the proceedings of our conference and try to consider your comments in greater fairness than I could possibly offer to do at this late moment. For now I would join Ian when he said, he learned a lot – so did I. Thank you.

Sir Ian Sinclair:

Ladies and gentlemen, I can do nothing other than to thank you all again for coming here. We wish you a good journey home. And, I now propose to adjourn.

Index